The Collected Essays of Asa Briggs

Volume I: Words, Numbers, Places, People

The Collected Essays of Asa Briggs
Volume II: Images, Problems, Standpoints, Forecasts

The Collected Essays of Asa Briggs

Volume I:
Words, Numbers, Places, People

Asa Briggs

Provost, Worcester College, Oxford

THE UNIVERSITY OF ILLINOIS PRESS
URBANA AND CHICAGO

© 1985 by Asa Briggs   *11523703*

First published in the United States of America by
University of Illinois Press, Urbana and Chicago

Manufactured in Great Britain

Library of Congress Cataloging in Publication Data

Briggs, Asa, 1921-
   The collected essays of Asa Briggs.

   Includes indexes.
   Contents: v.1. Words, numbers, places, people – v. 2.
Images, problems, standpoints, forecasts.
   1. England – Social conditions – 19th century – Addresses,
essays, lectures.   2. Social history – 19th century – Addresses,
essays, lectures.   3. Great Britain – History – 19th
century – Addresses, essays, lectures. I. Title.
HN385.B7577 1985   306′.0942   84-24484
ISBN 0-252-01216-X (v.1)
ISBN 0-252-01228-3 (set)
ISBN 0-7108-0094-0 (UK edition, Harvester)

$62.09
(2 v.)

The attitudes of individuals and groups of individuals to their own situation in society and the conduct these attitudes dictate are determined not so much by actual economic conditions as by the image in the minds of the individual groups.

Georges Duby, *Les Sociétés médiévales:*
une approche d'ensemble (1971)

But stay – the present and the future – *they* are another's; but the past – that at least is ours.

W.S. Gilbert, *The Gondoliers* (1889)

Contents

List of Illustrations

The Originals

'The Language of "Class" in Early Nineteenth-Century England' first appeared in A. Briggs and J. Saville (eds), *Essays in Labour History* (1960).

'The Language of "Mass" and "Masses" in Nineteenth-Century England' first appeared in D. E. Martin and D. Rubinstein (eds), *Ideology and the Labour Movement, Essays presented to John Saville* (1979).

'The Human Aggregate' first appeared in H. J. Dyos and M. Wolff (eds), *The Victorian City*, vol. I (1973). An earlier version, 'The Victorian City, Quantity and Quality', first appeared in *Victorian Studies*, vol. XI (1968). It was the text of a lecture delivered at the University of Indiana in 1967.

'The Sense of Place', now completely rewritten, first appeared in the *Smithsonian Annual*, vol. II, *The Fitness of Man's Environment* (1968).

'Press and Public in Early Nineteenth-Century Birmingham' was first delivered as a lecture to the Dugdale Society in 1948. It subsequently appeared in the *Occasional Papers of the Dugdale Society*, no. 8 (1949).

'Thomas Attwood and the Economic Background of the Birmingham Political Union' first appeared in the *Cambridge Historical Journal*, vol. IX (1948).

'The Background of the Parliamentary Reform Movement in Three English Cities' first appeared in the *Cambridge Historical Journal*, vol. IX (1948).

'Social Structure and Politics in Birmingham and Lyons, 1825-1848' first appeared in the *British Journal of Sociology*, vol. I, no. 1 (1950). It was based on a paper read to the first post-war Anglo-French Historians' Conference at All Souls College, Oxford, on 24 September 1949.

Preface

The essays and papers assembled in these volumes, most of them substantially revised, were written at various times, sometimes long ago, and were published in various places. Nonetheless, in retrospect at least, they have a unity. They are all concerned with social and cultural change and, equally important, with how it was perceived, particularly after the advent of steam-driven industry.

Because they were written at various times, the first of them long ago in 1948, they will be interesting, I hope, not only because of their content, but because they chart some of the most important changes which have re-shaped the study of social history between the late 1940s and the early 1980s. The only ones which I have not revised are included in their original form because they conveniently capsulate historical scholarship as it was at a particular time. I have also retained the shape and style of a number of lectures where there was a particular sense of occasion.

The extent of the transformation in the study of social history is well known to professional historians but is still not generally appreciated. From being at best one (among many) relatively neglected and often trivialised sub-branches of history, usually bracketed, at its most serious, with economic history, social history has moved more closely towards becoming an integrated history of particular societies and of 'society'; and other 'sub-histories' within social history have boomed, notably urban history and labour history. I have been deeply committed to both. They were seldom studied in depth during the late 1940s and early 1950s. Nor were they institutionalised. I was privileged to take them up at that point.

Doubtless my interest in these subjects can be explained in terms of my background and temperament. Yet it was more by accident than by design that in the late 1940s I embarked on the *History of Birmingham* which was published in 1952. My attention was first drawn to Birmingham when I planned to write a biography of Joseph Chamberlain. I never wrote it, but the desire to do so led me back first from Chamberlain to a far less well-known character, Thomas Attwood, and second – and in the long run, more important in terms of my own writing – from a man to a city. There was no boom in urban history then, and I had to explore *terra incognita* without maps when Birmingham Corporation invited me to write the second of two volumes on the history of the city covering the period from 1868 to 1938.

Sir Charles Grant Robertson, who had been commissioned to write it during the 1930s on the eve of the centenary of incorporation, had not produced one line, and I had a free hand. Nor was I influenced in my approach by Professor Conrad Gill, who had already written most of the first volume before I started. The two volumes are often referred to as Gill and Briggs, but, although I was on the friendliest terms with Gill, the volumes were not written on a collaborative basis.

My own volume was what I now realise was an ambitious attempt to deal with *all* identifiable relationships in a great industrial city and not with particular aspects of its life treated separately. I dared even to use the phrase 'total history' to describe my purpose long before reading Braudel or *Annales*. Moreover, I was drawn through the enterprise into a study of urban sociology in which I not only crossed disciplinary frontiers which had previously been closed to most historians, but the physical barrier – and it was greater then than now – of the Atlantic Ocean. I learnt much from the urban sociologists of the University of Chicago, a great school still looking back to Park, and with Louis Wirth still active; and this activity had a bigger influence on the development of my work (ultimately resulting in *Victorian Cities* (1963)) than the activity of French historians. Yet I met many of the latter at the time of the celebrations of the centenary of the 1848 Revolution in Paris, and I first read my paper on Birmingham and Lyons to a joint Anglo-French meeting.

Of the four Birmingham essays, the one which to me still seems to point to the future is my thoroughly revised comparative study of Birmingham and Lyons. With Braudel in mind – and other French historians, like Rude writing on Lyons, and Labrousse, whom I met and admired – I have always felt that we need far more comparative work on England and France in the nineteenth century. Yet I believe that the comparative work should be concerned less with two 'nations' than with two social and cultural configurations where there were many elements in common. The aim should be a richer synthesis.

The particular article among the Birmingham four which belongs most not to the future but to the present, however, is that on 'Thomas Attwood and the Economic Background of the Birmingham Political Union'. When I first wrote it in 1948, I had no intimation that forms of monetarism, often crude, which preoccupied Attwood so much in his own generation, would become keystones of contemporary economic policy. I had no intimation either that unemployment rates would

reach their present dimensions. Much that seemed then to be narrowly
'academic' now has its point. Social confrontation itself calls for
historians. So, too, do the pressures of technological change.

Having once produced my *History of Birmingham* and the bundle of
articles which preceded it, I have never lost my interest in the city or its
historiography and I have reviewed most of the new books about them
when they have appeared. Fashions change, as well as relevant topical
issues and it is now fashionable to stress what Birmingham has in
common with other cities. My task, I felt, was to explain what was
distinctive about it from Attwood to Chamberlain, and from
Chamberlain to the general election of 1945. Yet I soon felt that it
was not enough to look at Birmingham and other particular cities in
order to understand the nineteenth-century environment. It was
necessary, too, to consider problems which affected all cities – notably
public health – and through such considerations to assess what was the
part of public opinion – and expert opinion – in forcing through
change. The change, moreover, was often change in the mind,
particularly a major change in the attitudes towards 'fate' and 'social
control' (the latter a term which has more recently been used or
misused in far too many contexts). There were common features in the
response everywhere, although the timing was different; and these are
themes dealt with more fully in the second volume of these collected
essays.

Through public health I became more interested in people's
reactions to their environment than in physical data concerning it.
And with this shift in my own interests I passed increasingly willingly,
even eagerly, from social history as economic history with the politics
put in, to social and cultural history with the technology put in; and
rather than generalising more – on the basis of limited and often over-
exploited evidence – I began to pay particular and close attention to
the relationship between the distinctive perceptions of individual
writers and artists and the kind of culture which they shared.

Following this shift the first two essays in this volume, therefore, set
out to examine the new verbal frameworks or 'vocabularies' within
which experience, old and new, was expressed and communicated.
They consider words like 'classes' and 'masses', which have subsequently become part both of the specialised vocabulary of sociology
and of the general vocabulary of social and political action. In these, as
in many of the later essays in my second volume, I have drawn heavily
on newspapers and 'news' set out in other 'ephemeral' sources (one
essay deals with such evidence) and I have tried to draw too on
anthropology when I seek to relate the concepts (and images) of class
to the historical experience of it. I have drawn equally heavily,
however – and more, perhaps, than most historians – on 'literature',

noting both the opportunities and difficulties of doing so. I have always believed that the historian should be concerned both with the 'social sciences' (not least demography) and with literature, sensing that the gulf between writing in the 'social sciences' and 'literature' is as wide as the 'two-cultures' gulf between 'sciences' and 'the arts'.

One mode of perception was statistical, and my essay *The Human Aggregate* explores the preoccupation with numbers in the nineteenth century, a somewhat different preoccupation from that of the late twentieth century, and how it developed. It focuses mainly, but not exclusively, on the city as an 'aggregate', and should be related, therefore, to my book on *Victorian Cities* which was concerned both with generalisations about urbanisation and with profiles of individual cities. At the same time, in so far as it focused attention on differentials in the statistical fortunes of different social groups, it was directly related to public health.

As far as individual perceptions and values are concerned, it is important to grasp, first, that while we can trace patterns of perceptions and values through the experiences of individual people, there was no one single shared sense of what life was like, or what it might be like, after the advent of steam-driven machinery and, second, that ambitious attempts were made in the nineteenth century and have been made since both to discover one and to impose one. The reason why the attempts failed was not so much intellectual – a matter of 'science' – but social – a matter of 'experience'. There were such sharply contrasting varieties of experience after the advent of the steam engine – not least within the same factory or the same city – that neither the statistical nor the verbal frameworks of explanation received general assent.

Of course, there had been sharply contrasting varieties of experience in pre-industrial societies, but with the rise of industry new factors were brought into action and old factors given new weighting – individual and group aspirations, in particular, views of what life might be. These led to voluntary initiatives as well as to the formation of new public policies, local or national through often intricate processes. Shapes of the future flit through the changing past, as my essay on the 'Welfare State' in my second volume shows.

Shared or contrasting perceptions reflected, of course, shared or contrasting values, some traditional, although those were often under threat, some new values in the crucible. Neither of the articulated versions of 'individualism' and 'solidarity' in the middle years of the nineteenth century can be explained without searching back through the centuries before the rise of steam-driven industry. Nor can the late nineteenth-century 'revolt' be considered simply as a revolt against mid-Victorian values (and institutions); it was a revolt also against far older values (and institutions). An era was under assault, not a generation.

It is impossible to move through the nineteenth century, however, without recognising that this was a period when new 'scientific theories' were advanced (by the end of the century they had often been clustered into 'disciplines' with 'professional' practitioners) and new 'ideologies' (no earlier century had generated more *isms*, including one unique *ism* associated with the name of a monarch, 'Victorianism'). The relationship between 'theories' and 'ideologies' is complex. In particular, from the early nineteenth century onwards there were separated if related, versions of 'political economy', which some, at least, of their expositors and adherents considered to be the key to the 'science of society'.

I have never believed that it is, or at least that it is the only key, and for this reason several essays in my second volume are concerned with the approaches not of contemporaries but of historians. G. M. Young is the one historian with whom I have felt a close affinity, although not a political one. Trevelyan's *History of England* and his *Social History* I have introduced in their latest editions, and I know his work well. I used to listen to his lectures as an undergraduate in Cambridge, and I must have been among the first readers and reviewers of his *Social History*. It is not a coincidence that both these writers were as much interested in literature as in history.

It is a mistake, in my view – if a favourite one, even among academics – to treat history as 'background', and 'literature' as text. Both history and literature deal with human experience, common or individual, although some 'literature', of course, is 'escapist' and there is an element of fantasy even, perhaps not least, in the work of novelists like Trollope who endear themselves to historians. The word 'common' can relate either to the experience of a whole society or culture, or to social groupings and their 'sub-cultures' within it. Given the many divisions in nineteenth-century English society and culture, divisions determined by 'place' (a concept specifically considered in one of my essays) as well as by class, we have to identify rather than take for granted what was 'common' and to explain in each case how that which was inherited was eroded and how that which was new was secured.

Within this context, there is a need to explore the 'mental maps of the social scene', a term used, long before it became fashionable, by F. M. Martin in 1954 in Professor David Glass's important collection of papers *Social Mobility in Britain*. The statistical mode of perception was only one – and not the most common. It was through the study of cities rather than through the study of class that I became interested both in 'city scapes' and in people's very varied perceptions of them.

While I was influenced by Patrick Geddes' plea in his remarkable Columbo Plan of 1921 for the supplementation of 'verbal present-ments by the fullest possible use of accompanying plans and diagrams', I began to realise that this was not enough. I was ready, therefore, for Kevin Lynch's *The Image of the City* (1960), for the later studies in this country of Peter Smith, and for the 'new geography'.

We turn both to 'literature' and to 'art' for common experience, uncommonly depicted – the images carry meanings which might otherwise be lost through time – and for distinctive, often highly distinctive, individual experience communicated through the 'arts' to numbers of others who did not share it. In the latter case, indeed, we can tap the diversity of a society and a culture. There is some 'literature' and 'art', of course, which transcends such frameworks and bears new 'meanings' in new times, being both reinterpreted and reassessed in the process. There is much nineteenth-century 'escapist' literature, too, which illuminates many aspects of the century – not least 'nonsense' literature, often accompanied by sketches which are as revealing as the texts. We often seem to be untapping the unconscious here.

A curious element of fantasy can even creep into a volume of twentieth-century historical essays like mine when essays written at different times, in different places and for different readers are put together. Odd links appear. Mrs Thomas Attwood, for example, was a surprising ancestor of E. A. Freeman, the historian described at some length in my second volume in 'Saxons, Normans and Victorians'. Cholera, the subject of another essay in my second volume, did *not* strike in Lyons, although the Prefect feared that it would. And George Eliot herself the subject of another essay supplied me with a motto which I might have used as my motto for the whole of my collection:

> To live over other people's lives is nothing unless we live over their perceptions, live over the growth, the varying intensity of the same – since it is by these they themselves lived.

Instead, I chose my first motto for both volumes from a professional historian, but a historian concerned primarily with the middle ages and not a historian of the nineteenth century.

I have owed much in my endeavours to pupils and much to the University of Sussex, where I could encourage others as well as myself to cross the boundaries between disciplines. I had colleagues there with whom I could discuss all the issues raised in these papers while at the same time combining my delights as a historian with the labours of a Vice-Chancellor. And I also look back in time further still to the *Cambridge Journal*, where some of my first pieces appeared under the

tender editorial care of Michael Oakeshott. After that, my six years at
the University of Leeds were not an interlude. I wrote much then, and
it was good to be back in a Victorian city while it still was a Victorian
city. It is not only the pursuit of history which has changed during the
last thirty years. Most recently, a small group of colleagues in Oxford,
meeting informally in each others' homes, has kept alive not only my
personal pursuit of history but theirs.

I

WORDS AND NUMBERS

There are masses, and there are classes but the machine it is that has invented them both.

D. H. Lawrence

Instead of using only comparative and superlative Words, and intellectual Arguments, I have taken the course ... to express myself in Terms of *Number*, *Weight*, or *Measure*; to use only Arguments of Sense, and to consider only such causes, as have visible foundations in Nature; leaving those that depend on the mutable Minds, Opinions, Appetites, and Passions of particular Men, to the Consideration of others.

William Petty

1 The Language of 'Class' in Early Nineteenth-Century England

The concept of social 'class' with all its attendant terminology was a product of the large-scale economic and social changes of the late eighteenth and early nineteenth centuries. Before the rise of modern industry,[1] writers on society spoke of 'ranks', 'orders', and 'degrees' or, when they wished to direct attention to particular economic groupings, of 'interests'. The word 'class' was reserved for a number of people banded together for educational purposes[2] or more generally with reference to sub-divisions in schemes of 'classification'.[3] Thus, the 1824 edition of the *Encyclopaedia Britannica* referred to 'classes of quadrupeds, birds, fishes and so forth, which are again subdivided into series or orders and these last into genera'. It cross-directed its readers to articles on 'Animal Kingdom' and 'Botany'.

By 1824, however, the word 'class' had already established itself as a social label following the economic and social transformation, and although that transformation was not complete even ten years later, John Stuart Mill was then to remark:

> They revolve in their eternal circle of landlords, capitalists and labourers, until they seem to think of the distinction of society into those three classes as if it were one of God's ordinances not man's, and as little under human control as the division of day or night. Scarcely any one of them seems to have proposed to himself as a subject of inquiry, what changes the relations of those classes to one another are likely to undergo in the progress of society.[4]

The word 'class' has figured so prominently in the subsequent development of the socialist – and of other social – vocabularies that a study of the origins and early use of the term in Britain is not simply an academic exercise in semantics.[5] There was no dearth of social conflicts in pre-industrial society, many of them, particularly in the north-east, with a powerful momentum, but they were not conceived of at the time in straight class terms, but rather in terms of 'gentlemen', 'the people' and 'the mob'. The change in nomenclature in the late eighteenth and early nineteenth centuries reflected a basic change not only in men's ways of viewing society but in society itself. It is with the relationship between words and movements – in an English context – that this essay is concerned.

I

Eighteenth-century English society was hierarchical, and was often conceived of in terms of a pyramid with the 'common people', those without rank or 'dignity', at the base. The 'meer labouring people who depend upon their hands', as Defoe called them, were never without defenders,[6] but social orthodoxy had little use for 'the gross and inconsistent notion' of equality.[7] Skilled artisans had their own grades of 'superiority' and 'inferiority',[8] while between the 'nobility' and the 'commonalty' were the growing numbers of 'middling people' or 'middling sorts' whose praises were frequently sung in an age of increasing wealth and mercantile expansion. The most successful of them could be absorbed into the 'gentry', that most English of social groupings, and Chapter xxiv of Defoe's *Complete English Tradesman* (1726) was entitled 'Extracts from the genealogies of several illustrious families of our English nobility, some of which owe their rise to trade, and others their descent and fortunes to prudent alliances with the families of citizens'.[9]

That distinct element of mobility in the social system – based on what Adam Smith and Malthus after him called 'the natural effort of every individual to better his own condition'[10] – was often stressed by social commentators, particularly those who drew a sharp distinction between England and the continent. There were two other very different elements in the system however, which were given equal attention and were especially emphasised by the first generation of writers to condemn the social 'disintegration' consequent upon the rise of factory industry. The first of them was what Cobbett called 'the chain of connection' between the rich and the poor[11], and the second was what Southey described as 'the bond of attachment'.[12] The use of the nouns 'chain' and 'bond' is as eloquent (in retrospect) as the choice of 'connection' and 'attachment', but Cobbett and Southey in their different ways were praising the past in order to condemn the present. 'Connection' was associated not only with a network of social obligation but with gentle slopes of social gradation. It implied that every man had his place within an order, but that the order allowed for declensions of status as well as bold contrasts. To those who were willing to disturb that order Cobbett exclaimed, 'You are for reducing the community to two classes: Masters and Slaves'.[13] 'Attachment' was directly associated both with 'duty' – the 'duty' appropriate to 'rank' – and with dependence, and thereby with 'charity', 'deference', and 'subordination'. 'The bond of attachment is broken', wrote

Southey in 1829, 'there is no longer the generous bounty which calls forth a grateful and honest and confiding dependence.'[14]

Before the industrial revolution of the 1780s there were many signs of tension and contradiction both in society and in contemporary writings about it. The growth of population, the problem of 'indigence', the enclosure movement in the villages, the increase in home and foreign trade, and the emergence of 'radical' ideas in politics preceded the development of the steam-engine. It was the steam-engine, however, limited though its use may have been, which was the 'principal factor in accelerating urban concentration' and 'generalising' the labour force.[15] It was the steam-engine also which inspired both the optimistic panegyrics of man's 'conquest of Nature' and the critical analyses of the contradictions and conflicts of the new society. The extent of the contradictions and the conflicts was clearly appreciated long before the term 'industrial revolution' passed into general circulation. John Wade, the author of the *History of the Middle and Working Classes* (1833), one of the first attempts to put the facts of the recent past into historical perspective, wrote as follows:

The physical order of communities, in which the production of the necessaries of subsistence is the first want and chief occupation, has in our case been rapidly inverted, and in lieu of agricultural supremacy, a vast and overtopping superstructure of manufacturing wealth and population has been substituted. It is to this extraordinary revolution, I doubt not, may be traced much of the bane and many of the blessings incidental to our condition – the growth of an opulent commercial and a numerous, restless and intelligent operative class; sudden alternations of prosperity and depression – of internal quiet and violent political excitement; extremes of opulence and destitution; the increase of crime; conflicting claims of capital and industry; the spread of an imperfect knowledge, that agitates and unsettles the old without having definitely settled the new foundations; clashing and independent opinions on most public questions, with other anomalies peculiar to our existing but changeful social existence.[16]

The use of the word 'class' and the sense of class that made the use increasingly meaningful must be related to what Wade called both 'the bane' and 'the blessings' of the new society. The development of factory industry often broke 'the bond of attachment', substituting for it what Carlyle was to call a 'cash nexus'.[17] The continued existence of factory paternalism checked but did not reverse this process. At the same time, with the breaking of the bond there was increasing pressure to secure 'union' among the workers themselves. The demand not only for union at the factory or the local level but for 'general union' was directly related to the story of the emergence of a self-conscious 'working class'.[18] Cobbett, who was one of the most forthright advocates of the old social system operating in an ideal form, saw clearly that once that system had been destroyed, 'classes' would be ranged against each other:

> They [working men] combine to effect a rise in wages. The masters combine against them. One side complains of the other; but neither knows the *cause* of the turmoil, and the turmoil goes on. The different trades combine, and call their combination a GENERAL UNION. So that here is one class of society united to oppose another class.[19]

The same consequence followed on the growth of industrial cities, where the 'masses' were segregated and left to their own devices.[20] A few years before Disraeli used the phrase 'two nations', a distinguished preacher spoke in very similar terms at a chapel in Boston across the Atlantic:

> It is the unhappiness of most large cities that, instead of inspiring union and sympathy among different 'conditions of men', they consist of different ranks, so widely separated indeed as to form different communities. In most large cities there may be said to be two nations, understanding as little of one another, having as little intercourse, as if they lived in different lands ... This estrangement of men from men, of class from class, is one of the saddest features of a great city.[21]

It was a theme which was to be taken up frequently in nineteenth-century argument, and which dominated Engels's picture of Manchester in the 1840s. 'We know well enough', Engels wrote, 'that [the] isolation of the individual ... is everywhere the fundamental principle of modern society. But nowhere is this selfish egotism so blatantly evident as in the frantic bustle of the great city.'[22] But the disintegration of society into 'individuals' was accompanied by the carving out of classes. 'The cities first saw the rise of the workers and the middle classes into opposing social groups.'[23]

Forty years before Engels, Charles Hall had stressed the snapping of 'the chain of continuity' in society and stated, perhaps for the first time, the central proposition of a class theory of society:

> The people in a civilised state may be divided into different orders; but for the purpose of investigating the manner in which they enjoy or are deprived of the requisites to support the health of their bodies and minds, they need only be divided into two classes, viz. the rich and the poor.[24]

The sharp contrasts of industrialism encouraged the reinstatement of theories of society in these terms. So, too, did the pressures of popular politics, which often prompted a two-class set of images, like Hall's, rather than Mill's three-class set.[25] In one sense 'class' was a more indefinite word than 'rank' and this may have been among the reasons for its introduction. In another sense, however, employment of the word 'class' allowed for a sharper and more generalised picture of society, which could be provided with a historical and economic underpinning. Conservatives continued to prefer to talk of 'ranks' and 'orders' – as they still did in the middle of the nineteenth century[26] – and the old language coexisted with the new, as it did in the words of the preacher quoted above – but analysts of the distribution of the national income[27] and social critics alike talked increasingly in class terms. So too did politicians, particularly as new social forces were given political expression. The stormiest political decade of early nineteenth-century English history, that which began with the financial crisis of 1836 and the economic crisis of 1837, was the decade when class terms were most generally used and 'middle classes' and 'working classes' alike did not hesitate to relate politics directly to class antagonisms.

There was, however, an influential social cross-current which directed attention not to the contrasting fortunes and purposes of 'middle classes' and 'working classes' but to a different division in industrial society, that between 'the industrious classes' and the rest. Those writers who were more impressed by the productive possibilities of large-scale industry than afraid of social 'disintegration' dwelt on this second division. St Simon's demand for unity of 'the productive classes' against parasitic 'non-producers'[28] had many parallels as well as echoes inside England. Patrick Colquhoun, whose statistical tables were used by Robert Owen and John Gray,[29] attempted to divide industrial society into a productive class whose labour increased the national income and a 'diminishing class' which produced no 'new property'. When he argued that 'it is by the labour of the people, employed in various branches of industry, that all ranks of the community in every condition of life annually subsist',[30] he was not stating, as Gray later did, that manual labour created all wealth. He pointed also towards a social analysis which allowed for an 'intermediate class'.[31] Owen, who occasionally wrote in what were coming to be regarded as conventional terms of the 'upper', the 'middle', and the 'working classes', more usually conceived of society in the same terms as Colquhoun:

> There will be, therefore, at no distant period, a union of the government, aristocracy, and non-producers on the one part and the Industrious Classes, the body of the people generally, on the other part; and the two most formidable powers for good or evil are thus forming.[32]

The same conception influenced radical politics. The *Extraordinary Black Book*, also borrowing from Colquhoun and mixing up the language of 'class' and 'orders', maintained that

> The industrious orders may be compared to the soil, out of which every thing is evolved and produced; the other classes to the trees, tares, weeds and vegetables, drawing their nutriment, supported and maintained on its surface ... When mankind attain a state of greater perfectibility ... [the useful classes] ought to exist in a perfect state. The other classes have mostly originated in our vices and ignorance ... having no employment, their name and office will cease in the social state.[33]

Thomas Attwood, who in favourable social and economic circumstances in Birmingham, tried to unite 'middle' and 'working classes' in a single Political Union,[34] also believed that what he called 'the industrious classes' should secure political power. 'The ox is muzzled that treadeth the corn.'[35] It was only after the Reform Bill of 1832 had failed to satisfy his hopes – and only then for a short period of time – that he claimed that 'in a great cause, he was content to stand or fall with the workmen alone' even if the middle classes, to which he belonged, were against him.[36]

II

Before turning to 'working-class' critics of both Owen and Attwood and to the statement of class theory in specifically working-class perspectives, the terms 'upper class' and 'middle class' require more careful and detailed examination. The phrase 'higher classes' was used specifically by Edmund Burke in his *Thoughts on French Affairs* in 1791, significantly only when the position of the 'higher classes' seemed to be threatened not only in France but in England. It was an exhortatory phrase in much of the Evangelical literature of the last decade of the century. When the French Revolution challenged the power of aristocracies and in England traditional duties seemed to be in disrepair, there was a need to re-define them. It was in this mood that Thomas Gisborne, friend of William Wilberforce, published his *Enquiry into the Duties of Men in the Higher Rank and Middle Classes of Society in Great Britain* in 1795. There was much literature of this kind in the 1790s. Hannah More, Cobbett's 'old bishop in petticoats',[37] was an indefatigable supporter of the 'old order', and her tracts, some of which were specially addressed to 'Persons of the Middle Ranks', 'were bought by the gentry and middling classes full as much as by the common people'.[38]

The phrase 'middle classes', which antedates the phrase 'working classes' or 'labouring classes',[39] was a product, however, not of exhortation but of conscious pride. As early as the 1780s, attempts had been made to create new organisations which would uphold the claims of the new manufacturers. Pitt's commercial policy goaded manufacturers to set up the General Chamber of Manufacturers in 1785:

> Common danger having at length brought together a number of Manufacturers in various branches, and from various places, and their having felt the advantages resulting to each from unreserved conferences and mutual assistance, they are now persuaded, that the prosperity of the Manufacturers of this kingdom, and of course that of the kingdom itself, will be promoted by the formation of a general bond of union, whereby the influence and experience of the whole being collected at one common centre, they will be the better enabled to effect any useful purposes for their general benefit.

In eighteenth-century terms this was the mobilisation of a new economic 'interest', an interest which failed to maintain its unity in the immediate future. It was something more than that, however. 'The manufacturers of Great Britain', their statement began, 'constitute a very large, if not a principal part of the community; and their industry, ingenuity and wealth, have contributed no small share towards raising this kingdom to the distinguished and envied rank which she bears among the European nations.'[40] The word 'class' was not used, as it was used freely and unashamedly by the Anti-Corn Law League half a century later, but what was whispered in private in the 1780s was shouted on the platform in the 1840s.

There were several factors encouraging the development of a sense of middle-class unity where hitherto there had been a recognition of (imperfect) mutual interest. First in time was the imposition of Pitt's income tax, which entailed the common treatment of a group of diverse 'interests' by the government. Second was the impact of the Napoleonic Wars as a whole, which laid emphasis on the incidence of 'burdens', burdens which seemed to be of unequal weight for the owners of land and the owners of capital. Adam Smith had already distinguished clearly between these two 'interests' or 'orders' as he called them (and, indeed, a third 'interest', that 'of those who live by wages' as well), but he did not concede the claims of the merchants and 'master manufacturers': in his opinion, they were more concerned with their own affairs than with the affairs of society as a whole. 'Their superiority over the country gentlemen is, not so much in their knowledge of the public interest, as in their having a better knowledge of their own interest than he has of his.'[41] Between 1776 and 1815, however, the numbers and wealth of the 'owners of capital' increased, and both their public grievances and their public claims were advocated with energy and persistence.

It is not surprising that a sense of grievance stimulated talk of 'class', and there are many expressions of it in the periodicals of the day. 'Why rejoice in the midst of rivers of blood', asked a writer in the *Monthly Repository* in 1809, 'while the burden of taxation presses so heavily on the middle classes of society, so as to leave the best part of the community little to hope and everything to fear?'[42] Four years later, the same magazine demanded immediate peace 'for the relief of those privations and burdens, which now oppress every class in the community, including the poor and middle classes'.[43] The *Oxford Dictionary* gives 1812 as the first occasion on which the phrase 'middle class' was used – in the *Examiner* of the August of that year – and in the twentieth century the example has a very familiar ring – 'such of the Middle Class of Society who have fallen upon evil days'.

By 1815, however, statements about the 'middle classes' or the still popular term 'middle ranks' often drew attention not to grievances but first, to the special role of the middle classes in society as a strategic and 'progressive' group and, second, to their common economic interests.

As early as 1798, the *Monthly Magazine* had sung the praises of 'the middle ranks, in whom the great mass of information, and of public and private virtues reside'[44], and in 1807 the *Athenaeum* had eulogised 'those persons whom the wisest politicians have always counted the most valuable, because the least corrupted, members of society, the middle ranks of people'.[45] Such magazine comments had an element of editorial flattery about them, but beneath the flattery was a keen awareness of social trends. The growing reading public included large numbers of people who belonged to the 'middle classes',[46] and their views were considered to be the main expression of the new 'public opinion'. It was not difficult, indeed, to argue, as James Mill did in his *Essay on Government*, that 'the class which is universally described as both the most wise and the most virtuous part of the community, the middle rank', was the main opinion-making group in a dynamic society and would control politics 'if the basis of representation were extended'.[47] In the diffusion of Utilitarian ideas in the 1820s this case was frequently argued. The middle classes, 'the class who will really approve endeavours in favour of good government, and of the happiness and intelligence of men', had to unite to bring pressure upon the aristocracy. Their philosophy, like their wealth, depended on 'individualism', but their social action had to be concerted. 'Public opinion operates in various ways upon the aristocratical classes, partly by contagion, partly by conviction, and partly by intimidation: and the principal strength of that current is derived from the greatness of the mass by which it is swelled.'[48]

Politicians could not remain indifferent to this language, particularly when it was backed by wealth and increasing economic authority. One of the first to appreciate the need to win the support of the 'middle classes' was Henry Brougham. While the Luddites were engaged in what Engels later called 'the first organised resistance of the workers, as a class to the bourgeoisie',[49] the 'middle classes' were being mobilised in a campaign to abolish the Orders-in-Council.[50] Brougham, 'the life and soul' of the agitation, was later in his life to produce his celebrated equation of the 'middle classes' and 'the People'. 'By the people, I mean the middle classes, the wealth and intelligence of the country, the glory of the British name.'[51] During the Reform Bill agitation of 1830-2 many similar statements were made by Whig leaders who were anxious, in Durham's phrase, 'to attach numbers to property and good order'.[52] Even the aristocratic Grey, who feared the Political Unions with their propaganda for unity between the middle classes and the working classes, chose to appeal 'to the middle classes, who form the real and efficient mass of public opinion and without whom the power of the gentry is nothing'.[53]

The Whigs wished to hitch the middle classes to the constitution to prevent a revolution: a section of the extreme Radicals wanted to associate them with the working classes to secure a revolution. In the tense atmosphere of the years 1830 to 1832 it was not surprising that advocates of cautious change insisted that 'any plan [of Reform] must be objectionable which, by keeping the Franchise very high and exclusive, fails to give satisfaction to the middle and respectable ranks of society, and drives them to a union, founded on dissatisfaction, with the lower orders. It is of the utmost importance to associate the middle with the higher orders of society in the love and support of the institutions and government of the country.'[54] The language as much as the content of this statement reflects a traditionalist view not only of politics but of society.

The relationship between estimates of 'public opinion' and of the growing strength of the 'middle classes' was recognised even when there was an absence of political crisis. Sir James Graham, at that time an independent, but later a member both of the Whig committee which drafted the Reform Bill and of the Conservative Cabinet which proposed the repeal of the Corn Laws, remarked in 1826:

> I know no bound but public opinion. The seat of public opinion is in the middle ranks of life – in that numerous class, removed from the wants of labour and the cravings of ambition, enjoying the advantages of leisure,

and possessing intelligence sufficient for the formation of a sound judgement, neither warped by interest nor obscured by passion.[55]

The remark echoes Aristotle rather than Mill,[56] but it was one version of an extended argument. Another, more cogent, was set out in a historically important but neglected treatise *On the Rise, Progress, and Present State of Public Opinion in Great Britain and Other Parts of the World* (1828). Its author, W.A. Mackinnon, generalised from recent experience.[57] His book began with a 'definition' of the 'classes of society' and went on to describe how the rise of the 'middle classes' led to the growth of wealth and freedom:

> The extent or power of public opinion ... resolves itself into the question whether ... a community is possessed of an extensive middle class of society, when compared to a lower class; for the advantages called requisites for public opinion, cannot exist without forming a proportionate middle class ... In every community or state where public opinion becomes powerful or has influence, it appears that the form of government becomes liberal in the exact proportion as the power of public opinion increases.[58]

Mackinnon related the recent rise of the 'middle classes' to what was later called 'the industrial revolution':

> Machinery creates wealth, which augments the middle class, which gives strength to public opinion; consequently, to allude to the extension of machinery is to account for the increase of the middle class of society.[59]

In a footnote to this passage he drew attention to the magnitude of the changes in his own lifetime:

> That the results arising from the improvement of machinery and its increase, are almost beyond the grasp of the human mind to define, may seem probable from the change that has and is daily taking place in the world.

Finally he pegged class divisions to the distribution of property:

> The only means by which the classes of society can be defined, in a community where the laws are equal, is from the amount of property, either real or personal, possessed by individuals. As long as freedom and civilisation exist, property is so entirely the only power that no other means, or choice is left of distinguishing the several classes, than by the amount of property belonging to the individuals of which they are formed.[60]

Not only the amount of property was relevant in shaping class consciousness after 1815, but the kind. The prolonged but intermittent battle for the repeal of the Corn Laws encouraged social analysis in class terms: at the same time, particularly in its last stages, it sharpened middle-class consciousness and gave it highly organised means of expression.

The kind of social analysis set out in T. Perronet Thompson's *Catechism on the Corn Laws* (1826) was immediately popular for its content as much as for its style of exposition. The theory of rent was used to drive a wedge between the 'landlords' and the rest of the community, often with as much force as the labour theory of value was used in working-class arguments. Rent was defined as 'the superfluity of price, or that part of it which is not necessary to pay for the production with a living profit'. Adam Smith's argument that 'the landed interest', unlike the manufacturing interest, had a direct concern in 'the affairs of society as a whole' was turned on its head. The landlords were described by the repealers as selfish monopolists, who used the Corn Laws to protect their own selfish interest against the interests of the community. No vituperation was spared. There were two other particularly interesting questions and answers in the *Catechism*. 'Q. That we must reconcile conflicting interests. A. There can be no conflict on a wrong. When the question is of a purse unjustly given, it is a fallacy to say we must reconcile conflicting interests, and give the taker half. Q. That the relation between the landlords and others, arising out of the Corn Laws is a source of kindly feelings and mutual virtues. A. Exactly the same was said of slavery.'[61]

Between the publication of the *Catechism* and the formation of the Anti-Corn Law League in 1839 there was a lull in the agitation. The League, however, was a uniquely powerful instrument in the forging of middle-class consciousness. 'We were a middle-class set of agitators,' Cobden admitted; and the League was administered 'by those means by which the middle class usually carries on its movements'.[62] When the battle for repeal had been won, Cobden asked Peel directly and frankly –

> do you shrink from the post of governing through the *bona fide* representatives of the middle class? Look at the facts, and can the country be otherwise ruled at all? There must be an end of the juggle of parties, the mere representatives of tradition, and some man must of necessity rule the state through its governing class. The Reform Bill decreed it: the passing of the Corn Bill has realised it.[63]

Such a bold statement demonstrates that by 1846, not only had the phrase 'middle class' established itself as a political concept, but those people who considered themselves as representatives of the middle classes were prepared to assert in the strongest possible language their claim to political leadership.

Behind the League were middle-class wealth and what Disraeli in *Coningsby* (1844) called 'the pride of an order'.[64] There was also what had recently been called 'a strong belief in the nobility and dignity of industry and commerce', a kind of businessmen's romantic movement:

> trade has now a chivalry of its own; a chivalry whose stars are radiant with the more benignant lustre of justice, happiness and religion, and whose titles will outlive the barbarous nomenclature of Charlemagne.[65]

This kind of rhetoric was usually accompanied by attacks on 'aristocratic tyranny', 'hereditary opulence', and 'social injustice', and by the declaration that 'trade shall no longer pay a tribute to the soil'. At the same time, it was necessary to supplement it – for political purposes – by an appeal to the 'working classes' ('joint victims' of the 'monopolists') and by an attempt to win over tenant farmers and to draw 'a broad distinction ... between the landed and the agricultural interest'.[66] The case for repeal had to be stated in different terms from those employed in Manchester in 1815, when the narrow economic interests of the manufacturers were the main staple of the published argument.[67] In John Morley's famous words, 'class-interest widened into the consciousness of a commanding national interest'.[68] The argument was radically different in its tone and its implications from that advanced by the General Chamber of Manufacturers in the 1780s. Again Morley has caught the mood as the Leaguers themselves liked to interpret it:

> Moral ideas of the relations of class to class in this country, and of the relations of country to country in the civilized world, lay behind the contention of the hour, and in the course of that contention came into new light. The promptings of a commercial shrewdness were gradually enlarged into enthusiasm for a far-reaching principle, and the hard-headed man of business gradually felt himself touched with the generous glow of the patriot and the deliverer.[69]

III

The glow was not always infectious, and although the League had some success in attracting the support of 'the working classes of the more respectable sort',[70] it was confronted in the provinces with the first large-scale self-consciously 'working-class' movement, Chartism.

The forging of working-class consciousness was apparent before the drafting of the Charter. 'Are the working classes better satisfied with the institutions of the country since the change [of 1832] has taken place?' a witness before a parliamentary committee was asked in 1835. 'I do not think they are,' he replied. 'They viewed the Reform Bill as a pressure calculated to join the middle and upper classes to government and leave them in the hands of the government as a sort of machine to work according to the pleasure of government.'[71] The Charter, drafted in a period of growing economic distress, provided a lever to action, and although middle-class radicals played a major part in its drafting, relations between Chartists and Leaguers often demonstrated straight class antagonism. Mark Hovell quotes, as an example, the story of the relations between the two groups in Sunderland. The Leaguers asked the local Chartist leaders, moderate men who agreed that the Corn Laws were an intolerable evil, to join them in their agitation. They replied that they could not cooperate merely on the merits of the question:

> What is our present relation to you as a section of the middle class? – they went on – It is one of violent opposition. You are the holders of power, participation in which you refuse us; for demanding which you persecute us with a malignity parallelled only by the ruffian Tories. We are therefore surprised that you should ask us to co-operate with you.[72]

This attitude was not shared by all Chartists in all parts of the country – actual class relations, as distinct from theories of class, varied from place to place – but it was strong enough and sufficiently persistent to ensure that Chartists and Leaguers were as violently opposed to each other as both were to the government. Indeed, middle-class claims both of the rhetorical and of the economic kind helped to sharpen working-class consciousness, while fear of independent working-class action, tinged as it was with fear of violence, gave middle-class opinion a new edge. To men like Ebenezer Elliott, the Corn Law Rhymer, who as part of the same programme believed in repeal, suffrage extension, and class conciliation, the 'middle classes' were being assailed on two sides. On the one side was 'the tyranny of the aristocracy': on the other was 'the foolish insolence of the Chartists, which has exasperated into madness the un-natural hatred which the have-somethings bear to the have-nothings'.[73]

Chartist theories of class and expressions of class consciousness have recently been scrutinised.[74] They certainly alarmed those contemporaries who believed that while privation generated discontent, 'the classes into which England is divided are opposed to each other only because they are ignorant of each other'.[75] How was it possible to turn the notion of a dependent 'labouring class' into the notion of a militant 'working class?' as described, for example, by William Lovett and the London Working Men's Association in 1836, before the Marxist terminology of class had been developed?

Adam Smith had often showed considerable sympathy in his writings for the 'workman', but the sympathy was frequently accompanied by statements about the workman's powerlessness. 'Many workmen could not subsist a week, few could subsist a month, and scarce any a year without employment.' Nor did their 'tumultuous combinations' do them much good. 'The interposition of the civil magistrate', 'the superior steadiness of the masters', and 'the necessity which the greater part of the workmen are under of submitting for the sake of the present subsistence' were handicaps to concerted action.[76] In addition, Smith was impressed by the limitations of the effectiveness of political action on the part of the 'labourers':

> Though the interest of the labourer is strictly connected with that of the society, he is incapable either of comprehending that interest, or of understanding its connection with his own. His condition leaves him no time to receive the necessary information, and his education and habits are commonly such as to render him unfit to judge even though he was fully informed. In the public deliberations, therefore, his voice is little heard and less regarded, except upon some particular occasions, when his clamour is animated, set on, and supported by his employers, not for his, but their own particular purposes.[77]

Between 1776 and the time of the drafting of the Charter such a diagnosis, warmed as it was by human sympathy, began to be increasingly unrealistic. The combined effect of the French and industrial revolutions was to direct attention not to the powerlessness of the labourer but to the potential power of the 'working classes', whether hitched to the 'middle classes' or, more ominously, relying on their own leaders. During the early 1830s, when political radicalism was often blended with labour economics in a lively and heady brew, critics of 'working class' claims, like Peter Gaskell, talked of the dangers of the growth of a dual society hopelessly torn apart:

> Since the Steam Engine has concentrated men into particular localities – has drawn together the population into dense masses – and since an imperfect education has enlarged, and to some degree distorted their views, union is become easy and from being so closely packed, simultaneous action is readily excited. The organisation of these [working-class] societies is now so complete that they form an 'imperium in imperio'

of the most obnoxious description ... Labour and Capital are coming into collision – the operative and the master are at issue, and the peace, and well-being of the Kingdom are at stake.[78]

The same case was argued before and after the repeal of the Combination Acts in 1824 and 1825. The Acts had 'set the interests and feelings of two great classes in direct opposition to each other', one critic wrote in 1824, turning the masters into 'petty despots' and the workmen into 'treachorous and rebellious slaves'.[79] Yet ten years after the Acts had been repealed, Henry Tufnell in his extremely interesting study, *The Character, Objects and Effects of Trades Unions* (1834), could express horrified alarm at the ramifications of a secret and hidden system of trade-union authority, based on its own laws with 'no reference to the laws of the land'. Like Gaskell, Tufnell argued that

Where combinations have been most frequent and powerful, a complete separation of feeling seems to have taken place between masters and men. Each party looks upon the other as an enemy, and suspicion and distrust have driven out the mutual sentiments of kindness and goodwill, by which their intercourse was previously marked.[80]

Leaving on one side the merits of Tufnell's assessment of earlier industrial relations,[81] there has been a marked shift of emphasis since *The Wealth of Nations*. The shift was marked even in the far shorter period between the end of the Napoleonic Wars and the Reform Bill crisis. James Mill, who in his *Essay on Government* stated categorically that 'the opinions of that class of the people, who are below the middle rank, are formed, and their minds are directed by that intelligent and virtuous rank, who come the most immediately in contact with them ... to whom they fly for advice and assistance in all their numerous difficulties, upon whom they feel an immediate and daily dependence',[82] was bemoaning in 1831 the spread of 'dangerous doctrines' among 'the common people' which would lead to a 'subversion of civilised society, worse than the overwhelming deluge of Huns and Tartars'. In a letter to Brougham he exclaimed:

Nothing can be conceived more mischievous than the doctrines which have been preached to the common people. The illicit cheap publications, in which the doctrine of the right of the labouring people, who say they are the only producers, to all that is produced, is very generally preached, are superseding the Sunday newspapers and every other channel through which the people might get better information.[83]

A pamphlet published by an 'approved source', the Society for the Diffusion of Useful Knowledge, founded in 1827, warned that such doctrines, apparently 'harmless as abstract propositions', would end in 'maddening passion, drunken frenzy, unappeasable tumult, plunder, fire, and blood'.[84]

While James Mill was finishing off his *Essay on Government*, there had already been published what seems to be one of the first English working-class manifestos to talk straight language of 'class'. *The Gorgon*, published in London in November 1818, set out a series of four objections to an argument which was being frequently employed at that time that 'workmen must be expected to share the difficulties of their employers and the general distress of the times'. The language of the eighteenth and nineteenth centuries overlaps in the statement of their second objections, as it does in much of the socialist literature of the 1820s:

> To abridge the necessary means of subsistence of the working classes, is to degrade, consequently to demoralise them; and when the largest and most valuable portion of any community is thus degraded and demoralised, ages may pass away before society recovers its former character of virtue and happiness.[85]

Their other objections – the last of them related to the lack of political representation – were frequently reiterated by later working-class organisations. What Mill most complained of in 1831 – the spread of the doctrine of the right of the labouring people to the whole produce of labour – still needs a more systematic examination than historians have given it. The story of the development of formal labour economics in the 1820s is relatively well charted,[86] but, despite a number of recent studies, the story of popular social radicalism is as yet only partly explored. The two stories are related, but they are not the same. Cobbett's post-war demand for the restoration of the dignity of labour in a changing society[87] merged with Owen's demand for an end to 'the depreciation of human labour';[88] and theories of radical reform of Parliament and economic cooperation were often seen not as alternative ways to working-class emancipation but as pointers to complementary areas of working-class action. As early as 1826, a speaker in Manchester claimed that 'the purpose of parliamentary reform was to secure to the labourer the fruits of his own labour ... and to every British subject a full participation in all the privileges and advantages of British citizens'.[89] John Doherty and his supporters in industrial Lancashire continued to argue that 'universal suffrage means nothing more than a power given to every man to protect his own labour from being devoured by others' and urged that parliamentary reform would be of little value to the masses of the population unless it was accompanied by social action to guarantee to the workmen 'the whole produce of their labour'.[90] The same views were being canvassed in the London Rotunda in 1831 and 1832 and were often expressed in the pages of the *Poor Man's Guardian*.[91] During the agitation for the Reform Bill the National Union of the Working Classes, founded in 1831, identified political oppression and social injustice:

> Why were the laws not made to protect industry, but property or capital? Because the law-makers were compounded of fund and landholders, possessors of property, and the laws were made to suit their own purposes, being utterly regardless of the sources from which the property arose ... Had the producers of wealth been the makers of laws, would they have left those who made the country rich to perish by starvation?[92]

As far as the leaders and members of the National Union of the Working Classes were concerned – numerically they were extremely small, and on many points they were divided[93] – it did not need disillusionment with the results of the Reform Bill of 1832 to make them distinguish clearly between the interests of the 'middle classes' and the 'working classes'. The distinction was made on economic grounds before 1832. The 'working classes', the argument ran, were victims of the industrial system, yet they constituted a majority in society. They did not receive that to which they were legitimately entitled: the rights of property were the wrongs of the poor.[94] They could only secure their proper place in society, however, by concerted action, what was called in the language of the day – with both economic and political reference – 'union'. History could be employed to support their claims,[95] but the claims could be understood without difficulty in their immediate context, an industrial system founded on 'competition' instead of 'co-operation'. There was an urgent need for 'the elite of the working classes'[96] to communicate their ideas and solutions to the rest. As one popular lecturer on cooperation in Lancashire put it:

> About one third of our working population ... consists of weavers and labourers, whose average earnings do not amount to a sum sufficient to bring up and maintain their families without parochial assistance ... It is to this class of my poor fellow creatures, in particular, that I desire to recommend the system of co-operation, as the only means which at present, seem calculated to diminish the evils under which they live.[97]

Owen might be suspicious of the mixing of his doctrines with those of popular radical reformers[98] and continued to talk of the need to create an ideal class of 'producers' which included both workmen and employers, but the social and political situation was beyond his control. It was not only the National Union of Working Classes which talked in class terms. At the third Co-operative Congress held at the Institution of the Industrious Classes in London in 1832 several speakers described operatives and employers as separate and hostile forces,[99] while in the pages of the *Pioneer*, which first appeared in September 1833, there were many signs of differences of opinion between the editor, James Morrison, and Owen on questions of class. The first number of the *Pioneer* had a 'correct' Owenite editorial,[100] but Morrison soon proclaimed the independence of the 'working class' from the 'middle men'.[101] In one striking passage he declared: 'Trust none who is a grade above our class, and does not back us in the hour of trial ... Orphans we are, and bastards of society'.[102]

In writing the detailed history of working-class movements of the 1830s, culminating in Chartism, it is necessary to separate out different strands.[103] For the purposes of this essay, however, emphasis must be placed on the element of class consciousness which in various forms was common to them all. Bronterre O'Brien, who was identified with three of the main movements – the struggle for Reform in 1831 and 1832, trade unionism, and Chartism – described this element as follows:

> A spirit of combination had grown up among the working classes, of which there has been no example in former times ... The object of it is the sublimest that can be conceived, namely – to establish for the productive classes a complete dominion over the fruits of their own industry ... Reports show that an entire change in society – a change amounting to a complete subversion of the existing 'order of the world' – is contemplated by the working classes. They aspire to be at the top instead of at the bottom of society – or rather that there should be no bottom or top at all.[104]

In the bitter rivalry between Chartists and Leaguers there was class consciousness on both sides, although a section of the Chartists came to the conclusion that they would be able to accomplish nothing without middle-class support, the Leaguers were always compelled to look for working-class allies, and there were other claims on commitment besides the sense of class. Tory traditionalists disliked the language of 'class' from whichever quarter of society it came. Peel, Prime Minister in the critical years of the century, would have nothing to do with it. During the middle years of the century, the language of class was softened as much as social antagonisms themselves, but it burst out again in many different places in the years which led up to the second Reform Bill of 1867.

IV

There were some affinities, on the surface at least, between eighteenth-century views of society and those most frequently canvassed in the 1850s and 1860s. Attention was paid not to the broad contours of class division, but to an almost endless series of social gradations. The quest for individual – or family – status was usually more apparent than the solidarity of class. The role of deference, even in an industrial society, was stressed, and the idea of a 'gentleman', one of the most powerful of mid-Victorian ideas but an extremely complicated one both to define and to disentangle, was scrutinised by novelists as much as by pamphleteers. The case for inequality was as much a part of social orthodoxy as it had been a hundred years before. 'Almost everybody in England has a hard word' for social equality, wrote Matthew Arnold as late as 1878.[105] The language of 'interests' enjoyed a new vogue both in the world of politics and outside. It was perhaps a sign of the times that the Amalgamated Society of Engineers, founded in 1851, did not claim that it was its duty to secure the objects of a 'class' but rather 'to exercise the same control over that in which we have a vested interest, as the physician who holds his diploma, or the author who is protected by his copyright'.[106] The term 'labour interest' figured prominently in political discussion at all levels. A distinction was drawn even by radical politicians between the articulate 'labour interest' and the 'residuum', the great mass of the working-class population. The concept of the 'residuum', indeed, was useful to writers who wished to write off the 'condition of England question' of the 1840s as something dead and done with: it was the passive version of the 'mob'.

Against this background, 'class' came to be thought of as a rather naughty word with unpleasant associations. *The Times* in 1861 remarked that 'the word "class", when employed as an adjective, is too often intended to convey some reproach. We speak of "class prejudices" and "class legislation", and inveigh against the selfishness of class interest.'[107] One of the most influential of the people who inveighed was Herbert Spencer. In a chapter with the significant title 'The Class Bias' he wrote:

> The egoism of individuals leads to an egoism of the class they form; and besides the separate efforts, generates a joint effort to get an undue share of the aggregate proceeds of social activity. The aggressive tendency of each class thus produced has to be balanced by like aggressive tendencies of other classes.[108]

The word 'balance' was one of the key words of the period both in relation to politics and to society.[109]

It is not surprising that during these years three main points were made about 'class' in England. First, England was a country where there was a marked degree of individual mobility, and this made class divisions tolerable. Second, the dividing lines between classes were extremely difficult to draw. Third, there were significant divisions *inside* what were conventionally regarded as classes, and these divisions were often more significant than divisions *between* the classes. Taken together these three points constituted a description rather than an analysis. The description was compared, however, with descriptions of the state of affairs in other countries, the United States or France, for example, or even India.[110] Whereas during the 1840s both middle-class and working-class politicians (and most writers on society) had argued about 'class' in general terms, relating what was happening in England to what was happening in other countries,[111] during the middle years of the century most of the arguments were designed to show that England was a favoured special case.

The 'facts' of individual mobility were stated eloquently and forcefully by Palmerston in his famous speech during the Don Pacifico debate in the House of Commons in 1850:

> We have shown the example of a nation, in which every class in society accepts with cheerfulness the lot which Providence has assigned to it; while at the same time every individual of each class is constantly striving to raise himself in the social scale – not by injustice and wrong, not by violence and illegality, but by preserving good conduct, and by the steady and energetic execution of the moral and intellectual faculties with which his Creator endowed him.[112]

Only two years after the revolutions of 1848 and the waning of Chartism the language of politics was already changing. The values were the same as those described by Beatrice Webb at the beginning of *My Apprenticeship*:

> It was the bounden duty of every citizen to better his social status; to ignore those beneath him, and to aim steadily at the top rung of the ladder. Only by this persistent pursuit by each individual of his own and his family's interest would the highest general level of civilisation be attained.[113]

The rungs of the ladder did not move: it was individuals who were expected to do so. 'Individuals may rise and fall by special excellence or defects', wrote Edward Thring, the famous public school headmaster, 'but the classes cannot change places.'[114]

The metaphor of 'ladders' and 'rungs' proved inadequate for the many writers who wished to emphasise the blurring of class dividing lines in mid-Victorian England. 'Take any class of Englishmen, from the highest to the lowest', wrote the young Edward Dicey in a stimulating essay, 'and it will be found to mix, by imperceptible degrees, with the class below it. Who can say where the upper class ends, or where the middle class begins?'[115] Arnold, who was quick to catch the 'stock notions' of his age, some of which he believed in himself, referred in *Friendship's Garland* to 'the rich diversity of our English life ... the happy blending of classes and character'.[116] Other writers made the most of 'intermediate classes' bridging the chasms of class antagonism: they were said to include a wide range of people from shopkeepers to professional men.

Finally, divisions within classes – the presence of what were sometimes called 'sub-classes' – were stressed. The 'middle classes', which Cobden had struggled to pull together during the 1840s, separated out into diverging elements after 1846, and the plans of the more daring spirits of the Manchester School to carry through a 'middle-class revolution' were never realised.[117] To cross the 'moral and intellectual' gulf between the skilled workers and unskilled, wrote Henry Mayhew, was to reach 'a new level ... among another race'.[118] In some respects, at least, dividing lines seemed to be sharper at the base of the social pyramid than towards the apex.

The political debate which followed the death of Palmerston in 1865 and ended with the passing of the Second Reform Bill two years later led to a revival of interest in the problems and terminology of 'class', the Positivists leading the way. When Professor Beesly, a leading Positivist spokesman, was invited to join the Reform League in 1865, he replied sharply:

> So fast increasing is the divergence between the aims and (apparent) interests of the working class and the classes that have more or less wealth, that one of two things must happen before long – either the latter class will have to modify their present pretensions and adopt an entirely new attitude towards labour, or a vast convulsion will upturn society, in the course of which I would expect, and hope, to see political changes effected of a far more fundamental description than those put forward in your programme.[119]

This letter was written on the day Palmerston died. It was the change in economic circumstances in the 1870s and 1880s, however, and the disturbance of the mid-Victorian social balance which shifted the debate on to a wider front. An understanding of the new phase which was opening during the late Victorian years depends on a thorough examination of the phrase 'working classes' in a context of socialism, and from this point it begins to be impossible to ignore the ideological issues raised by Marx, but until then little discussed in Britain.[120] Yet the word 'class' was used very vaguely even by English Marxists. 'The word class is used in many ways,' wrote Belfont Bax and Harry Quelch in 1909. 'For instance, we speak of the professional class, the clerical class, the artisan class, the labouring class, etc., as well as of the upper and lower classes.'[121]

Whatever else may be said of the new phases, one development is incontrovertible. The language of 'ranks', 'orders', and 'degrees', which had survived the industrial revolution,[122] was finally cast into limbo. The language of class, like the facts of class, remained. So, too, did the new language of 'union' and 'movement'.[123] And so, finally, did the language of 'mass' and 'masses'.

NOTES

1   In its modern sense the word 'industry', used with reference not to a particular human attribute but to a segment of the economy, was itself a new word in the late eighteenth century. See R. Williams, *Culture and Society* (1958), p. xv. Adam Smith was one of the first writers to use the word in this way, although only occasionally. See my analysis of Smith's language in T. Wilson and A.S. Skinner (eds), *The Market Place and the State, Essays in Honour of Adam Smith* (1976), pp. 25-33. The Peel family chose the word 'industria' for its motto in 1792. Smith did not use the word 'class' in the sense discussed in this essay.

2   It was later used by the Methodists to refer to 'class' meetings, a usage which was later borrowed by early nineteenth-century 'Political Protestants' and Chartists.

3   Daniel Defoe, who usually wrote in terms of 'orders', 'ranks' and 'degrees', on a few occasions used 'class' in contexts where he was referring to social classification. See, for instance, *Review*, 14 April 1705, 21 June 1709. Smith also referred (incidentally) to 'classes of people' in his account of 'the three great orders of society' in his *The Wealth of Nations* (1776), Book I, Chapter 11. During the 1790s the word 'class' was applied increasingly to people in phrases like 'the lower class of inhabitants' or 'the inferior class of people'.

4   *Monthly Repository* (1834), p. 320.

5   This article is not concerned with non-British usage. The German division between 'Klasse' and 'Stand' is discussed, *inter alia*, in L. von Wiese, *Gesellschaftliche Stände und Klasse* (1950). For France and Belgium, see two important articles with a good bibliography of books and articles to that date by L. Moulin and Luc Aerts, 'Les classes moyennes, Essai de bibliographie critique d'une définition', in *Revue d'histoire économique et sociale*, vol. XXXII (1954).

6   For one of the most important strands in the defence, see C. Hill, 'The Norman Yoke', in J. Saville (ed.), *Democracy and the Labour Movement* (1954).

7   For an early eighteenth-century criticism of it and an alternative analysis of society, see D. Defoe, *Of Royall Educacion* (written 1728-9).

8   Francis Place complained in the early nineteenth century of the indiscriminate jumbling together of 'the most skilled and the most prudent workmen with the most ignorant and imprudent labourers and paupers' whenever the term 'lower orders' was used. 'The difference is great indeed', he went on, 'and in many cases will scarce admit of comparison.' (*Place Papers*, British Museum, Add. MSS. 27,834, f. 45.)

9   Cp. P. J. Grosley, *A Tour of London*, vol. II (1772): 'The mixture and confusion ... between the nobility and the mercantile part of the nation, is an inexhaustible source of wealth to the state, the nobility having acquired an accession of wealth by marriage, the tradesmen make up for their loss by their eager endeavours to make a fortune, and the gentry conspire to the same end by their efforts to raise such an estate as shall procure a peerage for themselves or their children.' There were many statements of a similar point of view earlier and later, but they were seldom factually based.

10 *Wealth of Nations*, Book IV, Chapter 9.

11 *Political Register*, 14 April 1821.

12 R. Southey, *Sir Thomas More: or Colloquies on the Progress and Prospects of Society* (1829), p. 47.

13 *Political Register, op. cit.*

14 *Sir Thomas More, op. cit.*

15 For the social impact of the change from water-power to steam-power, see G. D. H. Cole, *Studies in Class Structure* (1955), pp. 28-30. Marx, *Capital*, vol. I, Part IV, Chapter 13, quoted A. Redgrave, a factory inspector, who argued that 'the steam-engine is the parent of manufacturing towns'. (Everyman edn, vol. I (1930), p. 398.) See also A. Briggs, *The Power of Steam* (1982).

16 J. Wade, *History of the Middle and Working Classes* (1842 edn), Preface, p. 1.

17 This phrase, which was used by Disraeli, the authors of the *Communist Manifesto*, and many of the novelists and reviewers of the 1840s, was first used by Carlyle. As early as 1829 he wrote in his essay *Signs of the Times* that 'Cash Payment' was becoming the 'sole nexus' between man and man. Later, the shorter term became something of a slogan.

18 See G. D. H. Cole, *Attempts at General Union* (1953).

19 *Political Register*, 27 August 1825.

20 For the history of the term 'masses', see below, pp. 34-54.

21 W. E. Channing, *A Discourse on the Life and Character of Rev. Joseph Tuckerman* (1841), pp. 7-8.

22 *The Condition of the Working Class in England* (trans. W. O. Henderson and W. H. Chaloner, 1958), p. 31.

23 ibid., p. 203.

24   C. Hall, *The Effects of Civilisation on the People in European States* (1805), p. 3.

25   E. P. Thompson's *The Making of the English Working Class* (1963) was recognised as a seminal, if controversial, book from the date of its publication. For a Marxist critique of the three-class picture, see J. Foster, *Class Struggle and the Industrial Revolution* (1974), and for an alternative critique, R. S. Neale, *Class and Ideology in the Nineteenth Century* (1972). R. J. Morris, *Class and Class Consciousness in the Industrial Revolution* (1979), is a careful and perceptive summary of the main issues. See also R. Dahrendorf, *Class and Class Critics in an Industrial Society* (1959).

26   The *Quarterly Review*, which continued to refer to 'attachment' and 'continuity' in many of its articles on the social system even in the second half of the nineteenth century, referred in 1869 (vol. CXXVI, p. 450) to 'lower-middle class', adding hastily, 'We must apologize for using this painful nomenclature, but really there is no choice.'

27   Writers on the national income were among the first to have to consider how best to describe the various sections of the population. 'Political arithmetic' and social classification went together.

28   See G. D. H. Cole, *Socialist Thought, The Forerunners, 1789-1850*, pp. 42-3, for the distinction between *les industriels* and *les oisifs*. The word 'industry' itself had a special significance for St Simon (see his *L'Industrie* (1817)), and there were socialist undertones beneath many of the words derived from it. See the pioneering article by A. E. Bestor, 'The Evolution of the Socialist Vocabulary', in *Journal of the History of Ideas*, vol. IX (1948).

29   Owen constructed visual aids to illustrate Colquhoun's tables, a set of eight cubes exhibiting a 'General View of Society', the working classes being represented at the base by a large cube whilst the apex was formed by a small cube, representing the royal family and the aristocracy. See F. Podmore, *Robert Owen* (1906), pp. 255-6. John Gray's *A Lecture on Human Happiness* (1825) set out the case that labour received only one-fifth of its produce, the rest being appropriated by the 'unproductive' classes.

30   *A Treatise on the Wealth, Power and Resources of the British Empire* (1814). Colquhoun's attempt – in his own words – 'to show how ... New Property ... is distributed among the different Classes of the Community' – had socialist implications which he did not draw out. He believed that poverty was necessary in society, that Malthus's population doctrine was sound, and that improved 'social police' would hold society together. Yet just as Ricardian economics were used to develop a socialist theory of value, so Colquhoun's statistics were used to propound a socialist analysis of distribution.

31   The term is used in a *Quarterly Review* article on Colquhoun, vol. XII (1815).

32   'Address to the Sovereign', printed in *The Crisis*, 4 August 1832.

33   *The Extraordinary Black Book* (1831 edn), pp. 217-18. Colquhoun was

described as 'a bold, but as experience had proved, a very shrewd calculator'. (ibid., p. 216.)

34 See below, p. 237.

35 Report of the Proceedings of the *Birmingham Political Union*, 25 January 1830. The Declaration of the Union drawn up on this occasion claimed that the House of Commons 'in its present state' was 'too far removed in habits, wealth and station, from the wants and interests of the lower and middle classes of the people to have any just views respecting them, or any close identity of feeling with them'. It went on to complain of the over-representation of the 'great aristocratical interests', only nominally counter-balanced by the presence of a few 'rich and retired capitalists'. The National Political Union, founded in London in 1831, also proclaimed as one of its purposes, 'to watch over and promote the interests, and to better the condition of the INDUSTRIOUS AND WORKING CLASSES'. (*Place Papers*, Add. MSS. 27,791, f. 184.)

36 *Birmingham Journal*, 17 January 1836.

37 *Political Register*, 20 April 1822.

38 Letter to Zachary Macaulay, 6 January 1796, quoted by M. G. Jones, *Hannah More* (1952), p. 144. These tracts were regarded as 'antidotes to Tom Paine', 'Burke for Beginners'.

39 Gisborne's *Enquiry* was one of the first publications to use the term 'middle classes'. In 1797 the *Monthly Magazine*, founded by Richard Phillips and John Aikin to 'propagate liberal principles', spoke of 'the middle and industrious classes of society' (p. 397). The phrase 'working classes' seems to have been used for the first time by Robert Owen in 1813 in his *Essays on the Formation of Character*, later reprinted under the more familiar title *A New View of Society*, but it was a descriptive rather than an analytical term ('the poor and working classes of Great Britain and Ireland have been found to exceed 12 millions of persons'). He used the term frequently in letters to the newspapers in 1817 and in 1818 he published *Two Memorials on Behalf of the Working Classes*.

40 *Sketch of a Plan of the General Chamber of Manufacturers of Great Britain* (1785).

41 Smith's general account of the division of the 'annual produce' of land and labour is given at the end of the last chapter (11) of Book I of *The Wealth of Nations*.

42 The *Monthly Repository* (1809), p. 501.

43 ibid. (1813), p. 65.

44 The *Monthly Magazine* (1798), p. 1. It referred to the 'ignorant apathy' of the 'lowest classes'.

45 *The Athenaeum* (1807), p. 124.

46 See R. D. Altick, *The English Common Reader* (Chicago, 1957), p. 41.

47 *An Essay on Government* (ed. E. Barker, 1937), pp. 71-2. The essay was completed in 1820. There is a remarkable and significant contrast between the method and style of Mill's argument and the form of his dogmatic and defiant concluding sentence. 'It is altogether futile with regard to the foundation of good government to say that this or the

other portion of the people, may at this, or the other time, depart from the wisdom of the middle rank. It is enough that the great majority of the people never cease to be guided by that rank; and we may with some confidence, challenge the adversaries of the people to produce a single instance to the contrary in the history of the world.' (ibid. p. 73.)

48 James Mill in the *Westminster Review*, vol. I, October 1824.

49 Engels, *op. cit.*, p. 243.

50 For a novelist's approach to this agitation, see below, vol. II, pp. 80-1.

51 This quotation is given in the *Oxford Dictionary*. In introducing the Reform Bill Lord John Russell talked of changing the House of Commons from 'an assembly of representatives of small classes and particular interests' into 'a body of men who represent the people'.

52 Quoted by N. Gash, *Politics in the Age of Peel* (1953), p. 16.

53 Grey made this remark outside Parliament. See Henry, Earl Grey (ed.), *The Correspondence of the Late Earl Grey with His Majesty King William IV* (1867), vol. I, p. 376.

54 H. Cockburn, *Letters on Affairs of Scotland*, quoted by Gash, *op. cit.*, p. 15.

55 Sir James Graham, *Corn and Currency* (1826), p. 9. Graham appealed to the landed proprietors to unite as 'the manufacturing and commercial body' had done, and to frame their actions in accordance with 'public opinion' and 'the interest of the community'.

56 It also recalls a passage in Defoe's *Robinson Crusoe* – 'Mine was the middle state or what might be called the upper station of low life . . . not exposed to the Labour and sufferings of the Mechanick part of Mankind, and not embarrassed with the Pride, Luxury, Ambition and Envy of the Upper Part of Mankind.'

57 William Mackinnon was a Member of Parliament almost continuously from 1830 to 1865. His book on public opinion was rewritten in 1846 as a *History of Civilisation*.

58 W. Mackinnon, *On the Rise, Progress, and Present State of Public Opinion* (1828), pp. 6-7.

59 ibid., p. 10.

60 Mackinnon, *op. cit.*, p. 2.

61 For the background of the *Catechism* and its importance in the struggle for repeal, see L. G. Johnson, *General T. Perronet Thompson* (1957), Chapter 8, and D. G. Barnes, *A History of the English Corn Laws* (1930), pp. 210-12.

62 J. Morley, *The Life of Richard Cobden* (1903 edn), vol. I, p. 249.

63 ibid., pp. 390-7. In his reply Peel was careful to avoid all reference to 'class'.

64 Disraeli also referred to 'classes'. When Coningsby went to Manchester, 'the great Metropolis of Labour', he 'perceived that [industrial] wealth was rapidly developing classes whose power was imperfectly recognized in the constitutional scheme, and whose duties in the social system seemed altogether omitted' (Book IV, Chapter 2). In conversing with Milbank he had already 'heard for the first time of influential classes in the country, who were not noble, and yet were

determined to acquire power' (Book II, Chapter 6). He referred to 'the various classes of this country [being] arrayed against each other' (Book IV, Chapter 12). For Disraeli's use of the term 'masses', see below, pp. 34-5.

65 H. Dunckley, *The Charter of the Nations* (1854), p. 25.

66 A phrase of Cobden, quoted in ibid., p. 145.

67 The early advocates of free trade in 1815 'took the untenable and unpopular ground that it was necessary to have cheap bread in order to reduce the English vote of wages to the continental level, and so long as they persisted in this blunder, the cause of free trade made little progress'. (W. Cooke Taylor, *The Life and Times of Sir Robert Peel* (1842), p. 111.)

68 Morley, *op. cit.*, vol. I, p. 180.

69 ibid., vol. I, p. 182.

70 A phrase used in a letter from a repealer in Carlisle, quoted by N. McCord, *The Anti-Corn Law League* (1958), p. 97. There was strong working-class support in Carlisle for Julian Harney, who preached a very different gospel to that of the League. See A. R. Schoyen, *The Chartist Challenge* (1958), p. 72.

71 Quoted by Thompson, *op. cit.*, p. 832.

72 Quoted by M. Hovell, *The Chartist Movement* (1925 edn), pp. 215-16.

73 Quoted by Johnson, *op. cit.*, p. 233. For Elliott, see below, vol. II, pp. 36-49.

74 See Schoyen, *op. cit.*; A. Briggs (ed.), *Chartist Studies* (1959), Chapter 9.

75 *Westminster Review*, vol. 38 (1842).

76 *Wealth of Nations*, Book I, Chapter 8.

77 ibid., Book I, Chapter 9.

78 Gaskell to Lord Melbourne, 16 April 1834 (Home Office Papers 40/32). Gaskell, whose book *The Manufacturing Population of England* (1833) was freely used by Engels, had a diametrically opposed view of the correct answer to the 'social problem'.

79 *Edinburgh Review*, vol. 39 (1823).

80 H. Tufnell, *The Character, Objects and Effects of Trades Unions* (1834), pp. 2, 97.

81 Gaskell shared Tufnell's tendency to idealise social relations before the industrial revolution. 'The distinctions of rank, which are the safest guarantees for the performance of the relative duties of classes, were at this time in full force' (*op. cit.*, p. 20). Engels, who did not make use of this sentence, borrowed direct from Gaskell in the 'Historical Introduction' to his own book, and thereby overrated 'patriarchal relationships' and 'idyllic simplicity'. He broke sharply with Gaskell, however, in his conclusion. Workers before the rise of steam power 'knew nothing of the great events that were taking place in the outside world .... The Industrial Revolution ... had forced the workers to think for themselves and to demand a fuller life in human society' (*op. cit.*, p. 12).

82 *Essay on Government*, p. 72. He added the words 'to whom their children look up as models for their honour to adopt'.

83 Quoted by A. Bain, *James Mill* (1882), p. 365.

84 'The Rights of Industry' (1831), *passim.*

85 This statement in *The Gorgon* (28 November 1818) is printed in full in G. D. H. Cole and A. W. Filson, *British Working-Class Movements, Select Documents, 1789-1875* (1951), p. 159.

86 The road leads back before Adam Smith, but Ricardo's *Principles of Economics* (1817) was the greatest single milestone. Smith used the phrase 'the whole produce of labour' (Book I, Chapter 8), but claimed that the labourer had only been able to secure it in a primitive society and economy, 'the original state of things'. Ricardo (with important qualifications) based his general theory of value on 'the quantity of labour realised in commodities'. William Thompson (*An Inquiry into the Principles of the Distribution of Wealth, most Conducive to Human Happiness* (1824)) and Thomas Hodgskin (*Labour Defended* (1825)) anticipated Marx in using the theory as part of a socialist analysis.

87 *Political Register*, 2 November 1816. 'The real strength and all the resources of a country, ever have sprung and ever must spring, from the *labour* of its people.'

88 See 'Labour, the Source of All Value', in *A Report to the County of Lanark* (1820).

89 *Wheeler's Manchester Chronicle*, 28 October 1826.

90 Home Office 52/18. A letter from a Preston correspondent to the Home Secretary encloses a pamphlet, *A Letter from one of the 3730 Electors of Preston to his Fellow Countrymen.* See also Doherty's pamphlet, *A Letter to the Members of the National Association for the Protection of Labour* (1831).

91 e.g. 16 February 1833. 'Universal suffrage would give the power to those who produce the wealth to enjoy it.'

92 ibid., 24 December 1831.

93 For the division between 'Huntites' and 'Owenites', see ibid., 4 February 1832.

94 ibid., 26 January 1833.

95 The old Saxon/Norman theme (see above, p. 4, n. 6, and below vol. II, pp. 215ff.) was still raised. In a London debate in 1833 on the notion that 'until the laws of property are properly discussed, explored and understood by the producers of all property the wretched condition of the working classes can never be improved', more than one spectator referred to 'the misappropriation' of the Norman Conquest and its aftermath (ibid., 18 May 1833).

96 This phrase, which has often been used with reference to the London Working Men's Association, was employed in the *Poor Man's Guardian.* Describing the fourth Co-operative Congress, the newspaper reporter said that it was comprised of 'plain but intelligent workmen ... the very élite of the working classes' (ibid., 19 October 1833).

97 F. Baker, *First Lecture on Co-operation* (1830), p. 2.

98 He sharply condemned 'a party of Owenites of the Rotunda' as 'desperadoes' and said that he had never been to the London Rotunda (*Union*, 17 December 1831).

99 See *The Crisis*, 28 April 1832.

100 'The Union [the Grand National Consolidated Trade Union] is a well-organised body of working men, bound together by wise and discreet laws, and by one common interest. Its object is to affect the general amelioration of the producers of wealth, and the welfare of the whole community. Its members do not desire to be at war with any class, neither will they suffer any class to usurp their rights.' (*Pioneer*, 7 September 1833.)

101 ibid., 21 June 1834. 'The capitalist', he wrote (21 December 1833), 'merely as a property man, has no power at all, and labour . . . regulated by intelligence, will in a very few years, be the only existent power in this and in all highly civilised countries.'

102 ibid., 22 March 1834.

103 See for the various strands, *Chartist Studies*, esp. Chapter 1, 'The Local Background of Chartism'. It is important to note that at the local level many working-class activists joined several movements, caring less about doctrinal differences than leaders or writers.

104 *Poor Man's Guardian*, 19 October 1833.

105 Essay on 'Equality', in *Mixed Essays* (1878), p. 49.

106 Quoted in J. B. Jeffreys (ed.), *Labour's Formative Years* (1948), p. 30.

107 *The Times*, 10 August 1861.

108 H. Spencer, *Principles of Sociology* (1873), p. 242.

109 See W. L. Burn, *The Age of Equipoise* (1964).

110 See, for instance, Walter Bagehot's essays on Sterne and Thackeray, reprinted in *Literary Studies* (1873), where he distinguished between social systems founded upon caste and those founded upon equality. He argued that the English system of 'removable inequalities' was preferable to both.

111 The leaders of the London Working Men's Association, for example, had clearly stated in addresses to working men in America, Belgium and Poland that there were common interests among 'the productive millions' in all parts of the world and that it was 'our ignorance of society and of government – our prejudices, our disunion and distrust' which was one of the biggest obstacles to the dissolution of the 'unholy compact of despotism'. See W. Lovett, *Life and Struggles* (1876), p. 152.

112 Quoted in J. Joll (ed.), *Britain and Europe, Pitt to Churchill* (1950), pp. 125-5.

113 B. Webb, *My Apprenticeship* (1950 edn), p. 13.

114 Rev. E. Thring, *Education and School* (1864), p. 5.

115 *Essays on Reform* (1867), p. 74. Dicey added that 'in criticising a theory of class representation, the words "classes", "orders", or "interests", must be constantly employed'. Such employment, in his view, gave an undue advantage to the view criticised, for 'the very basis on which this view rests is not firm enough to support the conclusions grounded upon it'. For a parallel question of a later date about the social position of 'working men', see C. Booth, *Life and Labour of the People, East London* (1889), p. 99.

116 *Friendship's Garland* (1897 edn), pp. 49-50. One aspect of the blending,

which deserves an essay to itself, was the association of the industrial and agricultural 'interests'. 'Protection', wrote a shrewd observer, Bernard Cracroft, 'was the only wall of separation between land and trade. That wall removed, the material interests of the two classes have become and tend to become every day more indissolubly connected and inseparably blended.' (*Essays on Reform*, p. 110.) In other words, a two-class model was more convincing than a three-class one.

117   Cobden himself came to believe in the 1860s that 'feudalism is every day more and more in the ascendant in political and social life .... Manufacturers and merchants as a rule seem only to desire riches that they may be enabled to prostitute themselves at the feet of feudalism.'

(Quoted by Morley, *op. cit.* vol. I, Chapter 25.) He was very critical of the alliance of the industrial and the landed 'interest', and on one occasion in 1861 wrote to a friend, 'I wonder the working people are so quiet under the taunts and insults offered to them. Have they no Spartacus among them to head a revolt of the slave class against their political tormentors?' (quoted ibid., vol. II, Chapter 30).

118   H. Mayhew, *London Labour and the London Poor*, vol. I (1862), pp. 6-7. Cp. T. Wright, *Our New Masters* (1873): 'Between the artisan and the unskilled a gulf is fixed. While the former resents the spirit in which he believes the followers of "genteel occupations" look down upon him, he in his turn looks down upon the labourers' (p. 5).

119   E. S. Beesly to George Howell, 18 October 1865, quoted by Royden Harrison in A. Briggs and J. Saville (eds), *Essays in Labour History* (1960), p. 220.

120   Marx's view of the 'sum total of the relations of production' provides 'the real foundation on which rise legal and political super-structures and to which correspond definite forms of social consciousness' (Preface to *Zur Politik der Politisches Ökonomie* (1859)). He distinguished, however, between the major classes of industrial society and intermediate classes. The *Communist Manifesto* of 1848 had declared boldly that all previous history was the history of 'class struggle'.

121   E. Belfont Bax and H. Quelch, *A New Catechism of Socialism* (1909), pp. 7-8. For a recent account of the twentieth-century story, see B. Waites, 'The Language and Imagery of "Class" in early Twentieth-century England', in *Literature and History*, no. 4 (1976).

122   Traditionalists employed the old language in some of the mid-century debates about education, e.g. P. Peace, *An Address on the Improvement of the Condition of the Labouring Poor* (Shaftesbury, 1852), p. 15. 'Children must be instructed according to their different ranks and the station they will probably fill in the graduated scale of society.' A similar thought was expressed quite differently by Sir Charles Adderley in 1874. 'The educating by the artificial stimulus of large public expenditure, a particular class, out of instead of in the condition of life in which they naturally fill an important part of the community, must

upset the social equilibrium.' (*A Few Thoughts on National Education and Punishment,* p. 11.)

123   For 'movement', see my preface to A. Briggs and J. Saville (eds.), *Essays in Labour History,* 1886-1923 (1971), pp. 3-7.

2 The Language of 'Mass' and 'Masses' in Nineteenth-Century England

Out of the crucible of early industrialisation in England there eventually emerged not only a new language of social 'class', which had power both to express and to accelerate new ways of thinking and feeling about group consciousness and action, but a new language of 'masses'. Both languages have survived into the late twentieth century, with the latter sometimes supplanting the former and raising interesting and important questions of ideology in the process.

This article is concerned with origins and early development rather than with later usage, although it suggests first, that there are anticipations of later usage in the mid-nineteenth century and second, that our views of nineteenth-century development are often coloured by twentieth-century perceptions. 'Mass' and 'masses' were not completely new terms in 1800, but as late as 1837 Tom Moore could still refer not directly to 'the masses' but rather to '"the masses" as they are called'.[1] The quotation marks around the word 'masses' (though they had never been thought necessary around the word 'mass') did not completely disappear until the last decades of the century.

One of the most remarkable early nineteenth-century references to the term 'masses' within quotation marks – a passage from the Disraeli, written in 'Carlylese' – suggested that the term, which he disliked as much as the term 'the People', had only just been invented by 'Papineau writers and orators'. 'Who can resist the Masses? Mighty Masses, mighty mysterious?', Disraeli asked.

> Papineau writers out of Parliament concoct articles in reviews, specially in Sunday journals, about the Masses; would have no tax on pen, ink, or paper, or be supplied by the government *gratis*, that the Masses may read and believe their lucubrations, which all others do most heartily resist.

It was remarkable in the light of what was to come later that this early reference pointed to Canada. There were to be many cross-glimpses during the nineteenth century across the Atlantic to the United States and some across the seas to Australia when writers and politicians complained of the power of 'the masses', but it was not until the twentieth century when 'mass media' were under scrutiny that Canada was to produce the communications prophets Innis and McLuhan.

Disraeli on this early occasion was referring to Papineau, the leader of a Canadian 'reform party' which had been associated with the rebellion of 1837, and he feared contagion. Even his language had a touch of McLuhan about it.

> What if said Papineau orators and writers by some mischance of a *lapsus linguae* ... do but omit the initial letter of that name, wherewith they have defined, and in a manner baptized, their countrymen? And may not the next stage come even to this?
>
> | First | Public |
> | Second | People |
> | Third | Masses |
> | Fourth | Asses |
>
> O Richard! *O Mon Roi!* O England! O my country! Shall I live even to see this?'[2]

By the end of the nineteenth century, Englishmen had lived through many different 'stages' of political, economic and social evolution, and orators and writers were using the terms 'mass' and 'masses' far more than they had done during the 1830s. They were backed, too, by changing market forces, reflected in the rise of disposable incomes, the production of 'branded' goods, the growth of advertising, and the beginnings of 'mass entertainment'.[3] The 'masses' had become a target, and it could be stated in 1897, however misleadingly – before the term 'mass advertising' came into use – that 'the hoardings ... act as a pretty safe index to the taste of the masses'.[4] Although twentieth-century terms like 'mass entertainment' (or for that matter 'mass production' and 'mass distribution') were also not yet in use, men like William Lever or Alfred Harmsworth knew what they implied and built their growing enterprises on an appeal to 'the millions'.[5] There were occasional customers or readers, moreover, who knew exactly what was happening. Thus, a *Tit-Bits* reader in 1897 claimed that while 'the classes take in the daily newspapers ... the masses prefer to take in the weekly supplements, where the week's news is served up with a liberal seasoning of anecdotes, extracts from books, with instalments of one or two serial stories thrown in.'[6]

Meanwhile, the political uses of the term 'masses' were pointing not to manipulation but to militancy. When Thomas Kirkup noted in 1887 'a growing spirit of righteous discontent with our social and economic arrangements' among 'the mass of serious and thinking men',[7] the term 'masses' was already in widespread use in socialist circles. William Morris thought of himself and his comrades as

'instructors of the masses',[8] although he used the term rather
sparingly, and a little later Tom Mann set about arousing 'the inert
mass of workers with the old religious fervour'.[9]

It became possible by the early twentieth century to summarise
history in 'mass' terms, relating it to biological evolution.[10] 'The
conflicts and movements that make history', J. R. MacDonald wrote
in 1911, 'have been the conflicts and movements of masses and
organisations.' 'The colossal historical figure has been the man
endowed with the capacity to gather up in himself the life of his
time.'[11]

To try to trace the changing way in which the words 'mass' and
'masses' were used in the nineteenth century is no more of an academic
exercise than my earlier attempt to trace the language of 'class', for
developments in social nomenclature and vocabulary usually reflect
basic changes not only in men's ways of viewing society but in society
itself. Aspects of nineteenth-century history can be illuminated in the
process, not least developments in both political and in economic
systems. There is an added interest, however, in such an attempt in
that the language of 'mass' and 'masses', then rudimentary, has
displayed extraordinary vitality in the late twentieth century, com-
plemented as it is by the language of élites.[12] 'Orders', 'ranks' and
'degrees' have long seemed to belong to the past. 'Mass' concepts,
however, are felt to belong to the future, to 'post-industrial' as much
as to 'industrial' societies. The term 'mass society' is used at least as
much as the term 'class society', although the *Oxford Dictionary* cites
a date as recent as 1948 for its first recorded use – T.S. Eliot's *Notes
Towards a Definition of Culture*.[13]

I

In the early nineteenth century the idea of 'the mass' was related both
to number and to scale and to 'massing', the bringing together of
people in towns or in factories. 'The rapid progress of our manufactures and commerce', wrote a reviewer in 1833, 'has accumulated
great masses of population, in which society has assumed new relations
among its several classes.'[14] This review is interesting in that it
registers the confluence of different streams of language. 'The various
orders of society are mutually dependent,' the reviewer began. 'Their
interests are interwoven with a complexity which cannot be un-
ravelled; and natural connexions tend to diffuse throughout the mass
the happiness or misery suffered by any particular portion.'[15]

Already the words 'mass' and 'masses' were being treated as more
than numerical aggregates.[16] Like the words 'multitude' and 'mob',

which preceded them, they already had connotations of value. Just as the 'multitude' could be conceived of either as 'a many-headed monster' or as a source of popular strength,[17] so the terms 'mass' and 'multitude' and 'masses' could carry with them a sense either of fear (and mystery) or of power. Disraeli was not always thinking of Papineau when he used the term, and he could curdle the imagination of his readers as thrillingly as Papineau when he wrote of 'the mighty mysterious masses of the swollen towns'.[18] Like Carlyle, who also expressed sympathy towards 'the miserable millions ... fermenting into unmeasured masses of failure', 'the dumb millions born to toil',[19] he appreciated that they could be stirred.[20] 'The way to move great masses of men is to show that you yourself are moved,' Hazlitt had written in 1825.[21] But there was more than one way. 'Men who discern in the misery of the toiling complaining millions not misery, but only a raw-material which can be wrought upon, and traded in, for one's own poor hide-bound theories and egoisms', Carlyle claimed, were 'men of the questionable species.' They were demagogues 'to whom millions of living fellow-creatures with beating hearts in their bosoms, beating, suffering, hoping' were 'masses' – and he used quotation marks – 'mere "explosive masses for blowing down Bastilles with", for voting at hustings for *us*'.[22]

For Carlyle, as for Disraeli, demagogues were manipulators. Parents, teachers, supervisors, leaders, deserved 'obedience': they were part of a hierarchy, and *they* did not think in terms of 'masses'. Demagogues did. This argument was related first to Carlyle's profound interest in the French Revolution and in the *'sans culottism'* which he saw at the heart of it and, second, to his concern about *laissez-faire* society in England, which, as he conceived it, had been created by a parallel English industrial revolution. 'The people' needed proper 'governance'. 'How an Aristocracy, in these present times and circumstances could, if never so well despised, set about governing the Under Class. What they should do, endeavour or attempt to do? That is the question of questions.'[23]

Carlyle knew how to pose, but not how to answer it. Others believed that the answer could only be found in 'the masses' themselves. 'The spark of patriotism runs with electric until the whole mass vibrates in unison swiftness from pulse to pulse,' the Radical *Black Dwarf* exclaimed in what reads like late nineteenth-century language in 1819. 'Then, despots, tremble for the hour of retribution is at hand.'[24] In 1831 during the struggle for the Reform Act the more conservative *Manchester Guardian* could pin its faith not in revolution, but in reform, with a new electorate consisting of 'the great mass of the property, the knowledge, the moral energy and the respectability of the country'. A writer in the same issue, however, was aware

of the contrast between political hopes and economic facts and spoke
of 'the great mass of the lower classes' being obliged 'by the necessity
of earning a subsistence to submit to a daily and protracted toil'.[25]
Such contrasts were further sharpened after the passing of the Reform
Bill and during the political economic crises of the late 1830s and
1840s, when the language of 'class' was sharpened. 'What is the
prevailing cry of the Chartists and Universal Suffrage men? ... That
they have *not obtained the fruits of Reform.*'[26] Yet it was an apologist of
Peelite policy and of the new industrial system, W. Cooke Taylor, who
held that one day 'the masses' must 'like the slow-rising and gradual
swelling of an ocean ... bear all the elements of society aloft upon their
bosom'.[27]

One of the most interesting pieces of early writing on 'the
masses' – and one which exposes some of the difficulties in handling
the concept – is a remarkable early essay by John Stuart Mill, first
published in 1836.[28] As 'civilization' advances, Mill argued, 'power'
passes more and more from individuals, and small knots of individuals,
to 'masses'. Indeed, it is 'a law of human affairs' – and of 'progress' –
that in the process 'the importance of the masses becomes constantly
greater, that of individuals less'. Within the masses Mill included both
'a middle class' and 'operative classes', each benefiting – through
education and property – from the advance of 'civilization'. Like his
father before him, he did not suggest any possible conflict of interest
between them, and his conclusion – though he quoted de Tocqueville – was optimistic.[29] 'When the masses become powerful, an individual, or a small band of individuals, can accomplish nothing considerable except by influencing the masses.' He urged those 'who
called themselves Conservatives' to consider carefully 'whether, when
the chief power in society is passing into the hands of the masses, they
really think it possible to prevent the masses from making that power
predominant as well in the governing as elsewhere'.

Mill's main doubts about the future concerned not politics but
culture, and he got near to anticipating not only most of the arguments which he was to advance twenty years later in *On Liberty* but to
the twentieth-century arguments of David Riesman and even of
Ortega y Gasset.[30] With the rise of 'the masses', the individual got so
'lost in the crowd' – he repeated this phrase after a page or two and he
used it again in *On Liberty*[31] – that he was in peril of losing his
individuality. 'When the opinions of masses of merely average men are
everywhere become or becoming the dominant power', he wrote in *On
Liberty*, 'exceptional individuals, instead of being deterred, should be
encouraged in acting differently from the mass.' The 'danger' which
threatened 'human nature' was not 'the excess but the deficiency of
personal impulses and preferences'.[32]

Accusations have been made against Mill that he generalised too remotely and bookishly about 'social context',[33] and it is certainly remarkable how close to each other Mill's judgements on the 1830s and 1850s were, given the marked social, political and cultural differences between the two decades. Yet the judgements had a prophetic flavour to them. Already, indeed, the young Mill was discerning during the 1830s the shapes of problems concerning what came to be called in the twentieth century 'mass advertising' and 'public relations'. As people ceased to know everybody, he maintained, 'quackery' and 'puffing' became more commonplace and corrupting. He pointed too to what in the twentieth century were to become thought of as problems of 'mass culture'. 'This is a reading age; precisely because it is so reading an age, any book which is the result of profound meditation is, perhaps, less likely to be duly and profitably read than at a former period.' Similar points were to be taken up by Matthew Arnold in *Culture and Anarchy* in 1869, although his philosophical and cultural approach was different from that of Mill, as was the political context in which he was writing.[34] 'Our society is probably destined to become more democratic', Arnold wrote in 1861, going on to ask 'Who or what will give a high tone to the nation then?'[35] 'The question is not about individuals', he went on. 'The question is about the common bulk of mankind, persons without extraordinary gifts or exceptional energy.'[36]

Mill had ended his 1836 essay with a provocative but bracing appeal for individualism. 'The main thing which social change can do . . . – and it is what the progress of democracy is insensibly but certainly accomplishing – is gradually to put an end to every kind of unearned distinction, and let the only road open to honour and ascendancy be that of personal qualities.' This was a not dissimilar message to that of Samuel Smiles, whose *Self Help* appeared in the same year as *On Liberty*. Smiles summarised the essence of his message most succinctly not in 1859 but in 1880, however, on the eve of a socialist upthrust:

> Men cannot be raised in masses as the mountains were in the early geological states of the world. They must be dealt with as units; for it is only through the elevation of individuals that the elevation of the masses can effectively be secured.[37]

By then, Mill had been dead for seven years. His chapters on 'socialism', however, written in 1869, had only just been published for the first time. They recognised more explicitly than Mill had ever done before that distinctive 'working-class' claims were being and would increasingly be put forward – and resisted – in a way which would transform politics. Mill no longer used the word 'mass' or implied an

identity of interest. 'The classes, which the system of society makes
subordinate, have little reason to put faith in any of the maxims which
the same system of society may have established as principles.'[38]
Already in revisions of his *Political Economy*, first published in 1848,
he had asked whether under 'communism' there would be 'any asylum
left for individuality of character', and whether 'public opinion would
not be a tyrannical yoke?'[39]

II

Before turning to the development of a socialist or communist
vocabulary of 'mass' and 'masses', it is necessary to consider more fully
the middle years of the nineteenth century, when the ideas of 'mass'
and 'masses' were related not only to arguments about individualism
and individuality but to arguments about 'brains and numbers', what
we would now call the role of élites.[40] 'The extreme advanced party is
likely for the future to have on its side a great portion of the most
highly cultivated intellect in the nation', wrote John Morley in 1867,
'and the contest will be between brains and numbers on the one side,
and wealth, rank, vested interest, possession in short, on the other.'[41]

The issue of franchise reform stimulated intellectual discussion of
such subjects between 1865 and 1874, but the discussion did not start
or end there. It ranged widely over the long period of history since the
'dual revolutions', political and industrial, in France and in England in
the late eighteenth century – with occasional references back to the
ancient world and over countries as different from each other and as
widely separated as the United States, Australia and Germany. Thus,
Morley related his speculations to those of Burke and de Maistre,[42]
while in his notebooks for 1868 Arnold quoted a letter of Baron
Bunsen, written in 1815, 'it is too true that our own class, the guild of
the studious, does too little with the object of working upon the
nation'.[43]

Both the 'nation' and 'humanity' had their disciples during the mid-
Victorian years. Matthew Arnold, like Mazzini, drew attention to
'the fermenting mind of the Nation'[44], and the Positivists, 'the party
of Humanity', with Beesly at the fore, looked to the 'working classes',
what Frederic Harrison, one of the most active English followers of
Comte called 'the horny handed millions'.[45] On his first visit to the
industrial north Harrison was awed rather than frightened by 'the
enormous weight, mass and power of the manufacturing districts'.[46]
'The working class is the only class which (to use a paradox) is not a
class,' he generalised. 'It is the nation.'[47]

It was not only the Positivists who shared this conviction: it runs through many of the essays written for the remarkable volume of 1867, *Essays on Reform*,[48] many of them inspired by a deep distaste for the speeches and writings of the most intellectually brilliant of the anti-reformers, Robert Lowe. And once reform had been accomplished – the Second Reform Act of 1867 – John Morley could write with delight of the transfer of power 'from a class to the nation'.[49] For Morley, as for several of the essayists, 'class' and 'nation' (they did not use the term 'masses') were in opposition. Yet 'classes' were not conceived of in Marxist or proto-Marxist terms. 'What is a "class"?', G.C. Brodrick, the first of the essayists asked, 'but a purely artificial aggregate, which may consist of hundreds, thousands or millions, according to the fancy or designer of its framer?'[50] The 'educated classes' might ally themselves with 'the masses' serving as vanguards or élites, but the 'privileged classes' would inevitably stand in the way.[51]

This was a way of viewing society which reached its classic climax in a famous Gladstone speech of 1886 when he told a Liverpool crowd that 'all the world over' he would 'back the masses against the classes'.[52] Already by 1870, however, Gladstone's future biographer, Morley, looked forward to a day 'when all this talk about classes shall be at an end and when every citizen shall be able to rise to the conception of a national life'. Meanwhile, he insisted, 'in the multitude you have the only body whose real interests can never, like those of special classes and minor orders [note the linking], become anti-social'.[53]

This view, strongly opposed by Lowe, lost some of its point for educated 'liberal' sympathisers with the 'masses' when the Conservative Party, not the Liberal Party, won the general election of 1874. It seemed then, indeed, however justly, that the strongest 'mass' element in the 'masses' – what John Bright had called 'the residuum'[54] – was more willing to respond to bribes than arguments. The demand for popular education, so eloquently advanced by Morley, was as urgent for him as it was for Lowe. Disraeli, of course, saw things differently, believing that the attraction of his anti-egalitarian philosophy of life saved civilised society from being reduced 'to human flocks and herds'.[55] Meanwhile, Walter Bagehot, who had maintained in 1867 that 'the mass of uneducated men' could not be expected to 'choose' their rulers, put his trust not in philosophies of life but in working men's continuing 'deference'. 'If you look at the mass of the constituencies, you will see that they are not very interesting people.' 'The mass of the people yield obedience to a select few.'[56]

Such assessments were based partly on observation, partly on speculation. Both the observation and the speculation changed, as Lowe predicted that they would, by the end of the century.[57] The further extension of the franchise in 1884 guaranteed that the new electorate would be 'a great seething and swaying mass'.[58] It was at the noisiest during the last years of the century, when 'mass meetings' – and much 'mass entertainment' – turned jingoistic, provoking anti-imperialist Liberals to complain bitterly of a decline in political behaviour.[59] This was not surprisingly the decade of Gustave Le Bon, who could state categorically in 1895 that 'the destinies of nations are elaborated at present at the heart of the masses, and no longer in the councils of princes'.[60]

Already within two years of the passing of the 1884 Reform Act, Salisbury, who had been opposed to the 1867 Act, was writing to Lord Randolph Churchill, a very different kind of Conservative, that 'while the "classes and the dependants of class" are the strongest ingredients in our social composition . . . we have so to conduct our legislation that we shall give some satisfaction to both classes and masses.'[61] This was explicit if private. For the Liberals there was nothing private in acknowledging the need to 'blend' the traditions of 'the older Liberalism' with 'the new aspirations of the labouring masses out of which the party of the future must spring'.[62]

While statistically-minded political economists were noting with satisfaction a continued material improvement in the position of 'the masses',[63] Liberal politicans were drawn inevitably into the politics of poverty. An active minority of them held that they had a special duty to deal with matters affecting food, health, housing and amusement of the working classes, 'the mass of the citizenry',[64] although it still would be exaggerated to say, as it was said in 1891, that 'the whole theory of modern Liberals is that the State is to take in hand the control of the masses'.[65] There were competing theories about the actual and desirable relationship between the individual and the state, not all of them expressed in 'mass terms', when once the rich and long legacy of 'liberal individualism' began to be thoroughly re-examined.

A few progressive (and realistic) Liberals, like J.A. Hobson, denied that mass appeals to the working classes represented any transcendence of class on the part of the Liberal Party. 'The labour movement', Hobson insisted at the end of the century, 'even in its widest significance is still a class movement.' It had to be considered, he went on, both as a sectional interest, the biggest of such interests, and as 'the largest form of individualism'.[66] Hobson's views are always stimulating, whether he was writing about the psychology of mass meetings during the Boer War, or about the vested interests which he believed inspired it.

III

The labour movement had certainly been transformed between 1880 and the end of the century. The socialist upthrust of the 1880s began with the revolt of a few, the 'pioneers', against the presuppositions and conventions, economic, political and otherwise, of mid-Victorian England. As the decade went by, however, large numbers of trade unionists and unemployed workers were drawn into what was soon described as 'the movement'. There was a strong sense of threat in the air and the language of politics was often the language of threat:

> A million of starving people, with another million on the verge of starvation, represent a potential of destructive force to measure which no dynometer has yet been made, but which will, if suddenly liberated, assuredly and absolutely destroy every vestige of nineteenth-century civilization so-called.[67]

Economic forces and a sequence of unprecedented political events, culminating in the Liberal split of 1886, were in the background. Yet once again the perspectives were large. Socialists and anti-socialists alike scanned the centuries. William Morris and Belfont Bax's *Socialism: its Growth and Outcome* (1893) began with 'ancient society' and ended with an appendix on the ancient city, Greek, Roman and Hebrew. It did not touch, however, on the language of social thought (of analysis or threat) in the ancient world which provided a starting point for many nineteenth-century thinkers.

A sense of identification of the 'mass' or 'masses' with the 'working class' had never been entirely absent at the grass-roots level during the middle years of the century, when there was often a wide gap between social practice and social thought. Two of the most remarkable examples of the mid-century sense of identification have been noted by G.D.H. Cole and A.W. Filson. Faced with what it called 'the mass of factory tyranny', *The People's Paper* wrote in 1852 of the continuation of 'the social war'.[68] Two years later, a 'Labour Parliament' in Manchester set out to organise what it called 'The Mass Movement'.[69] Yet, in general, throughout the 1850s and early 1860s 'the masses' proved 'singularly unwilling to move'. As the *National Review* put it in 1863, 'if not contented they did not feel that they were wilfully injured'. Yet already there was a sense that the proletariat was the majority, and although most English socialists were to put their trust in the ballot box rather than in revolution, revolutionaries and non-revolutionaries alike realised in the 1880s and 1890s that they would have to turn to the 'masses' in the social struggle.[70] In the social context of the age not all of them found their own identification with the 'masses' easy,[71] but in the process of mobilisation enough working-class socialists emerged to speak not on behalf of but as 'members' of 'the masses'.

It is interesting to trace the language of 'mass' and 'masses' in the two early socialist journals *Justice* (1884-) organ of the Social Democrats, and *Commonweal* (1885-), organ of the Socialist League. The first issue of the latter – a monthly until April 1886 – referred to the 'mass of workers' (as did the fifteenth, eighteenth and twentieth) and the second to 'the great masses of working people' and 'the working masses of the town'.[72] The eighth mentioned 'the masses of people out of work'.[73] *Commonweal* recognised, like *Justice*, that 'the masses' had to be awakened or activated.[74] Otherwise, they might be 'deluded' as well as 'oppressed'.[75] Because they 'might not understand their position', they needed both to be 'educated' and 'inspired'.[76] There was always a danger it was argued too, that they might split into 'factions' or 'sectional' interests.[77] Distinctions were often drawn – and they were relevant to the whole history of trade unionism – between the specific interests of a union and the general interests of 'the masses' as a whole.[78]

'A trades society', it had been noted long before, when trade unionism was restricted mainly to skilled workers, was necessarily confined to the interests of one special class, although it may heartily sympathize with the objects of all the industrial classes.'[79] As the unskilled began to become organised, they sometimes thought of themselves as 'masses' as opposed to 'trades'. This was a new distinction, and their perception of their own interest, economic and political, was to influence both the politics of the ballot box and the related development of industrial trade unionism in the late nineteenth and early twentieth centuries.

It was not only socialists who were interested in reaching 'the masses' during the 1880s and 1890s. When unemployed workers began to organise parades to the churches, including St Paul's Cathedral, in 1887, Thomas Hancock, a Christian Socialist, was delighted on two counts. 'The non-churchgoing "masses", have taken to churchgoing,' he said in a famous sermon, subsequently printed. 'We have seen what journalists of Mammon and Caste call an "invasion of the Churches" by the poor socialists. We have seen nothing else like it in our generation.'[80]

If socialists often talked of socialism in terms of religion, religious leaders sometimes approached the task of reaching 'the masses' in very similar ways to the socialists. Even before the Religious Census of 1851 established facts, opinions were expressed that 'the masses' did not attend church.[81] 'Most of the neglecters', the Census showed, belonged to 'the masses of our working population … never or but seldom seen in our religious congregations'.[82] Social reasons were often given. Bishop Fraser of Manchester spoke in 1872 of a 'huge mass of ignorance, poverty and wretchedness' in the 'manufacturing towns'[83] and there were many similar statements about 'the metropolis'.[84] F.D. Maurice welcomed the increasing signs of working-class organisation – including trade union organisation – as a way of getting rid of 'a wild floating mass of atoms'.[85]

The phrase 'the lapsed masses' was sometimes used.[86] It suggested that there had once been a social order more favourable to religious attendance than the social order of the nineteenth century. Occasionally the language of 'classes' and 'masses' was employed. The clergy must 'take the side of the masses against the classes', Stewart Headlam urged.[87] 'The Church is mostly administered and officered by the classes', wrote a headmaster in 1898,

> her influential laity belong almost wholly to the class. She is doing a great and growing work among the masses, but the deep sympathies of the clergy with the poor are largely obscured to the eyes of the masses by the fact that social rank and social position secured by wealth and tradition, still count for so much in her service, both amongst clergy and laity.[88]

At least once, it was suggested that socialists and Christians faced the same problems. 'The overwhelming majority of the masses of the people no more want the economic ideals of the "Labour Programme" than either the classes or the masses want the distinctive message of the Church.'[89]

IV

It has been the purpose of this article to explore the use of language, not to examine the value of the freight which the language carried. 'Men grope in a kind of linguistic bewilderment until the phrase-monger comes along, and gives them a proper form of expression,' a late nineteenth-century journalist remarked. 'Then they are as if a great light had suddenly beamed upon them. The lucky words relieve a strain, and enthusiasm follows.'[90]

It is not only 'enthusiasm' which may follow, however. The language of 'masses' created and still creates many difficulties, since it raises awkward separations – between 'them' and 'us'; 'above' and 'below'; 'brains and numbers'; 'individuals and crowds'. 'Mass is not only a very common but a very complex word in social description,' Raymond Williams begins his article on 'Masses' in *Keywords*, and he has explored some of the complexities himself in several places.[91]

Gladstone might appreciate 'the sense of justice, which abides tenaciously in the masses',[92] but for many people who used such a generalised term it could carry with it both condescension and confusion – even contempt – during the nineteenth century, as it has done since. Thus, *The Economist* in 1846 'had no hesitation' in 'pronouncing' that 'because the masses are suffering, and have long been suffering, without amending their condition, they are greatly to blame .... Nature made them responsible for their conduct – why should not we?'[93]

A few people were aware of the dangers of the term, as dangerous as the term 'hands' when applied to all 'working men, women and children'. In the same decade as *The Economist's* statement, a Leeds minister, the Rev. R.W. Hamilton, properly complained that 'our judgements are distorted by the phrase [the masses]. We unconsciously glide into a prejudice. We have joined a total without thinking of the parts. It is a heap, but it has strangely become indivisible.' Hamilton recognised that industrialisation had brought with it 'a new order of men' – he did not call it a 'class' (or 'classes') – yet he was right to see latent power in the mass.

> Who are the labouring poor? Are they an excrescence or a surplus or an evil, of which we might rid ourselves? ... Let us not sneer at their mental influence .... Their intellectual nature, though feebly developed cannot be extinguished. It is now, at least, earnestly awake.[94]

'Thinking of the parts', as Hamilton recognised, involves thinking about relations. So does all social history.[95] Use of the word 'class' necessarily entails an understanding. The novelist George Eliot should perhaps have the last word. She began a review written in 1856 with these words, 'It is an interesting branch of psychological observation to note the images that are habitually associated with abstract or collective terms – what may be called the picture-writing of the mind.' Her conclusion, however, was that those who use terms like 'the people', 'the masses', 'the proletariat' or 'the peasantry' reveal as much concrete knowledge of the actual social world as a mere passenger might have grasped of the workings of a railway.[96]

NOTES

1 Quoted by Raymond Williams in *Keywords* (1976), p. 160.
2 'Nation-cries', one of a series of 'Old England' articles written for *The Times* in January 1838. Disraeli used the pseudonym '*Coeur de Lion*'.

The articles are reprinted in W. Hutcheon (ed.), *Whigs and Whiggism* (1913), pp. 415-16.

3 See my Joseph Fisher Lecture, 'Mass Entertainment: the Origins of a Modern Industry' (Adelaide, 1960).

4 *Illustrated London News*, 10 July 1897.

5 For Harmsworth's interest both in the attitudes of 'the millions' and in the exact size of magazine and newspaper circulations – one of the first deliberate exercises in 'mass measuring' – see R. Pound and G. Harmsworth, *Northcliffe* (1959), esp. pp. 128, 130, 138, 165. For Lever, see C. H. Wilson, *The History of Unilever*, vol. I (1954). By 1892, four years before the founding of the *Daily Mail*, Harmsworth publications were claimed to have 'the largest circulation in the world'. The word 'masses' or 'mass circulation' does not seem to have been used by Northcliffe before 1900, however, nor did Lever (or Lipton) talk of 'mass distribution'. Jeffreys, *Retail Trading in Britain, 1850-1950* (1954) was uninterested in the contemporary language of retailing, and I was not able to note any use of the term myself in *Friends of the People* (1856), a study of Lewis's founded in Liverpool.

6 *Tit-Bits*, 10 April 1897.

7 T. Kirkup, *An Inquiry into Socialism* (1887), p. 20.

8 A statement of 1885, quoted in E. P. Thompson, *William Morris* (1976 edn), p. 465. The title of his chapter 'The Socialists make Contact with the Masses', suggests a more frequent use of the term 'the masses' than was the case. The word 'masses' does not appear in the anthology of contemporary texts concerning the labour movement, edited by E. J. Hobsbawm, *Labour's Turning Point* (1948).

9 T. Mann, *Memoirs* (1923), p. 49. For religion and 'the masses', see below, pp. 44-5.

10 See J. R. MacDonald, *Socialism and Society* (1905); P. M. Ferri, *Socialism and Positive Science* (1905), the first volume in 'the Socialist Library'.

11 J. R. MacDonald, *The Socialist Movement* (1911), p. 15.

12 See vol. II of *A Supplement to the Oxford Dictionary* (1976), p. 849, which lists more than forty examples, described as 'a selection', of nouns prefixed by 'mass', some of them what H. W. Fowler would have called 'vogue words' (see *Modern English Usage* (1962 edn, p. 697). 'Every now and then a word emerges from obscurity, or even from nothingness or a merely potential and not actual existence, into sudden popularity.'

13 For 'mass society', see *inter alia*, D. Bell, 'America as a Mass Society', in *The End of Ideology* (1960); E. Shils, 'The Theory of Society', in *Diogenes*, vol. 39 (1962), pp. 45-66; W. Kornhauser, 'Mass Society', in the *International Encyclopaedia of the Social Sciences*, vol. 10 (1968), pp. 58-64; A. S. Cohen, 'The Theory of Mass Society', in *Theories of Revolution* (1976); and S. Giner, *Mass Society* (1976). Giner's bibliography reveals how much of the relevant literature is foreign.

14 *Westminster Review*, vol. 18 (1833), p. 382.

15 ibid., p. 380. The author was reviewing J. P. Kay's *The Moral and*

Physical Condition of the Working Classes in Manchester (1833). P. Gaskell in his parallel book on *The Manufacturing Population of England* (1833) observed in Chapter VI how 'the steam engine has drawn together the population into dense masses'.

16 For nineteenth-century argument about aggregates (and statistical approaches to measuring them), see below, pp. 55ff.

17 For the word 'multitude' (with cross-references, as in Rudé, to the word 'mob'), see Christopher Hill, 'The Multitude: The Many-Headed Monster', in *Change and Continuity in Seventeenth-Century England* (1974). For the possibility of standing anti-popular rhetoric on its head, note how Paine, Cobbett and others turned Burke's term 'the swinish multitude' into a battle cry. See, for example, pamphlets like *Rights of Swine* (1794), *A Rod for the Burkites by one of the 'Swinish Multitude'* (1794), and the *Political Register*, 2 November 1816. 'With [a] correct idea of your own worth in your minds, with what indignation must you have heard yourselves called the Populace, the Rabble, the Mob, the Swinish Multitude?'

18 *Sybil* (1845) Chapter IV. Disraeli was always anxious, nonetheless, to maintain – and even to extend – the concept of 'gradation of ranks' in an industrial society.

19 T. Carlyle, *On Heroes, Hero-Worship and the Heroic in History* (1841), Lecture VI; *Past and Present* (1843), Chapter XIII.

20 He compared Thomas Attwood of Birmingham with Tamburlaine. See below, p. 224.

21 W. Hazlitt, Essay on 'Mr. Horne Tooke', in *The Spirit of the Age* (1825).

22 Carlyle, *Chartism* (1840), Chapter IX.

23 ibid., Chapter VII. Cp. *Past and Present*, Chapter V, 'Aristocracy of Talent'.

24 *Black Dwarf*, vol. III (1819), p. 695.

25 *Manchester Guardian*, 5 March 1831.

26 *Blackwood's Magazine*, vol. 46 (1839).

27 W. Cooke Taylor, *Notes of a Tour in the Manufacturing Districts of Lancashire* (1842); *The Natural History of Society* (1844).

28 J. S. Mill, 'Civilization', originally published in the *London and Westminster Review* (April 1836), and reprinted in *Dissertations and Discussions*, vol. I (1859), the year of the publication of his famous essay *On Liberty*.

29 For James Mill's belief in the identity of interests, a matter of passion to him as well as of logic, see his *Essay on Government* (1819), sec. X. See also G. Duncan, *Marx and Mill: Two Views of Social Conflict and Social Harmony* (1973). De Tocqueville, who is of major importance in any study of the international ramifications of 'mass' analysis, shared John Stuart Mill's belief that England was becoming a 'mass' society. He commented in his notes on his *Journey to England* (1958 edn, ed. J. P. Mayer, pp. 59-61) on the strength of the aristocracy; but believed nonetheless that 'in due time' England, like other countries, would become 'democratic' (ibid., pp. 66-7). 'The masses' had not developed

very radical ideas about property (ibid., p. 72), but there was a 'general movement common to humanity the world over' towards 'democracy'. 'The century is primarily democratic.' De Tocqueville's attitude towards 'class', but not towards 'mass', is explored in S. Drescher, *Tocqueville and England* (1944). See also for the ambiguities of the word 'democracy', A. J. Maess and K. Kral, *Democracy, Ideology and Objectivity: Studies in the Semantics and Cognitive Analysis of Ideological Controversy* (1956).

30 Although David Riesman, the American sociologist, quoted Mill several times in his remarkable and widely-read book, *The Lonely Crowd* (1950), he did not quote any of the most relevant passages from Mill. The only nineteenth-century writers mentioned by Ortega y Gasset – and then cursorily – in his influential but muddled *The Revolt of the Masses* (1930), were Hegel, Comte and Nietzsche. R. Williams, in *Culture and Society*, limits the range of his discussion of Mill in Chapter 3 by restricting it to Mill's essays on Bentham and Coleridge.

31 *On Liberty*, chapter 3: 'individuals are lost in the crowd'.

32 *On Liberty*, chapter 3, which he called 'Of Individuality, as being one of the Elements of Well-Being'. By then de Tocqueville was less willing to generalise about England. In his *Ancien Régime* (1856), vol. I, p. 146, he observed that in England 'common interests had closely knit together the various social classes ... but liberty, which enjoys that admirable power of creating among all citizens necessary relations and mutual ties of dependence, does not always make them similar.'

33 See J. Vincent, *The Formation of the British Liberal Party* (1972),p. 288.

34 For Mill and Arnold compared, see E. Alexander, *Matthew Arnold and John Stuart Mill* (1965).

35 M. Arnold, 'Democracy', the introduction to *The Popular Education of France* (1861). Williams does not refer to this important essay which also draws on de Tocqueville. He does refer, however, to the other important contribution of Arnold to this subject, *Friendship's Garland* (1871). See also P. J. McCarthy, *Matthew Arnold and the Three Classes* (1964).

36 'Democracy', p. 7. For the twentieth-century American development of the argument (with no debts acknowledged to Arnold), see, *inter alia*, D. Macdonald, *Against the American Grain: Essays on the Effects of Mass Culture* (1960), the first essay a brilliant study of 'mass-cult and mid-cult', first published in 1960; B. Rosenberg and D. M. White (eds.), *Mass Culture* (1957); N. Jacobs (ed.), *Culture for the Millions?* (1961); H. J. Gans, *Popular Culture and High Culture* (1974); and S. Sontag, *Against Interpretation* (1976).

37 S. Smiles, *Duty* (1880), p. 26. For the background see A. Briggs, 'Samuel Smiles and the Gospel of Work', in *Victorian People* (1954).

38 H. Taylor, 'Chapters on Socialism. By John Stuart Mill', in the *Fortnightly Review*, vol. XXV (1879). They are reprinted in J.S. Mill, *Essays on Economics and Society* (1967), vol. V of his *Collected Works*.

39 *Political Economy* (3rd edn, 1856), pp. 64-8.

40 The study of political élites is relatively recent in this country, although

it has become better known since the Open University began to work with this language. (See C. T. Harvie, 'Concepts of Élites' and 'Intellectuals and Society', in *British Élites*, 1750-1870 (1974).) Élitism was not a nineteenth-century word, and the two classic Italian texts – those of Mosca, whose study of 'the ruling class' first appeared in 1896 in his *Elementi de scienza politica*, and Pareto, who wrote on the subject in many places – were little studied until the 1930s and not related to English practice until the 1950s and 1960s. See W. L. Guttsman, *The British Political Élite* (1963); T. B. Bottomore, *Elites and Society* (1964); J. H. Meisel, *The Myth of the Ruling Class: Gaetano Mosca and the Elite* (1962); P. Bachrach, *The Theory of Democratic Elitism, A Critique* (1967); and the article on 'Élites', in the *International Encyclopedia of the Social Sciences*, vol. V (1968), pp. 26-9.

41   J. Morley, Review of *Essays on Reform*, in the *Fortnightly Review*, vol. II (1867), p. 492.

42   J. Morley, *Burke, A Historical Study* (1847) and an essay on De Maistre written in 1868, reprinted in *Miscellanies* (1886).

43   H. F. Lowry, K. Young and W. H. Dunn (eds), *The Note-Books of Matthew Arnold* (1952), p. 83. Cp. p. 37 for an 1866 note, '"the feeling between classes" but the distinction of classes should die away and we should be one people.' This followed a quotation from a speech by John Bright.

44   See above, p. 21.

45   M. Arnold, *Culture and Anarchy*: an 1856 reference, quoted in C. Kent, *Brains and Numbers* (1978), p. 71.

46   Quoted ibid., p. 73.

47   Quoted ibid., p. 68. 'Reform' meant 'the placing of ultimate control of the State in the hands of the mass of the people.' 'A Scheme of Reform' in *Commonwealth*, March 1866.

48   See, in particular, R. H. Hutton's essay 'The Political Character of the Working Classes'. For Lowe, see A. Briggs, *Victorian People*, chapter IX, 'Robert Lowe and the Fear of Democracy' and J. Winter, *Robert Lowe* (1976). Lowe, who thought in terms of a 'top' and 'bottom' to society, related the struggle for 'democracy', which he deplored, to the struggle for trade union power and protectionist changes in economic policy which he equally strongly deplored. He feared that the working classes, once given the vote, would launch themselves in 'one compact mass' on all British institutions (*Speeches and Letters on Reform* (1867), p. 55).

49   J. Morley, 'Political Prelude', in the *Fortnightly Review*, vol. X (1868).

50   G. Brodrick, 'The Utilitarian Argument against Reform', in *Essays on Reform*, p. 7.

51   For Comte's views on élites and mass, see H. B. Acton, 'Comte's Positivism and the Science of Society', in *Philosophy*, vol. XXVI (1951), and G. Lenzer (ed.), *Auguste Comte and Positivism* (1975). For the Oxford and Cambridge background of the English 'educated classes', see C. Harvie, *The Lights of Liberalism* (1976).

52   Speech at Liverpool, 28 June 1866, quoted in *The Times*, 29 June 1866.

53 *Fortnightly Review*, vol. XIV (1870). This was the year of the Commune, stoutly defended by the Positivists. See R. Harrison, *The English Defence of the Commune* (1971). For a Tennysonian vision of the end of 'class', see *Macmillan's Magazine*, vol. XX (1885), where the poet wrote

> 'Of knowledge fusing class with class,
> Of civic hate no more to be,
> Of love to leaven all the mass
> Till every soul be free.'

54 See Briggs, *Victorian People*, Chapter 7, 'John Bright and the Creed of Reform' for the idea of a 'residuum' unworthy of the right to vote. See also above, p. 21.

55 A speech of November 1873 at the University of Glasgow, quoted in G. Watson, *The English Ideology* (1973), p. 166. See also Chapter 10 of this book, 'Class and Rank'. Ruskin, like Carlyle, believed that 'all forms of government are good just so far as they attain this one vital necessity of policy – that the wise and kind, few or many, shall govern the wise and unkind', E. T. Cook and A. Wedderburn (eds), *The Works of John Ruskin*, vol. XVII, p. 248.

56 W. Bagehot, *The English Constitution* (1867), reprinted in its second edition (1872) form in N. St. John-Stevas (ed.), *The Collected Works of Walter Bagehot*, vol. 5 (1974), pp. 369, 378. The second passage follows a famous reference to public opinion as 'the opinion of the bald-headed man at the back of the omnibus'. Cp. *Reynolds News*, which claimed to represent that opinion, 23 August 1885: 'Toryism is today what it always was – exclusiveness. It is a representation of privileges and vested interests.'

57 'They [the working classes] will soon possess the secret of their own power, and then what is to prevent them from using it? What are the restraints that you propose? I know that very pretty metaphors have been given us; we are told, for instance, that society is divided into vertical instead of horizontal strata, but nevertheless, when men have power conferred upon them, infallibly they will employ it for their own purpose.' (Lowe, *op. cit.*, p. 53.)

58 A phrase of Lord Randolph Churchill, quoted by W. S. Churchill, *Lord Randolph Churchill*, vol. I (1906), p. 294.

59 See J. A. Hobson, *The War in South Africa* (1900), and *The Psychology of Jingoism* (1901). The theme is well handled in R. Price, *An Imperial War and the British Working Class: Attitudes and Reactions to the Boer War* (1972), esp. Chapter 4, 'The Jingo Crowd'.

60 G. Le Bon, *The Crowd: A Study of the Popular Mind* (English edn, 1903), p. 15. 'Crowds had their own psychology,' Sidney Webb had explained in *Fabian News*, November 1896. In the same year *Science Siftings* (1 August) referred to 'the spontaneous phenomena which the Germans call *Massenpsychosen* – a word denoting a state of mind shared by all a people at once'. For the development of 'collective behaviour' themes in relation to crowds, see E. Canetti, *Crowds and Power* (1960); G. Rudé, *The Crowd in the French Revolution* (1959) and *The Crowd in History* (1964): R. A. Nye, *The Origins of Crowd Psychology* (1975)

and the extremely illuminating article by R. J. Holton, 'The Crowd in History: some Problems of Theory and Method' in *Social History*, vol. 3 (1978).

61 W. S. Churchill, *op. cit.*, p. 224.

62 *Manchester Guardian*, 11 May 1894.

63 Sir Robert Giffen is the best source. See his collected papers, *Economic Inquiries and Studies* (1904).

64 G. W. E. Russell, 'The New Liberalism: A Response', in the *Nineteenth Century*, vol. 26 (1889), p. 496. See also R. B. Haldane, 'The New Liberalism', in the *Progressive Review* (1896), pp. 145-60.

65 R. A. Woods, *English Social Movements* (1891), p. 9.

66 J. A. Hobson, 'Of Labour', in J. E. Hand (ed.), *Good Citizenship* (1899), p. 105. See M. Freeden, *The New Liberalism. An Ideology of Social Reform* (1978), esp. Chapter IV, 'The Nature of Liberal Social Reform', sec. 5, '"The Masses verses the Classes"' – the striving for Non-Sectionalism'.

67 H. Halliday Sparling, *Men versus Machinery*, quoted in Thompson, *op. cit.*, p. 292.

68 *The People's Paper*, 13 November 1853.

69 See G. D. H. Cole and A. W. Filson, *British Working-Class Movements, 1780-1875* (1951), pp. 418-21.

70 Although Engels devoted a paragraph in his introduction to social and political terms, the words 'mass' and 'masses' were not on his list. In his chapter on 'Labour Movements', however, he stated that the object of the trade unions was 'to deal, *en masse*, as a power, with the employers'. The words *'en masse'* were very generally used by writers then and later.

71 George Gissing, whose *New Grub Street* (1891) has rightly been noted as a key novel in the history of 'mass culture' (which he perceptively described), said through one of his characters in *The Unclassed* (1880) that his 'zeal on behalf of the suffering masses was nothing more nor less than disguised zeal on behalf of my own starved passions'. This could be one difficulty in 'identifying'. Another difficulty was that of communication. Gissing's *Demos* (1886) is a fascinating novel in this context.

72 *Commonweal*, February, March 1885. The second March number included an article by Engels, 'England in 1845 and in 1885', which was later included as the Preface to the first English edition of *The Condition of the Working Class in 1844*.

73 *Commonweal*, September 1885.

74 The word 'apathetic' was used in relation to 'the masses' in *Commonweal*, September 1886. Cp. a Morris letter of 1886, cited in Thompson, *op. cit.*, p. 411, and the Fabian election manifesto of 1892, which included a section on 'Political Apathy of the Workers'. For 'apathy' as a concept, see S. Yeo, 'On the Uses of "Apathy"', in *Archives Européennes de Sociologie*, vol. XI (1974).

75 *Commonweal*, July 1885, September 1886.

76 ibid., August 1886, December 1886.

77 For 'factions', see a note by J. L. Mahon in ibid., October 1887. Mahon

often used the language of 'masses'. For 'sectional interests', represented particularly in the trade union structure, see ibid., September 1889.

78 See, for example, the Socialist League's *Strikes and the Labour Struggle*, cited in Thompson, *op. cit.*, p. 436, and a comment by Morris in *Commonweal*, September 1889 on 'class jealousy among the workers themselves'.

79 *The Beehive*, 2 June 1866.

80 T. Hancock, 'The Banner of Christ in the Hands of the Socialists', reprinted in *The Pulpit and the Press* (1904). See also M. B. Reckitt, *Maurice to Temple* (1946), Chapter II.

81 See, for example, Engels, *op. cit.*, p. 125.

82 *Religious Worship in England and Wales* (1954), p. 93. Horace Mann, who conducted the Census, liked to talk of the 'myriads', and the phrase 'the thronging myriads' was also used by a Methodist minister in 1883. (E. Smith, *The Great Problem of the Times* (1883), p. 3.)

83 J. Fraser, *Charge* (1872), pp. 76-7, quoted in K. S. Inglis, *Churches and the Working Classes in Victorian England* (1963), p. 25.

84 See ibid., p. 68.

85 F. D. Maurice, *On the Reformation of Society* (1851), p. 36.

86 Inglis, *op. cit.*, p. 83.

87 S. Headlam, *The Clergy on Public Leaders* (n.d.), p. 13.

88 T. C. Fry in C. Gore, *Essays in Aid of the Reform of the Church* (1898), p. 303. (Quoted ibid., p. 60.)

89 Rev. Ambrose Shepherd, *The Gospel and Social Questions* (1902), quoted in S. Yeo, *Religion and Voluntary Organisations in Crisis* (1976), p. 291.

90 *Science Siftings*, 3 April 1897. This magazine often used the language of 'the masses'. Thus, it suggested (31 July 1897) that public opinion was 'not dictated by leaders and adopted by the masses, but evolved by the masses, and accepted by the leaders'. The problem was taken up more seriously by James Bryce, one of the essayists on reform of 1867, in his *The American Commonwealth*, vol. 2 (1900), pp. 247-54: 'Sometimes a leading statesman or journalist takes a line to which he finds that the mass of those who usually agree with him are not responsive. He perceives that they will not follow him and that he must choose between isolation and a modification of his own views. A statesman may sometimes venture on the former questions ... a journalist, however, is obliged to hark back if he has inadvertently taken up a position disagreeable to his *clientèle*, because the proprietors of the paper have their circulation to consider ... he tries to feel the pulse of the average citizen and, as the mass look to him for initiative, this is a delicate process .... This mutual action and reaction of the makers or leaders of opinion upon the mass, and of the mass upon them, is the most curious part of the whole process by which the formation of opinion is produced.'

91 T. Williams, *Keywords*, p. 158. See also *Culture and Society*, esp. pp. 297-319; *The Long Revolution* (1961), p. 95 (an interesting dis-

cussion of 'individualism' and 'individuality'), pp. 110-11 (which touched on the problem of élites), and p. 334; and *Communications* (revised edn, 1966). There is also a good discussion in A. Smith, *The Shadow in the Cave* (1973), 'The Riddle of the Masses'.

92   Quoted in Sir Philip Magnus, *Gladstone* (1954), p. 323.

93   *The Economist*, 21 November 1846, quoted in J. D. Rosenberg, *The Darkening Glass* (1961), p. 127. See also S. Gordon, 'The London *Economist* and the High Tide of *Laisser Faire*' in the *Journal of Political Economy*, vol. LXIII (1975).

94   R. W. Hamilton, *The Institutions of Popular Education* (1845), p. 8.

95   The use of the word 'class', as E. P. Thompson points out – and the related sense of 'class consciousness' – depends on a sense of social relationships. 'Class happens when some men, as a result of common experiences (inherited or shared), feel and articulate the identity of their interests as between themselves, and as against other men whose interests are different from (and usually opposed to) theirs.' E. P. Thompson, *The Making of the English Working Class* (1963 edn), p. 9.

96   G. Eliot, *Essays and Leaves from a Note-Book* (Edinburgh, 1884), pp. 229-30, quoted by Watson, *op. cit.*, p. 181. See also vol. II, p. 51.

3 The Human Aggregate

To understand the nature of Victorian civilisation it is necessary to understand not only words but artefacts and environments. In particular, it is necessary to understand Victorian cities – visually, through their forms and formlessness; socially, through their structures and the chronology of their processes of change, planned and unplanned; symbolically, through their features and images, as expressed in literature and the arts; together for the light they throw on the processes of urbanisation, separately and comparatively in order to understand particularity and the sense of place. The world of Victorian cities was fragmented, intricate, eclectic, messy; and no single approach to their understanding provides us with the right questions and answers or leads us to all the right available evidence.

In studying such complex questions there is a danger in following singly one or other of two different kinds of approach, which all too seldom are considered together – the approach through 'qualitative' evidence derived from a wide range of sources, documentary, and non-documentary, public and private, and the approach through the accumulation and analysis of 'quantitative' evidence – the vast store of measurable data which the men of the nineteenth century produced in greater and greater quantities. Historians of literature and architecture usually adhere to one approach, and economic historians and historical demographers to the other. On both sides there are far too many abstractions. A few social and economic historians and a few general historians straddle the divide. The dangers of this situation do not lie simply in failures of interdisciplinary communication: they prevent us from understanding many problems which are key problems in Victorian studies.

The fact that the quantitative approach is now becoming increasingly feasible and increasingly fashionable is of the utmost significance in this context. By an analysis, with the help of modern statistical techniques, of factual material which the Victorians collected simply for immediate purposes, by the intelligent use of social indicators, and by asking questions which for various reasons the Victorians themselves did not ask, at least in precise form, about their own society and culture, we can go some way towards 'measuring' the quality of life in nineteenth-century cities.

I

Before exploiting our own approaches, it is as wise to turn back to the attitudes of the Victorians themselves as it is when we study the history of vocabularies or of tastes and styles. There is little doubt that throughout the whole period, early, middle and late, the Victorians approached the growth of their cities first and foremost in terms of *numbers*. They were aware – either with fear or with pride – that they were living through a period of change of scale – change in the size of industrial plant, change in the size of social organisation, change, above all, in the size of towns and cities. They liked to collect facts about all these phenomena – sometimes for reasons of curiosity, sometimes for reasons of what we would now call 'social control' – and they developed machinery for doing so.

The facts which they collected were set out in trade directories and brochures for local Chambers of Commerce as well as in the national Census reports and blue books: alongside successive editions of vast treatises like George Porter's *Progress of the Nation*, the first edition of which appeared in 1836, or J. R. McCulloch's *Descriptive and Statistical Account of the British Empire*, against which Dickens reacted so sharply when he wrote *Hard Times*, there were detailed guides, heavy with statistics concerning what were often called 'the large towns and populous districts'. One of the contributors to McCulloch's *Account* (1837), William Farr, became the first Registrar-General in the same year. It is interesting that the very year that Victoria came to the throne marked what Professor M. W. Flinn has called 'a major turning point in the history of demography in England'.[1] It was the 'business' of the 1830s, G. M. Young has suggested, 'to transfer the treatment of affairs from a polemical to a statistical basis, from Humbug to Humdrum.'[2] In 1837 there were still few figures to work on: by 1951 there were too many.

Some of the facts, zealously assembled by the Victorian statisticians, were crude indicators of what the Victorians themselves thought of as 'material progress', aggregates derived from the success stories of economic individualism. Other facts dealt with the unplanned collective problem areas – with fertility or mortality rates for example, with crime, or with the supply of houses and schools. Others were set out side by side in order to relate demography to social class, to economic structure, or to moral behaviour.[3] From the outset the facts were collected because many of the social statisticians were anxious not merely to present information but to propound a message, sometimes a gospel. Even when they were employed by the government as inspectors or servants of commissioners, they were seldom merely agents of the state. Moral instructors like Charles Kingsley eagerly translated the facts into the language of the sermon and the lecture. For example, in his lecture on 'Great Cities and their Influence for Good and Evil' delivered at Bristol in October 1857, Kingsley deliberately crossed the frontier between statistical and non-statistical methodology, stating that 'the moral state of a city depends – how far I know not, but frightfully, to an extent as yet uncalculated, and perhaps incalculable – on the physical state of that city; on the food, water, air, and lodging of its inhabitants.'[4]

As I have argued in *Victorian Cities*, there was no agreement on the implications, moral or social, either of the acknowledged facts or of the general laws which Victorians liked to derive from them.[5] In the most general terms, on the one side was fear – fear of change in the pattern of social relationships as the scale of the city changed; fear of the emergence and of the mounting pressure of new social forces which were difficult to interpret, even more difficult to control; fear that society would not deal quickly enough with urgent problems before the social fabric of society was torn apart. On the other side was pride – pride in achievement through self-help and, through self-help, in economic growth; pride in local success, often through rivalry with other places; pride not only in the tokens of wealth and in the symbols of prestige, but also in the means of control – mileage of sewers, numbers of water-taps and water-closets, numbers of school places, or numbers of policemen.

There was sometimes no give-and-take in this clash of values: the smoke from the chimneys spoke for itself. Yet there was usually ambivalence, with the ambivalence stretching to the statistical method itself. Dickens was not attacking all statistics in *Hard Times*, but rather a naïve reliance on certain kinds of statistics and on nothing more.[6] *Punch* regularly made fun of statistics, particularly 'useless' statistical research, but nonetheless recognised that the great utility of some kinds of research and calculation was so obvious that it need not point out the value of the labours of contemporary statisticians. Wordsworth, of all people, wrote to H. S. Tremenheere, the 'classic' Victorian inspector, that 'we must not only have knowledge, but the means of wielding it, and that is done infinitely more through the imaginative faculty assisting both in the collection and application of facts than is generally believed.'[7]

Given such ambivalence, much of which pivots on the Victorian idea of 'fact' itself, it is necessary to explore the statistical mode of enquiry as a way to reform, not to take it for granted. It may be true that 'statistics was to industrialism what written language was to earlier civilisation'.[8] Yet we can trace back to the 'pre-industrial' eighteenth century the origins of statistical preoccupation. The word 'statistics' itself does not seem to have been used in English before 1770, the year of the English translation (from the German in three volumes) of J.F. von Bielefeld's *The Elements of Universal Erudition*,[9] and twenty-seven years later the *Encyclopedia Britannica* was still describing 'statistics' as a 'word recently introduced to express a view or survey of any kingdom, county or parish'. Not surprisingly, an early English advocate of statistics was Jeremy Bentham who suggested a population register in 1782 and twenty years later was working on a new statistical vocabulary.[10]

The main thrust of the early 'statistical movement' was concern to explore (and to compare) the statistics of parish, town, city and county.[11] 'Great cities', J.C. Lettsom had written in 1774, 'are like painted sepulchres; their public avenues and stately edifices seem to preclude the very possibility of distress and poverty: but if we pass beyond this superficial, the scene will be reversed'.[12] Statistics pierced the veil not only in new industrial cities like Manchester, where as early as 1772 Dr Thomas Perceval was collecting and interpreting local health statistics, but in pre-industrial communities like Chester and Carlisle.[13] There was an actuarial impulse too.[14] Even without 'industrialism' the development of insurance provided it.

Although 'abstract' classical political economy, as developed in the early nineteenth century by Ricardo, was by its very nature non-statistical (like the developing natural sciences), this does not mean that political economists were uninterested in statistics. Ricardo himself agreed that 'speculation' had to be submitted to the 'test of fact', and the first Fellows of the Statistical Society of London, founded in 1834, included Nassau Senior, Malthus, and McCulloch. They were doubtless as sceptical as Dickens concerning the proposition that everything could be reduced to 'Two and Two are Four', 'Simple Arithmetic', or 'A Mere Question of Figures', the possible titles for *Hard Times* – and McCulloch among them rejected the idea that 'everything in statistics may be estimated in figures'.[15] Likewise, the first President of the British Association, William Whewell, the Master of Trinity College, Cambridge, deprecated the extension of statistical enquiries 'into regions where they would touch on the mainsprings of feeling and passion'. By 1838, however, members of the society were expressing the hope that 'the study of Statistics will, ere long, rescue Political Economy from all the uncertainty in which it is now enveloped'.[16]

The purposes which the Statistical Society of London was established to serve were set forth in a prospectus of 1834 as 'procuring, arranging, and publishing "Facts calculated to illustrate the Condition and Prospects of Society"'.[17] It expressed the hope that other societies would be founded outside London, and its provincial counterpart, founded a year earlier in Manchester, a city of unbridled economic individualism, certainly had from the start a distinct social leaning.[18] Businessmen might be concerned in their daily affairs with the statistics of the counting-house, but the little formative group of people who created the Manchester Society, related by kinship and religion as well as by common interest, were from the beginning preoccupied with the statistics of social relevance. They were anxious above all to show that Manchester was being misrepresented in official reports. The first complete available paper (1834) of the society was entitled 'An Analysis of the Evidence taken before the Factory Commissioners, as far as it Relates to the Population of Manchester and the Vicinity Engaged in the Cotton Trade'. The paper, prepared by the Greg brothers – one of whom was to clash with Mrs Gaskell on her interpretation of social relationships in Manchester[19] – was a secondary analysis of data gathered by a parliamentary committee. It had five sections dealing, not with 'the facts of progress' as registered in profits and wages, but with health, fatigue, alleged cruelty towards factory children, education, morals, and poor-rates. The first completely original survey produced by the Society dealt with the provision of education,[20] and the first annual report of the Society spoke of 'a strong desire felt by its projectors to assist in promoting the progress of social improvement in the manufacturing population by which they are surrounded'.[21]

In the case of some of the other early statistical societies, all of them expressions of the great burst of provincial intellectual and social energy during the 1830s and 1840s, the purposive emphasis was even more marked.[22] Thus, the full title of the Birmingham Society was 'The Birmingham Statistical Society for the Improvement of Education'; while the Glasgow Society spoke of collecting 'facts illustrative of the condition and prospects' of the community 'with a view to the improvement of mankind'; and the Liverpool Society chose as its first three papers the condition of the agricultural classes, the causes of crime and the building operatives' strike of 1833. The London Society itself referred to the 'careful collection, arrangement, discussion and publication of facts bearing on and illustrating the complex relations of modern society in its social, economical, and political aspects', with the adjective 'social' being placed first. By 1838, the fourth annual report of its Council noted that 'the spirit of the present age has an evident tendency to confront the figures of speech with the figures of arithmetic; it being impossible not to observe a growing *a priori* assumption that, in the business of social science, the principles are valid for application only inasmuch as they are legitimate deductions from facts accurately observed and methodically classified'.[23]

II

Such a statement was at the opposite end of the scale from romantic styles of social criticism; it was at some distance, too, both from generalised Owenite social science and Benthamite reasoning. Yet the Owenites sometimes used statistics, and Bentham followed through an early interest in statistics by arguing powerfully that the systematic collection and annual publication of returns would furnish valuable data for the legislator. Influenced by Bentham, whom he served as secretary, Edwin Chadwick was an energetic member of the Statistical Society of London, and though the limitations of his statistical methods were to be emphasised later in the century,[24] he told the Political Economy Club in 1845 that of two types of economists – 'the hypothesists' who reasoned deductively from 'principles' and those who believed in 'the school of facts' and worked inductively – he belonged to the second.[25] Nor was he alone. By the time of the tenth report of the Statistical Society of London in 1844, the Council was claiming that 'the pursuit of statistical enquiries has already made such progress ... as henceforth be a necessity of the age, and one of its most honourable characteristics.'

The statistical method was deliberately employed during the 1830s and 1840s to identify 'problems', to spread knowledge of 'social facts', and to educate 'opinion'. It was because the pioneering statisticians of this period were thought of as explorers of society – and, particularly, of urban society within which the statistical societies were created – that they were able to influence both the collective will and the individual literary imagination. Their chief merit seemed to be that they discovered 'facts' at first hand: Mill, thus, deferred to Chadwick on the grounds that Chadwick, for example, got his information direct while he (Mill) 'could only get it second hand or from books.'[26]

The notion of 'exploration' which recurs time and time again in the imagery of early urban studies carried with it a sense of adventure. It also carried with it the sense that nineteenth-century cities, in parti-cular, were 'mysterious places' where one section of the community knew very little directly about the rest. 'Why is it, my friends,' the great American Unitarian preacher W. E. Channing asked in Boston in 1841 – in a sermon in which he anticipated Disraeli in speaking of 'two nations coexisting side by side in the same community' – 'that we are brought so near to one another in cities? It is, that nearness should awaken sympathy; that multiplying wants should knit us more closely together; that we should understand one another's perils and suffer-ings; that we should act perpetually on one another for good.'[27] In reality, however, the nineteenth-century city, with all its varieties of

Plate 1: The Human Aggregate

Plate 2: Thomas Attwood

Plate 3: 'The Gathering of the Unions' on Newhall Hill, 7 May 1832

Plate 4: View of the Birmingham Bull Ring, *c.* 1835

experience, did not permit this intuitive understanding: it was difficult to grasp it as a whole. There was a striking contrast between
ought and *is* which the statistician could expose. At his best, indeed, he
could be a mediator as well as an explorer, not dwelling on the 'mystery
of the city' – or exploiting it, as G. M. W. Reynolds and some of the
purveyors of romantic fiction did – but rather on the dissipating of it.

Beyond a certain point it was clearly impossible to talk of 'numbers',
the starting point of urban exegesis, without also talking about
'relationships', social and geographical. Most pre-industrial cities had
been places which were small enough and, for all their complexities,
simple enough to generalise about or about which to moralise as
'wholes' or to satirise in terms of galleries of urban 'types'. It was far
more difficult in socially and geographically segregated cities with
unequal spatial densities and with manifestly unequal conditions of
'class', segregated district by district, to identify the 'problems' of the
city – or at least to suggest ways of solving them – except through the
collection and deployment of statistics. Doctors, who were particularly prominent in the deliberations of the Manchester Statistical
Society, might be in a more favourable position than most to move
easily from one area to another, relying on knowing directly rather
than knowing at second-hand. So also might at least an active minority
of ministers of religion. Yet with the separation of work-place and
home, the growth of single-class living areas and the decline in what
later urban sociologists were to call primary or 'face-to-face' relationships, statistics as a mode of enquiry easily came into its own.[28]

It was because 'numbers' could be used not simply for the purpose
of rhetoric but for purposes of disclosure – exposure in many cases is
not too strong a word – that journalists as well as 'men of good will'
were deeply concerned with statistics – the famous articles in the
Morning Chronicle in 1849 and 1850, written in the aftermath of
Chartism and in the alarming presence of cholera, provide the out-
standing example[29] – or that novelists also used statistics when they
presented social comment in fictional form during the 1840s. As
Arnold Kettle has pointed out, they were often addressing 'the
downright factual ignorance of the middle class'.[30] 'The facts – the
facts are all in all; for they are facts' wrote the reviewer of Mrs
Gaskell's *Mary Barton* in *Fraser's Magazine* in 1849.[31]

There were obvious difficulties when 'disclosure' was extended to
'analysis' and 'analysis' was related to 'action'. First, despite Mill's
comment on Chadwick, there was a problem of knowledge. The
statisticians were observers who often started their enquiries not only
in ignorance of what facts they would find but also with different
values from those of the people they were observing. At best, they
were able to display the need for sympathy which Channing empha-

sised. At worst, they were handicapped by their lack of the kind of personal knowledge that Mrs Gaskell, for instance, possessed, whatever the social limitations which restricted her approach, of how working-class families thought and felt. They might even be dogmatic, as Chadwick was, and for all their interest in statistics, attached more to preconceived theory than to observation. In general, they were more concerned with the facts of the city than with the facts of the factory. It was urbanisation, not industrialisation, which fascinated them most.

Henry Mayhew, who throughout his work deliberately interposed individual vignettes and statistics (many of his statistics related to people whom he was not directly describing – employers, customers, and clients), sometimes seemed to be trying to move one or two steps beyond the position of an observer. He took the trouble, for example, to provide written answers to queries he received from individuals mentioned in his surveys, and he was willing to hold public meetings. He also appeared freer from many of the stifling inhibitions and restraining 'value frames' which limited the social comment of most of his contemporaries. Yet even in Mayhew's case, as E. P. Thompson has remarked, it would be 'ludicrous' to suggest that he 'discovered Victorian poverty'. 'The poor had long before discovered themselves, and the *Northern Star* contained a part of their own testament.'[32] Their testament, moreover, necessarily had policy implications written into it which diverged from the policy implications of social statisticians like Chadwick.[33] The work of the statisticians was important, in Mayhew's opinion, in that it encouraged a questioning of untested middle-class assumptions and prejudices, and he complained bitterly, if a little too comprehensively, that 'economists', from Adam Smith down, 'have shown the same aversion to collect facts as mad dogs the touch of water'.[34]

There was more, however, to the question of 'values' than this. Not every middle-class critic of society was impressed by statistical exposure or by the conclusions which statisticians were prone to reach about the viability of the 'social system' and its inherent possibilities for 'improvement'. The kind of people who turned for guidance to Thomas Carlyle, the prophet of his age, spurned statistics, as Ruskin was to spurn them. What could be more 'general' than the opening sentences of Carlyle's *Past and Present* (1843) – 'England is full of wealth, of multifarious produce, of supply for human want in every kind', or Ruskin's remark in *Unto this Last* (1862) that 'our cities are a wilderness of spinning wheels ... yet the people have not clothes ... Our harbours are a forest of merchant ships, and the people die of hunger'? This kind of writing always appealed, and it encouraged satire of the statisticians. 'Where men formerly expended their energy on scholastic quibbles,' the *Edinburgh Review* complained during the late 1850s, 'they now compile statistics, evincing a mental disease, which may be termed the colloquative diarrhoea of the intellect, indicating a strong appetite and a weak digestion'.[35]

The preference for 'generality' was reinforced by the feeling, first that statistics was something of a 'fad', second that there could be more evasion and misrepresentation than disclosure in the work of statisticians, and third that individuals counted for more than 'averages'. 'It is astonishing', *Punch* wrote in 1848, having regularly satirised such pursuits,

> what Statistics may be made to do by a judicious and artist-like grouping of the figures; for though they appear to begin with a limited application to one subject, there is no end to the mass of topics that may be dragged in collaterally on all sides. A few facts on mendicancy, introduced by one of the members [of the British Association for the Advancement of Science] became the cue for an elaborate calculation of how many meals had been given to Irish beggars in the last twenty years; and this was very near leading to a division of the meals into mouthfuls, with a table showing the number of teeth, subtracting the molars and taking out the canine, employed in the mastication of these twenty years' returns of meals.[36]

There are innumerable satirical references to statistics in *Punch*, where the quality of life in London was a subject of frequent pictorial comment, but it was the novelist, in particular – and given the educational and social patterning of the time, perhaps the woman novelist even more than the rest – who made the most of the inadequacies of 'averages'. There appeared to be something misleading as well as arid in constructing systems of classification and statistical tables. One man's death was more 'real' than a statistic in a bill of mortality or what Mr Gradgrind called 'the laws which govern lives in the aggregate'. The preacher shared this same preoccupation with the individual (real-life even more than fictional) and the plot. 'We may choose to look at the masses in the gross, as subjects for statistics', wrote Kingsley in 1849, 'and, of course, where possible [he went on characteristically], of profits.' Yet there was 'One above who knows every thirst and ache, and sorrow, and temptation of each slattern, and gin-drinker, and street boy. The day will come when He will require an account of these neglects of ours not in the gross.'[37] For Kingsley and those who thought like him, 'the Sanitary Idea' might depend for its ammunition on statistics relating to the unhealthy environment, but its force as a 'gospel' rested on an appeal to deeper forces within the individual, through the operations of the conscience, and, possibly unconsciously, through psychological pressures which the men of the nineteenth century did not understand. It is interesting to compare

Elizabeth Barrett Browning with Kingsley when she wrote in her verse-novel, *Aurora Leigh* (1856), the lines

> A red-haired child
> Sick in a fever, if you touch him once,
> Though but so little as with a finger-tip
> Will set you weeping; but a million sick ...
> You could as soon weep for the rule of three
> Or compound fractions.[38]

Ruskin went far beyond 'the Sanitary Idea' in his writings on political economy, drawing an explicit general distinction between questions of quality and quantity: it was not the sum of products but the quality of a people's happiness which constituted the wealth of the community, he argued. 'But taken as a whole', he wrote, throwing statistics to the winds, 'I perceive that Manchester can produce no good art, and no good literature; it is falling off even in the quality of its cotton.'[39]

III

In any discussion of the approach of statisticians and the response of contemporaries to their methods and conclusions it is important to bear in mind that there were changes in statistical preoccupations from one part of the century to another. The earliest statistical surveys of city populations, some of which were based on questionnaires or what Kay-Shuttleworth called 'tabular queries', were already giving way in the late 1840s to less controversial analyses of more narrowly defined specific questions, with at least one precocious pre-Le Play essay on family budgets pointing the way forward to new modes of enquiry.[40] 'We are somewhat embarrassed by the extent of our subject,' William Whewell had told Quételet in 1834, and one way of dealing with the embarrassment was to circumscribe its boundaries. The papers of the Statistical Society of London read during the 1840s were 'concentrated on a smaller number of topics and ... on a smaller range within these topics'.[41]. By the 1850s and 1860s, substantial city surveys based on original exploration had been almost completely replaced by social-science essays concerned with secondary material: they were being debated by the members of the National Association for the Promotion of Social Science, founded in 1857,[42] with the aged Brougham, a link with Bentham, as first President, but they received far less widespread public attention from contemporaries than the surveys of ten to fifteen years before. The title of the Statistical Section of the British Association, which had been created in 1833, was changed to

'Statistical Science' in 1857 and in 1863 to 'Economic and Statistical Science', and the proportion of papers devoted to economics increased significantly.

During the late nineteenth century the social survey was to come into its own again, but by then some of the older provincial statistical societies had disappeared, the Royal Statistical Society had acquired its prestigious adjective (in 1875), and statisticians had developed an embryonic professional sense. 'We have learned', William Newmarch was once quoted as saying, 'that in all questions relating to human society ... the only sound basis on which we can base doctrines ... is not hypothetical deductions, however ingenious and subtle, but conclusions and reasoning, supported by the largest and most careful investigation of facts.'[43] Likewise, in 1894 the President of the Society, Lord Farrer, insisted on 'abjuring *a priori* methods and artificial systems'. The greatest mistakes which economists have made might have been avoided if they had relied less on *a priori* reasoning, and had paid greater attention to the facts of human society which it is the business of Statistical Science to furnish.'[44] It was Charles Booth who moved the vote of thanks to him.

The middle years of the century belonged to the National Association for the Promotion of Social Science, which on its visit to Manchester in 1866 inspired the *Manchester Examiner and Times* to comment that 'the mass of miseries which afflict, disturb or torment mankind have their origin in preventable causes. They can be classified just as drugs are classified and they may be employed with almost the same certainty of operation. It is to social science that we are indebted for a knowledge of their character, and it is to its progress we must look for the amelioration of our home miseries.'[45] On the same occasion the *Manchester Guardian* noted how social science thrived in a city atmosphere just because of the multiplicity of urban problems. 'Nowhere are the social changes which are now in progress and which are viewed with hope or fear according to the temper of the observer, more manifest than among the teeming population of which this city is the centre and metropolis.'[46]

Some statistical enquiries dealt with specific places, notably such cities, and with specific issues, notably during the late 1860s education. Some dealt with historical sequences – mainly 'tendencies' and 'trends' in production, consumption, distribution and related economic activities. A few of the most interesting were comparative, a few of the most daring exploratory. Yet increasingly the subject became more associated with 'learned papers' than with ideological battle cries.[47]

Characteristic of the new style of 'learned' paper in 'social science' was Dr William Ogle's fascinating piece on 'Marriage-Rates and Marriage-Ages with special reference to the Growth of Population',

read before the Royal Statistical Society in 1890.[48] This paper, which
neatly sets out a problem – why had the nineteenth-century marriage-
rate fluctuated in 'a very irregular manner'? – first disposed of a fallacy
propounded by, amongst others, J. S. Mill and Henry Fawcett, who
had not bothered to give the actual figures on which their statements
were based, that the marriage-rate varied inversely with the price of
wheat. Second, it went on with the aid of graphs to correlate the
marriage-rate with the value of exports per head of the population.
Third, it explored the relationship between export data and the very
patchy trade union statistics relating to employment and unemployment. Fourth, it developed a theory on the basis of the statistical
evidence, explaining why there were marked variations of marriage
rates in different registration counties (arguing that marriages were
more numerous in those counties where women earned independent
wages). Fifth, it looked at age and occupation structure. Sixth, it
related historical evidence to anticipations of the future. The limitations of statistical method were noted, even if they were not fully or
critically investigated. This kind of article needed ingenuity and skills
of the highest order, far removed from Dickens' 'Simple Arithmetic',
and Dr Ogle certainly could not be placed in the camp of those who
saw 'figures and averages and nothing else'.

There is still much to sort out in relation to the detailed history of
the use of statistics. As late as 1887, Wynnard Hooper, the writer on
Statistics in the ninth edition of the *Encyclopaedia Britannica*, had to
devote much of his limited space to the dispute between those who
believed that there was a science of statistics – with its own specific
content – and those who believed that there was only a statistical
method, a convenient aid to investigation in the majority of sciences.
The former group was still of strategic significance – not surprisingly
so, perhaps, when thinking in the natural sciences remained for the
most part non-statistical. It had moved from political to social
arithmetic, with some of its members following Maurice Block and
anticipating Louis Chevalier in giving a new name to their branch of
study – 'demography'. The President of the Royal Statistical Society
argued boldly and passionately at the jubilee meeting in 1885 that
statistics was superior in method to social science or sociology and
that it amounted to 'the science of human society in all its relations'.
Statistics *was* sociology.[49]

Hooper was more cautious, as he had every right to be when the map
of both natural and social sciences was changing as significantly as it
was at that time. After noting – and how common a note it was
becoming in so many areas of English life – that there had unfortunately so far been 'no attempt in England to deal with the subject of
statistics ... in a systematic way', although 'the practice of statistical

inquiry of scope and method has been carried on in England with a high degree of success', he refused to identify all sociology with statistics:

> The statistical method is essentially a mathematical procedure, attempting to give a quantitative expression to certain facts; and the resolution of differences of quality into differences of quantity has not yet been effected even in chemical science. In sociological science the importance of differences of quality is enormous, and the effect of these differences on the conclusions to be drawn from figures is sometimes neglected, or insufficiently recognized, even by men of unquestionable ability and good faith.

The term 'values' was not used in this context. 'Society is an aggregate', wrote Hooper, 'or rather a congeries of aggregates.' And he went on to draw an 'expert' conclusion, concerned solely with statistical techniques – a conclusion which was sharply different from that current in the statistical societies during the pioneer amateur phase of the 1830s and 1840s before the rise of professionalism: 'the majority of politicians, social "reformers" and amateur hoarders of statistics generally were in the habit of drawing the conclusions that seem good to them from such figures as they may obtain, merely by treating as homogeneous and comparable qualities which are not comparable. Even to the conscientious and intelligent inquirer the difficulty of avoiding mistakes in using statistics prepared by other persons is very great.'[50]

This cautious conclusion, set out two years after Charles Booth had started his huge statistical enquiries by challenging Hyndman's simple, unsophisticated, and politically-orientated figures of London poverty, should be set alongside Booth's ambition, far-reaching in scope, to prepare a detached and impartial presentation of the social situation through the use of statistics. 'A framework can be built out of a big theory and facts and statistics run in to fit it, but what I want to see instead is a large statistical framework which is built to receive accumulations of facts.'[51] Seebohm Rowntree likewise turned to statistics because they provided a less 'sentimental' foundation for policy recommendations than straight appeals to human feeling or to political prejudice.[52] It was Mrs Webb who wrote of Booth's study that 'prior to this enquiry, neither the individualist nor the Socialist could state with any approach to accuracy what exactly was the condition of the people of England. Hence the unreality of their controversy.'[53]

The problem of relating quantity to quality, which Booth never tried to baulk in the same way as he baulked most questions of theory, could be tackled, he said, 'given sociological imagination':

The statistical method was needed to give bearings to the results of
personal observation and personal observation to give life to statistics ...
It is this relative character, or the proportion of facts to each other, to us,
to society at large, and to possible remedies, that must be introduced if
they are to be of any value at all in social diagnosis. Both single facts, and
strings of statistics *may* be true, and demonstrably true, and yet entirely
misleading in the way they are used.[54]

Booth added to the list of questions for full quantitative examination
those relating to poverty, seeking 'to connect poverty and well-being
with conditions of employment'. And, in this attempt to connect, he
was to query (like Rowntree later) and with the blessing of the great
neo-classical political economist of late Victorian England, Alfred
Marshall, the non-quantitative basis of much of earlier nineteenth-
century political economy. It was not only sociology that had to be
statistical. Economics, as Lord Farrer emphasised, had to be statistical
too, as it had been for Porter earlier in the century, and as it was at the
time for Robert Giffen.[55]

However great the changes in mood and context, in one important
respect Booth followed directly in tradition from writers of the 1830s
and 1840s. He never concerned himself vey much with the state. Nor
did he restrict his attention to published economic facts. The city was
still *the* place to study if you wished to understand society, and you had
to explore it, not simply produce an inventory. 'It is not in country',
he wrote in a famous passage,

but in town that 'terra incognita' needs to be written on our social map. In
the country the machinery of human life is plainly to be seen and easily
recognized: personal relations bind the whole together. The equipoise on
which existing order rests, whether satisfactory or not, is palpable and
evident. It is far otherwise with cities, where as to these questions we live in
darkness, with doubting hearts and ignorant unnecessary fears, or place
our trust with rather dangerous consequences in the teachings of empiric
economic law.[56]

Booth's own preferences – subjected to searching self-criticism and
criticism by others – quickened inquiry. London was a stage, not a
laboratory: it had its drama, and the drama was perpetually interesting, as it was for Henry James, who while complaining of London's
'horrible numerosity', nonetheless concluded that it offered 'on the
whole the most possible form of life'.[57] H. L. Smith, one of Booth's
assistants, emphasised that among the attractions of London was 'the
contagion of numbers' and that, taking into account all the problems
of the city, it was 'the sense of something going on ... the difference
between the Mile End fair on a Saturday night, and a dark and muddy
country lane' which drew the young in particular into the 'vortex'.

The 'human aggregate' had to be broken down, and number and quality had to be related to each other in a sophisticated way.

'New York's the place for me,' Booth himself once wrote to his wife. 'There seems something subtle, an essence, pervading great metropolitan cities and altering everything so that life seems more lively, busier, larger, the individual less, the community more. I like it. It does me good. But I know it has another aspect and I am not surprised when people feel crushed by the wickedness of it, the ruthlessness, heartlessness of its grinding mill, as you did in Paris.[58]

By the end of Queen Victoria's reign, very much in English life had been measured. The great official inquiries into environment at the beginning of the reign – in the name of 'the Sanitary Idea' – had their counterpart at the end of the reign in the great unofficial inquiries into poverty. In between, while the cities grew, as did the proportions of the population who were city-dwellers, the collection of many of the relevant statistics ceased to be a major exercise in difficult and uncharted social investigation and became, like so much else in Victorian life, an institutionalised routine with decennial Census reports, annual Medical Officer of Health reports, financial returns, and so on. There were still big gaps in relation to both economic statistics (including the statistics of employment) and social and cultural statistics (including the statistics of crime), but there were now statistical experts who were taking over or seeking to take over previously debatable areas of policy and administration. Thus, from its inception in 1889 the London County Council appointed a full-time statistical officer to collect such data for the use of its various committees.[59] As for the dedicated non-experts, they were moving again from urban detail to more general schemes of social regeneration, to the nature of what Sir John Simon had called earlier in the century the 'underframework of society',[60] from issues related to municipal action within the particular city to national welfare policy which would iron out some of the differences between cities.[61]

It is interesting to note in the light of this story that the writer on the history of statistical method in *The International Encyclopaedia of the Social Sciences* states that 'if we have to choose a date at which the modern theory of statistics began, we may put it, somewhat arbitrarily, at 1890'. Pointing to the work of F. Y. Edgeworth, Karl Pearson, Walter Weldon, and G. U. Yule, he notes also that this was the birth year of R. A. Fisher. 'Life was as mysterious as ever,' he goes on, 'but it was found to obey laws. Human society was seen as subject to statistical enquiry, as an evolutionary entity under human control'.[62] This realisation, as we have seen, came early in studies of the Victorian city, but the refinements of statistical analysis came later. Full sophistication was a twentieth-century achievement.

IV

Before turning briefly from what the Victorians themselves did or failed to do with their limited techniques and the quantitative evidence at their disposal to what we in the twentieth century can and should do with statistics in our interpretation of the past, it is important to make two basic points. The first concerns the rates of measurable change in relation to qualitative evidence offered by or available to the Victorians themselves. The second concerns the relationship between facts and theories centred specifically on the city and facts and theories relating to the constitution and development of society as a whole.

On the first point, it is obvious from history, particularly that of urban public health, that the noisiest and most exciting periods of debate or political conflict did not necessarily coincide with the periods of greatest demographic and social change. Because rates of measurable progress did not reflect the power of language or of argument, qualitative evidence by itself may often be misleading. Fierce propaganda on behalf of the sanitary idea during the 'age of Chadwick', when he and others were fascinated by deviations from national or local averages, did little to force down crude death rates. Indeed, they did not fall substantially until the 1870s when, on the whole, questions of public health stirred contemporaries less. What William Farr, the statistical genius behind the mid-Victorian censuses, described as 'one of the most important series of facts relating to the life of a nation ever published' was the revelation that the annual mortality for all ages in the population had scarcely altered throughout the period 1838-71.[63] The infant mortality rate, rightly considered in the twentieth century to be one of the critical indices of social control, remained more or less constant around 150 per thousand live births until the new century began.

The first historians of public health concentrated on the study of qualitative materials relating to 'the age of Chadwick'.[64] Confronted with the mid-Victorian inability to bring down death-rates and infant mortality rates, the social historian of today with quantitative interests would seek to explain such statistics in one or all of four ways: (i) qualitatively by pointing to the fact that it was not until the 1870s that advances in bacteriology and medicine began to produce results and that the limitations of 'environmentalism' were overcome in an age of increasing concern for personal health and housing; (ii) qualitatively by examining those changes in the economy 'in the administrative system', and in society which distinguished late Victorian from early Victorian England and permitted effective 'amelioration'; (iii) quantitatively by breaking down national aggregate rates in particular places, for particular groups or for particular diseases; and (iv) counter-factually, by seeking to analyse what would have happened if there had been no health legislation, local or national, during the 1840s and 1850s.

There is little doubt that, in this field, quantitatively-based urban history enables us to know far more and to understand what we do know far more clearly and in greater depth than if we rely, as did whole generations of historians, on the colourful and rhetorical Victorian debate on sanitary matters. The 'qualitative' evidence ranges from the propaganda of the Health of Towns Association to an article by the Bishop of Bedford on 'Urban Populations' in the *Fortnightly Review* as late as 1893 which did not give one single precise statistic.[65] The 'new history'[66] forces attention to local variations in the period from the 1830s to the 1870s, gives added interest to the late Victorian years when rates actually did fall, and provides the basis for a not unfavour-able assessment of the mid-Victorian achievement. 'Stable death rates,' it has been argued, 'conceal a considerable victory; for by holding in check the powerful forces against health which swiftly growing population and rapid urban agglomeration naturally gener-ated, the sanitary pioneers could congratulate themselves on a valu-able, if negative, achievement.'[67] Finally, it leads to a new evaluation (but not to a dismissal) of the qualitative evidence itself. The early language of 'civic economics', the kind of language Chadwick talked naturally – and some of it was couched almost in terms of cost-benefit analysis[68] – gave way to the specialist language of doctors, engineers, and housing economists. At the same time, the fervour of the first novelists and poets when they took up 'the Sanitary Idea' disappears, and with it until the 1880s most of the sense of drama.

The second important point is related to the first. The local element in initiative for health improvement during the mid-Victorian years, which sometimes led to fierce battles between 'clean' and 'dirty' parties at the city level, changed in relative significance from 1870 onwards as the demand for a 'national' health policy gained in strength. Statistical information was a necessary, and, as time went by, an uncontroversial instrument in the reforms achieved through legis-lation and administration between 1869 and the foundation of the Ministry of Health at the end of the First World War. Indeed, it was through a detailed consideration of health statistics (along with statistics of education) that the balance between local and national action began to change. The significance of what was happening can be well illustrated also from a brilliant review of Rowntree's *Poverty* by C. F. G. Masterman, who was to make his reputation as author of the

Edwardian classic, *The Condition of England*. Masterman, who was a
master of qualitative argument and a brilliant coiner of original
phrases which still stick, was forced by Rowntree's bleak and un-
garnished statistics on poverty in York to this conclusion. 'The social
reformer, oppressed with the sense of the ... poverty of London',
Masterman pointed out, 'is apt to turn with envy towards the ideal of
some flourishing provincial town.' What better town than York, he
might ask, an ancient community revitalised by the railway in recent
Victorian history, a community contrasting in every way with the
homogeneous matrix and sheer immensity of the aggregation of
London? Would it not be desirable, he might go on, to break up the
giant city of six million into sixty cities of 100,000 each, 'not too large
to cause congestion nor too small to prevent the intertwining of varied
industries necessary for permanent stability'?

Such an approach, Masterman concluded, was quite wrong. Rowntree's demonstration that the proportion of primary poverty in York
was the same as in Booth's London was a devastating answer – 'a
thunder-clap', Masterman called it – to such social reformers. A
national policy was needed to tackle poverty, not a series of local urban
expedients, however enlightened. From this angle, Masterman found
Rowntree's detailed statistical work far more persuasive than Booth's,
for at the end of reading Booth's 'nine bulky volumes' with their mazes
of statistics and their picturesque maps, what was left was 'a general
impression ... of something monstrous, grotesque, inane: something
beyond the power of individual synthesis; a chaos resisting all attempts
to reduce it to orderly law.'[69] By contrast, Rowntree's 'definite and
limited material' was manageable enough and comprehensible enough
to guide policy – and, we can add in retrospect, to guide it towards the
peculiarly English twentieth-century balance between the urban and
the national, a balance never fixed but always expected, at least until
the 1980s.

There are more than administrative implications to this second
important point. It is easy for writers on the Victorian city or for that
matter on Victorian urbanisation to concentrate so much on the city
or on what happened in all cities that they forget that urbanisation is a
'societal' process which not only precedes the formation of particular
cities but also shapes their role as agencies in a developing society.[70]
Quantitative analysts have rightly pointed to other implications of
this process, relating changes in cities to changes in the countryside –
this was beginning to be a favourite late Victorian theme, very dear, it
may be noted, to Rowntree – or to the map of world trade. They have
also qualified conceptions of urban causality by looking more closely
at the components of class behaviour and at the logic of industrialisation.[71] In this context, it is not strange that studies which begin

with the Victorian city end with the twentieth century state. The quantitative investigation generation by generation of rates of change and differentials between cities, of tilts in the balance between local and national finance, and of shifts in politics and communications – is a necessary element in the approach to a fuller understanding of a wide range of welfare issues which cannot easily be grasped in terms of the available qualitative evidence taken by itself.

V

Any account of the approach of different generations of Victorians to statistics and the way in which they handled quantitative evidence must be qualified and supplemented in the light of recent historical scholarship. Yet the wisest of the Victorians themselves knew that their evidence was in places incomplete and in other places defective. Some of them even anticipated recent social scientists who have argued that 'both quality and quantity are misconceived when they are taken to be antithetical or even alternative. Quantities are *of* qualities and a measured quality has just the magnitude expressed in its measure.'[72] In Britain, as in France, current research, in Louis Chevalier's words, is 'a continuation of earlier interpretative efforts which have gone on as long as urbanization itself'.

Different kinds of quantitative enquiry have been carried out in Britain in recent years. In particular, historical demographers have related data about birthplace and migration to occupational data, family size, and varieties of environment within the same urban community, with W. A. Armstrong, for example, using enumerators' books for nineteenth-century Censuses to explore urban social structure through 'still glimpses of a moving picture'. Following in the footsteps of Rowntree in exploring York, he has been explicitly concerned not with the social pathology of the city – the subject which has always captured most attention, qualitative and quantitative – but with 'normal' communities and classes. He has interested himself in the relationship at the family base between conditions in Victorian urban society and conditions before.[73] Such sophisticated use not of the Censuses themselves but of the raw materials used in their compilation has carried into the nineteenth century some of the same methodologies adopted by historians of parish registers in examining periods before the introduction of the Census.[74]

Other methodologies are directly related to the nineteenth-century context. Thus, H. J. Dyos, with the assistance of computers, sought to define and explain the social changes which occurred in the making of Camberwell, a suburb of Victorian London. His interest, tragically cut short, lay not in 'still glimpses' but in processes – 'how particular neighbourhoods came to be occupied, held, or vacated by different social families and households'. His conclusions, however, were cautious: that while 'quantitative techniques can give precision to history, they do not seem capable of formulating new hypotheses, much less of bringing to it objectivity.'[75] So, too, were those of J. R. Kellett, who, after examining urban railway statistics, advanced new hypotheses and pointed out how the techniques of enquiry into the social effects of railway building on the urban way of life had become far more sophisticated by the beginning of the twentieth century than they had been during the 1840s. His study, which explains why parts of towns actually looked the way they did, is useful also in underlining that even in twentieth-century cost-benefit studies 'the most adequate and detailed statistical analysis tends to become only one of several factors moulding final decisions'.[76]

In relation to political decision-making in nineteenth-century cities, where studies of city 'personalities', attempts at 'city biography' and, most recently, 'Namierised' collections of data about mayors and councillors have dominated a largely underdeveloped field, J. R. Vincent has directed attention to the analysis of poll-book material, making generalisations on the way about political statistics and the political motivation which lies behind them. A number of other writers have collected statistics about the social composition of town councils – here, as in occupational studies, there are very real difficulties in categorisation – in an effort to relate leadership to class and occupational structure.[77] Other studies have focused on minority groups and sub-cultures. So far, however, it is obvious that the note of caution sounded by H. J. Dyos is particularly necessary in any consideration of 'the behavioural aspects of urban communities', and L. F. Schnore has even argued – surely, however, too gloomily – that quantitative studies are 'practically impossible'. 'We shall have to continue depending', he concludes, 'upon impressionistic accounts concerning the attitudes and values of our urban forebears.'[78]

Finally, on one subject where quantitative approaches seem possible and inevitable, very little statistical work has been carried out on local finance, where there are complicated issues centring on rateable values and annual rates in the pound (there were for long, of course, whole clusters of urban rates) and the relation of rating statistics to land values, building, and economic activity. What work has been started points to the difficulty of making even simple comparisons. Yet for political reasons the subject is alive.

How far is it feasible to go beyond all these individual studies and produce a Victorian counterpart for the useful study of C. A. Moser and W. Scott, *British Towns: A statistical study of their social and economic differences* (1961)? In *Victorian Cities* I suggested that 'a whole Victorian urban typology could be constructed on these lines'. In pursuing the matter a little further – and some historians should pursue it a lot further – it is useful to start with Moser and Scott's conclusion about 'the striking diversity' of the 157 English towns with a population of more than 50,000 in the middle of the twentieth century. Some are more or less self-contained towns with rural districts at their limits: others are grouped together, with no obvious boundaries, in the tangle of conurbations. 'Between the extremes ... lie every variety of urban species both simple and complex' so that 'no single formula can describe them all'. The statistical diversity even after decades of national social policy-making was extremely striking. One household in five in Gateshead lived in overcrowded conditions, for example, as against one in sixty in Coulsdon: infant mortality rates in Rochdale were three times as high as in Merton and Morden.

Moser and Scott followed eight main lines of statistical inquiry – into population size and structure; demographic change over twenty years; household and housing; economic characteristics; social class; voting; health; and education. Yet what they left out was just as interesting as what they put in – local government finance, on the grounds that it 'needed more detailed treatment' than they 'had time to give'; employment statistics, on the grounds that these were collected from different units; all cultural data, because the statistics were too patchy; all information on crime, religion, and 'the physical characteristics of the town and its amenities'.[79] Given the superiority of twentieth-century statistical sources over those of the nineteenth century, the omissions look unduly discouraging to the historian.

Indeed, the historian of Victorian cities, fascinated as he would be by the diversity of his communities – there were twenty-one of them (plus London) in 1901 – would not be happy on historical grounds about most of these exclusions or with the authors' statement that while 'the change of population between 1931 and 1951 is, on the whole, an inadequate index of the age of a town' they did not feel that they could delve further back into history. As a minimum he would wish to introduce chronological tables setting out the timetables of change in different cities as far, at least, as the creation of new institutions or activities was concerned – a necessary counterpart to statistical studies – and more ambitiously he would want to go on to relate classificatory systems to urban 'profiles' or 'images'.[80] He could, nonetheless, experiment happily with schemes of urban classification both in terms of Moser and Scott's list of primary variables, and, if he had the skill, with component analysis.

It is apparent at the outset that there are fascinating contrasts of experience between the nineteenth and twentieth centuries, with no Victorian town ever containing, as Worthing did in the period covered by Moser and Scott, 58·8 per cent of its population over the age of sixty-five. Bradford, for instance, never had more than 4 per cent at any census between 1841 and 1901, while the town with the lowest proportion in Moser and Scott's account – Dagenham – had 4·9 per cent in 1951. Middlesbrough had 36 per cent of its population below the age of fifteen in 1841 and 1901, a significantly higher figure than the English town with the highest 1951 figure – 31·1 per cent – Huyton-with-Ruby. Bradford had as high a figure as 45 per cent in 1841. The male/female ratio is also particularly interesting to compare. Middles-brough, with more males than females both in 1851 and 1901, stood out in this connection as much as in its remarkable statistics of growth, a matter of civic rhetoric and one of the topics covered qualitatively in my *Victorian Cities*. It was, in fact, described in 1885 by the statistician E. G. Ravenstein as a town which by 'its rapid growth, the hetero-geneous composition of its population, and the preponderance of the male sex, recalls features generally credited only to the towns of the American west.'[81]

Statistical series of many of Moser and Scott's social indicators are missing for the nineteenth century, but far more can be done with the nineteenth-century 'mix' of the population and the relationship bet-ween 'native' and 'extraneous' elements than they have tried to do. There would be value, too, through econometric and other network studies, in relating recent urban experience to that of the nineteenth century. Of Moser and Scott's urban groups 1, 2 and 3 in 1951 – mainly resorts, administrative, and commercial towns – five out of thirty-seven were already towns of over 50,000 in 1851 and thirteen in 1901; whereas of their groups 4, 5, 6, 7 and 8 – mainly industrial towns – six-teen out of sixty-seven were in the 1851 list and forty-seven in that of 1901. Of the fifty-one towns in their groups 9, 10, 11, 12, 13 and 14 – suburbs and suburban-type towns – there were no towns in the 1851 list and only seven in 1901.

Much of the history of Victorian urbanisation can be studied in such terms, although full explanations of historical change depend on relating statistics to evidence of a qualitative kind derived from impressions of particular places as seen by inhabitants, visitors and 'experts'. Such evidence must be accumulated from a wide variety of sources, local and national. No urban history can afford to neglect the 'sense of place' which must be a main theme of all studies of Victorian cities, or fail to consider the distinctive and the 'unusual' as well as the general and the commonplace. It was Henry James, writing of London, who commented aptly that 'when a social product is so vast and various, it may be approached on a thousand different sides, and liked and disliked for a thousand different reasons.'[82]

All such visions illuminate the city as it actually is or was. In the famous third chapter of Macaulay's *History of England* (1848), the historian drew an unforgettable picture of seventeenth-century London which relied heavily, through contrast, on the character of mid-Victorian London. 'The town did not, as now, fade by imperceptible degrees into the country. No long avenues of villas, embowered in lilacs and laburnums, extended from the great centre of wealth and civilization almost to the boundaries of Middlesex and far into the heart of Kent and Surrey.' By the middle of the nineteenth century, 'the fireside, the nursery, the social table' were no longer in the City of London: 'the chiefs of the mercantile interest are no longer citizens'. The use of space had changed. 'He who then rambled to what is now the gayest and most crowded part of Regent Street found himself in a solitude, and was sometimes so fortunate as to have shot at a woodcock.' Relations had changed, too, along with the ecology. Unimproved London was less socially segregated: 'In Covent Garden a filthy and noisy market was held close to the dwellings of the great.' At the same time, there was a more absolute difference between the metropolitan and the Londoner. 'A Cockney in a rural village was stared at as much as if he had intruded into a Kraal of the Hottentots. On the other hand, when the Lord of a Lincolnshire or Shropshire manor appeared in Fleet Street, he was as easily distinguished from the resident population as a Turk or a Lascar.'

Macaulay had little to say about statistics – far less, for instance, than Mayhew, writing soon afterwards, or Henry Buckle – yet his picture holds and illuminates. He set out less to explain or to interpret than to describe and to evoke. Quantitative approaches to social history do not destroy the value of this kind of writing. What they do, indeed, is to sharpen the appeal of the artist's vision, enabling us to relate special experience or special ways of viewing common experience to common experience itself.

NOTES

1 M. W. Flinn (ed.), Introduction to *The Sanitary Condition of the Labouring Population of Great Britain, 1842* (1965), p. 27. See also

J. M. Eyler, *Victorian Social Medicine. The Ideas and Methods of William Farr* (1979).

2   G.M. Young, *Victorian England, Portrait of an Age* (1963 edn), p. 32.

3   See, for example, R.W. Rawson, 'An Enquiry into the Statistics of Crime in England and Wales', in the *Journal of the Statistical Society of London*, vol. II (1839-40), and J. Fletcher, 'Moral and Educational Statistics of England and Wales', ibid., vol. XII (1847).

4   The address is printed in C. Kingsley, *Sanitary and Social Lectures and Essays* (1880), pp. 87-222.

5   *Victorian Cities* (1963), pp. 57-8.

6   'My satire is against those who see figures and averages, and nothing else ... the addled heads who would ... comfort the labourer in travelling twelve miles a day to and from his work, by telling him that the average distance of one inhabited place from another in the whole area of England, is not more than four miles.' From a letter to Charles Knight, 30 January 1855, quoted in the Norton Critical Edition of *Hard Times*, ed. George Ford and Sylvère Monod (1966), p. 277. Dickens admired H. T. Buckle's *History of Civilization in England* (2 vols, 1857-61) with its statistical preoccupations, although later Lord Acton complained that for Buckle nothing could 'withstand the rules of simple arithmetic' (*Historical Essays and Studies* (1908), p. 31).

7   His letter of 16 December 1845 is quoted in H. S. Tremenheere, *I was There: Memoirs* (ed. E. L. and O. P. Edmonds, 1905), p. 54.

8   H. Perkin, *The Origins of Modern English Society, 1780-1880* (1969), p. 326.

9   See Dr Guy, 'On the Original and Acquired Meaning of the Term "Statistics"', *Journal of the Royal Statistical Society*, vol. XXVI (1845). The original use of the term is attributed to Gottfried Achenwal (1749). See also M. J. Cullen, *The Statistical Movement in Early Victorian Britain* (1975), p. 10, who goes back to a German contemporary of William Petty.

10 See M. P. Mack, *Jeremy Bentham: An Odyssey of Ideas* (1962), pp. 237-40.

11 Statistical surveys of 'regions' were also to become fashionable. See, for example, the introduction to Sismondi's unpublished *Statistique du Département de Léman* (ed. H. O. Pappé, 1971). Quantitative statistics were only one element in such surveys. See also Sir John Sinclair's *Statistical Account of Scotland* (1791).

12 J. C. Lettsom, *Medical Memoirs of the General Dispensary in London* (1774), p. x.

13 See L. S. Marshall, *The Development of Public Opinion in Manchester* (1946) for an account of the work of the local Board of Health. Perceval's *Observations on the Population of Manchester and Salford* (1772) and his *Further Observations* (1774) are not only of interest to social statisticians, but reveal how closely he related statistical method to what would now be called quality of life. He also corresponded with James Watt on means to avoid smoke pollution. See E. Robinson and

A. E. Musson, *James Watt and the Steam Revolution* (1969), p. 125.

14 See, for example, the use made of vital statistics in 1825 by John Finlaison, actuary of the National Debt Office of the Treasury, in *First Report of the Select Committee on the Laws respecting Friendly Societies*, Parliamentary Papers, 1825, vol. IV, Appendix B_1, pp. 125-6. Finlaison discussed changes in expectation of life between the early eighteenth and the early nineteenth centuries.

15 W. T. Brande, *A Dictionary of Science, Literature and Art* (1842), p. 1150.

16 J. E. Portlock, Review of *An Address of the Objects and Advantages of Statistical Enquiries* (1838-9).

17 See [J. Bonar and H. W. Macrosty], *Annals of the Royal Statistical Society, 1834-1934* (1934), p. 22. The first meeting took place on 15 March 1834. In June 1833 the British Association for the Advancement of Science had decided at its third meeting to set up a Statistical Section, and Charles Babbage, advised by the French statistician, Adolphe Quételet, had gone on to press for the formation of the new society. Its history is well covered in F. J. Mowat, 'History of the Statistical Society of London' in the *Journal of the Royal Statistical Society*, Jubilee Volume (1885), pp. 14-60. See also V. L. Hilts, '*Aliis exterendum* or the Origins of the Statistical Society of London' in *Isis*, vol. 69 (1978).

18 The story is well told in T. S. Ashton, *Economic and Social Investigation in Manchester, 1833-1933* (1934). See also D. Elesh, 'The Manchester Statistical Society' in the *Journal of the History of Behavioural Sciences*, vol. 8 (1972).

19 W. R. Greg (1809-81) critically reviewed Mrs Gaskell's *Mary Barton* in the *Edinburgh Review*, vol. LXXXIX, in April 1849, calling it unfair to mill-workers. Mrs Gaskell in her preface stated that she was concerned to show how things *seemed* to the poor. See A. Pollard, *Mrs Gaskell, Novelist and Biographer* (1965), pp. 59-60, and E. Wright, *Mrs Gaskell* (1965), pp. 231-2.

20 *Report of Committee of the Manchester Statistical Society on the State of Education in the Borough of Manchester, in 1834* (1835). The Committee comprised seventeen men, and the main object of the report was to show that Parliament had underestimated the number of schools in Manchester. A second edition containing 'a more minute classification' appeared in the same year.

21 Quoted in Ashton, *op. cit.*, p. 13. For a brief critique of the approach and the relationship of the method to an ideology, see P. Abrams, *The Origins of British Sociology* (1968), p. 19.

22 See 'Provincial Statistical Societies in the United Kingdom', *J.S.S.*, vols I (1838-9) and II (1839-40).

23 Appendix to Chapter 2, 'The Origins of the Royal Statistical Society'.

24 See A. Newsholme, *The Elements of Vital Statistics* (1889), pp. 111-12; Cullen, *op. cit.*, Chapter 4.

25 MS. Draft, June 1845, quoted in R. A. Lewis, *Edwin Chadwick and the Public Health Movement 1832-54* (1952), p. 12.

26 Quoted in Lewis, *op. cit.*, p. 15.

27 William E. Channing, *A Discourse on the Life and Character of the Rev. Joseph Tuckerman, D.D.* (1841), p. 4. For Dickens's view of Channing, see *American Notes* (1842), Chapter 3.

28 There are many passages in English which anticipate the systematic distinction of Ferdinand Tönnies in 1887 between *Gemeinschaft* (community) and *Gesellschaft*. A twentieth-century classic statement widely reprinted, of urban sociology in terms of numbers and relationships, is that of Louis Wirth, 'Urbanism as a Way of Life', in *American Journal of Sociology*, (1938) vol. XLIV, pp. 1-24. See also a critique by R. N. Morris, *Urban Sociology* (1968), and R. E. Park, E. W. Burgess and R. D. McKenzie, *The City* (1925).

29 The first *Morning Chronicle* article by Mayhew on what was later incorporated in his *London Labour and the London Poor* (1861-2) appeared in October 1849.

30 Arnold Kettle, 'The Early Victorian Social Problem Novel', in Boris Ford (ed.), *The Pelican Guide to English Literature*, vol. VI. *The Nineteenth Century* (1958), p. 171. For the novel as a favourite form of social commentary during the 1840s, see Kathleen Tillotson, *Novels of the Eighteen-Forties* (1954).

31 *Fraser's Magazine*, vol. XIX (1849), p. 430.

32 E. P. Thompson, 'The Political Education of Henry Mayhew', *Victorian Studies*, vol. XI (1967).

33 For Chartist attacks on Chadwick, see, for example, *Charter*, 28 April 1839, 23 June 1839. Yet in 1848 Chadwick wrote to the Bishop of London that he did not see 'how any one could get up in the Commons and contend that where there was a heavy infantile slaughter, or where the working classes are ravaged by epidemics, there shall be no intervention except on the initiation of the middle classes.' (Quoted in Lewis, *op. cit.*, p. 170.)

34 Henry Mayhew, *Answers*, July 1851, quoted in Thompson, *op. cit.*, p. 56.

35 Quoted in Ashton, *op. cit.*, p. 51.

36 *Punch*, vol. XV (1848), p. 92; it added, more succinctly, a misquotation from Pope's line from his 'Epistle to Dr Arbuthnot': 'They lisped in numbers, for the numbers came.' For other examples of this theme, see A. Briggs and S. Briggs, *Cap and Bell* (1973), pp. 122-3.

37 *Charles Kingsley, His Letters and Memories of his Life*, edited by his wife (1892 edn), p. 88. Compare the speech of Dickens with that of Lord Carlisle at a Festival of the Metropolitan Sanitary Association in 1851 as described in the *Illustrated London News*, 7 May 1851: K. J. Fielding (ed.), *The Speeches of Charles Dickens* (1960), pp. 127-33. The occasion is briefly described in Humphry House, *The Dickens World* (1942 edn), pp. 195-6. See also the account of the implications of Tom-all-Alone's 'filth and slime', with its retribution theme, in *Bleak House* (1853).

38 Book II.

39 John Ruskin, *Fors Clavigera*, Library edn, vol. XXIX (1905), p. 224.

40 Henry Ashworth, 'Statistics of the Present Depression of Trade at

Bolton', in vols. IV/V *J.S.S.* (1842-3). See also T. C. Barker, D. J. Oddy and J. Yudkin, *The Dietary Surveys of Dr. Edward Smith, 1862-3* (1970).

41 See B. Rogers, 'The Social Science Association, 1857-1886', in *The Manchester School of Economics and Social Studies*, vol. XX (1952).

42 Cullen, *op. cit.*, p. 104.

43 F. J. Mouat, 'History of the Statistical Society, of London', Jubilee Volume (1885).

44 Inaugural address, ibid., vol. LVII (1894).

45 *Manchester Examiner and Times*, 5 October 1886.

46 *Manchester Guardian*, 1 October 1866.

47 See M. Sturt, *The Education of the People* (1967), pp. 296 ff., for a useful summary of the statistical inquiries leading up to the Education Act of 1870.

48 *Journal of the Royal Statistical Society*, vol. LIII (1890).

49 Sir Rawson W. Rawson, *Royal Statistical Society*, Jubilee edition (1885).

50 *Encyclopaedia Britannica*, vol. XXII, pp. 461-6.

51 Quoted in T. S. Simey and M. B. Simey, *Charles Booth, Social Scientist* (1960), p. 77.

52 B. Seebohm Rowntree, *Poverty, A Study of Town Life* (1901), pp. 133-4. For the method and its implications, see Asa Briggs, *Social Thought and Social Action: A Study of the Work of Seebohm Rowntree* (1961), Chapter 2.

53 Beatrice Webb, *My Apprenticeship* (1926), p. 216.

54 T. S. Simey and M. B. Simey, *op. cit.*, p. 78.

55 T. W. Hutchison, *Review of Economic Doctrines, 1870-1929* (1953), p. 426. See also Alfred Marshall, *Principles of Economics* (1920 edn), p. 492: 'No doubt statistics can be easily misinterpreted, and are often very misleading when first applied to new problems. But many of the worst fallacies involved in the misapplications of statistics are definite and can be definitely exposed, till at last no-one ventures to repeat them even when addressing an uninterested audience.'

56 Charles Booth, *Life and Labour of the People of London*, 2nd series: *Industry* (1903), vol. I, p. 18.

57 *The Notebooks of Henry James*, ed. F. O. Matthiessen and Kenneth B. Murdock (1961), pp. 27-8. James wrote this in a Boston hotel in 1881.

58 H. Llewellyn Smith, 'Influx of Population', in C. Booth, *Life and Labour of the People in London*, vol. III (1892), p. 75. There is something of the same sense in Ruskin's *Praeterita* (1886).

59 T. S. Simey and M. B. Simey, *op. cit.*, p. 80.

60 See *London Statistics*, 1889 onwards.

61 *City Reports* (1849), pp. 44-57, quoted in Royston Lambert, *Sir John Simon* (1963), p. 150.

62 M. G. Kendall, 'The History of Statistical Method', in *The International Encyclopaedia of the Social Sciences*, vol. XV (1968).

63 Infant mortality of males was 23·3 per 1000 for 1838-54, as for the whole period 1838-71. For females the figures were 21·6 and 21·5. See W. Farr, *Vital Statistics* (1885), p. 183.

64 See below, vol. II, p. 135.

65 *Fortnightly Review*, new series, vol. LIII (1893).

66 For quantitative approaches in general see E. A. Wrigley (ed.), *Nineteenth-Century Society: Essays in the Use of Quantitative Methods for the Study of Social Data* (1972). The approaches, which also cover questions of 'class', are discussed, too, in S. Thernstrom and R. Sennett (eds.), *Nineteenth-Century Cities: Essays in the New Urban History* (1969), an interesting American study. See also R. W. Vogel, 'The New Economic History, Its Findings and Methods', in the *Economic History Review*, 2nd series, vol. XIX (1966), and D. K. Rowney and J. Q. Graham (eds), *Quantitative History* (1969).

67 Lambert, *op. cit.*, p. 602.

68 See, for example, Lord Morpeth's speech in the debate on the Public Health Act of 1848. *Hansard*, vol XCVI, cols 385-428, and vol. II, pp. 138-9.

69 C. F. G. Masterman, 'The Social Abyss', *Contemporary Review*, vol. LXXI (1902), pp. 23-35.

70 See Eric E. Lampard, 'Historical Aspects of Urbanization', in Philip M. Hauser and Leo F. Schnore (eds.), *The Study of Urbanization* (1965), pp. 519-54.

71 A. Kaplan, 'Measurement in Behavioral Science', from *The Conduct of Inquiry* (1964), reprinted in M. Brodbeck (ed.), *Readings in the Philosophy of the Social Sciences* (1968), pp. 601-8.

72 Louis Chevalier, *Classes laborieuses et classes dangereuses à Paris pendant la première moitié du xixe siècle* (1958). See also his article 'A Reactionary View of Urban History', in *The Times Literary Supplement*, 8 September 1966.

73 See W. A. Armstrong, 'Social Structure from the Early Census Returns', in E. A. Wrigley (ed.), *An Introduction to English Historical Demography* (1966), pp. 209-38, and 'The Interpretation of the Census Enumerators' Books for Victorian Towns', in H. J. Dyos (ed.), *The Study of Urban History* (1968), pp. 67-85; and M. Anderson, *Family Structure in Nineteenth-Century Lancashire* (1971).

74 See R. S. Schofield, 'Historical Demography: Some Possibilities and Some Limitations', in *Transactions of the Royal Historical Society*, 5th Series, vol. 21 (1971).

75 H. J. Dyos and A. B. M. Baker, 'The Possibilities of Computerising Census Data', ibid., pp. 87-112. See also H. J. Dyos, *Victorian Suburb: A study of the growth of Camberwell* (1961).

76 J. R. Kellett, *The Impact of Railways on Victorian Cities* (1969). See also A. R. Prest and R. Turvey, 'Cost-Benefit Analysis, A Survey', *Economic Journal*, vol. LXXV (1965).

77 J. R. Vincent, *Poll-Books: How Victorians Voted* (1967).

78 L. F. Schnore, 'Problems of Quantitative Study', in H. J. Dyos (ed.), *The Study of Urban History*, pp. 189-208.

79 C. A. Moser and W. Scott, *British Towns: A Statistical Study of their Social and Economic Differences* (1961), p. 8.

80 See, *inter alia*, the pioneering study by K. Lynch, *The Image of the City*

(1960), and A. L. Strauss, *The American City: A Source Book of Urban Imagery* (1968). There is no equally good pair of studies for Britain.

81 E. F. Ravenstein, 'The Laws of Migration', in the *JRSS*, vol. XLVIII (1885).

82 H. James, *English Hours* (1963 edn), p. 10. The article first appeared in 1888.

II

PLACES AND PEOPLE

Cities and towns, the various haunts of men
Defy the pencil, they require the pen.

George Crabbe

The name of Watt will be known while that of every warrior and
monarch and statesman of his day has perished ... Science and the arts
are renovating the constitution of society. The destiny of nations
cannot be much longer held by political gamblers, wealthy dolts, titled
buffoons, and royal puppets: these no longer sustained by factitious
aids must descend to their own level.

Thomas Ewbank

4 The Sense of Place

Discussions on the quality of man's environment have revealed at least as much diversity of approach to the study of the subject as there is diversity in the actual environments which men have tried to fashion for themselves. And what holds for study holds also for the problems of environmental planning. Planning cities, like understanding them, requires a combination of insights and techniques and a convergence of disciplines. It is fitting to recall the words of Patrick Geddes in his plan for Colombo, Ceylon in 1921, that 'neither the most practical of engineers nor the most exquisite of aesthetes can plan for the city by himself alone, neither the best of physicians nor of pedagogues, neither the most spiritual nor the most matter-of-fact of its governing classes'.[1] Neither the necessary combination of insights and techniques nor the convergence of disciplines is usually there.

Another difficulty, more recently articulated, springs from the use of the word 'environment', a general term which became popular during the 1970s and which can relate either to the neighbourhood or to the biosphere. Much writing about environmental issues is so general (and so thick with jargon) that it loses all contact with particular people in particular places at a particular moment of time. We need poets and novelists even more than psychologists (or anthropologists) to restore the sense of experience through a particular place: their verse and prose illuminates the attachments.[2]

Recently a new generation of geographers has contributed to the exploration. Yi-Fu Tuan's *Space and Place* (1977) considered 'the intimate use of space' as well as the spatial map of a city or a country, stressing that 'space is transformed into place as it acquires definition and meaning' and that 'distance is a meaningless spatial concept apart from the idea of goal or place'. 'Space' is more abstract than 'place', Yi-Fu Tuan goes on. 'What begins as undifferentiated space becomes place as we get to know it better and endow it with value.'[3] The eloquent title of a more recent collection of specialist papers is *Timing Space and Spacing Time*.[4]

Historians have their role, too, as explorers, an older role, which goes back to the beginnings of history, their distinctive contribution being, perhaps, to concern themselves with the sense of place and what has made and still makes it. Many, perhaps most, historians have strongly *felt* a sense of place: Trevelyan, following Macaulay, was one, but so, too, was a very different historian, Edward Gibbon. Where historians have been less successful is when they have set out to *explain* it. Geographers have been better, and among British writers David Canter has shown by experiment that planners (and other 'environmental specialists') may experience a place quite differently from 'laymen'.[5]

My own efforts to explain 'place' were provoked by Lewis Mumford's confident generalisation about nineteenth-century cities – and Mumford was an admirer of Geddes[6] – which he described as the same places with different aliases and as warrens rather than communities. I was concerned from the start, therefore, with the comparative profiles of particular cities as well as with the processes of urbanisation. I became interested, too, in the images of cities, how people perceive or have perceived them.[7] It was necessary to establish structures and chronologies and to consider in detail the tangled nexus of private and public conflicts, compromises and decisions (many of them by default) which have fashioned 'places'. Yet this did not seem to be enough: the visual and the social had to be related to the psychological, to how people shared or did not share common responses. Our urban environments have been characterised by manifest inequalities – of education, of income, of health, of opportunity: in such circumstances both deprived and privileged groups often find it impossible to think and feel outside the limits of their own 'sub-environment'. There is no enclosing homogeneity, therefore, in the group of people called 'laymen' by professionals or in what civic leaders call 'citizens'.

Yet the images of places are often sharp and clear, provoking bold and controversial statements, like V.S. Pritchett's remark that 'if Paris suggests intelligence, if Rome suggests the world, if New York suggests activity, the word for London is experience'.[8] Writers' comparisons of this kind are an invitation to argument. At the same time, conflicting declarations have been made by different people about each particular city. Mrs Siddons, the actress, thought Britain's Leeds 'the most disagreeable town in His Majesty's dominions', and Dickens, two generations later, described it as 'a beastly place, one of the nastiest places I know'; yet G. S. Phillips, a local writer strongly influenced by Emerson, called it 'one of the grandest poems which has ever been offered to the world'.[9] Behind the literature of each particular city – and there often is a literature as well as a collection of texts and documents – there is divergent experience, reflected in divergent response.[10]

I always like to start, however, with 'whole' environments – their interrelatedness and coherence (or lack of it) – and not with lists of individual buildings or inventories of separate features, however impressive. Such a start should always involve seeing and feeling as well as reading. A directness of approach is a precondition of understanding. Rasmussen emphasises this point in the twentieth century when, for example, he writes that the many tourists who visit Sta. Maria Maggiore in Rome on sightseeing tours 'hardly notice the unique character of the surroundings. They simply check off one of the starred numbers in their guide-books and hasten on to the next one. They do not experience the place.'[11] Long ago Hazlitt rightly made fun of the painter Benjamin West who when asked if he had ever been to Greece replied, 'No, but I have read a descriptive catalogue of the principal objects in that country, and I believe I am as well conversant with them as if I had visited it.'[12]

I

There are at least four good reasons for introducing a historical dimension into a symposium devoted to the quality of man's environment, even when – perhaps because – we are living in a period when we have visions of a future vastly different from our past. First, since until relatively recently, there has been relentless pressure to consider questions concerning the contemporary environment exclusively in functional and quantitative terms, by introducing such a dimension we extend our range and strengthen our perspectives. We are provoked as well as stimulated when we select from the past as well as the present revealing examples from many different societies and cultures of 'successful' and 'unsuccessful' human environments, including not only 'planned' but what may be called 'spontaneous' environments, both successful and unsuccessful, which owed little or nothing to expert guidance or to deliberately planned design.[13] At the same time, past examples may be less interesting for 'their historicity' than for 'the many useful similes and analogies they offer for the contemporary architect and designer'.[14]

Second, there is more to be gained from comparing actual experience, past and present, common or distinctive, and the factors which moulded it, than from thinking of environmental problems in either an over-systematised fashion or in a utopian mould (Utopia means 'no place') as they often have been and still often are considered. In this context the study of relationships in the past can be just as useful an analytical exercise as the study of relationships in the present, particularly when an attempt is made to set out all the relevant relationships: technical, social, political, and visual. Third, many of our environments, particularly in Europe, cannot be thought of at all, let alone 'planned', without bringing the past into the reckoning; the ambivalent past, which carries with it both a rich heritage of buildings and vistas and a depressing legacy of blight, squalor and decay. We do not begin afresh. How to deal with this inheritance poses us with not one problem or with one choice but with a whole series of interrelated problems and options, and fortunately we have become more aware of these in recent years. Fourth, the study of history enables us to understand more fully some aspects of contemporary experience in developing countries which are undergoing strains and tensions in their contemporary processes or urbanisation. The stresses and strains of a developing nation often have more in common with nineteenth-century or earlier urban strains and tensions in what are now developed or overdeveloped countries than they have with twentieth-century strains and stresses of contemporary American cities as described in articles and features in widely-read current periodicals. Where there are differences – as there often are – these, also, often lend themselves to historical analysis.

II

I regard places, as Susanne Langer does in her *Feeling and Form*, as 'creative things', 'ethnic domains made visible, tangible, sensible'. In this connection, a ship, constantly changing its location, is nonetheless a self-contained place, and a gypsy camp is far different from an Indian camp, although geographically it may be where the Indian camp used to be.[15] Given this approach, it is essential to reiterate that cities are collections of places as well as places in themselves. While there has been only one Paris, one Rome, one New York, one London – to go back to the great quartet identified by Pritchett – each of these cities in itself has been a collection of distinct places, each with its own ecology and history, sometimes with its own sub-culture. There have always been some citizens who have thought primarily within the context of the city of a part rather than the whole. It is not only power or deprivation which determines communication. London's East-enders in the late nineteenth century may not have visited the West End because they had neither the time nor the money to do so, but when in the twentieth century Professor de Jouvenel deliberately does not visit the Champs Elysées, although he knows that it exists, it is certainly not because he is deprived. Yet in consequence, his 'experience' of Paris is quite different from that of people who do.

This phenomenon of disassociation has been a subject sometimes of amusement, sometimes of concern. 'I have often amused myself', wrote James Boswell in 1741 – and he is quoted with approval by Jane

Jacobs in *The Death and Life of Great American Cities* – 'with thinking how different the same place is to different people.'[16] In the nineteenth century, emphasis switched from disassociation to segregation, which has remained a twentieth-century preoccupation. Most people were shocked rather than amused by the fact that within the great cities populations coexisted in separation from each other, some 'belonging', some 'alienated'. Social changes had taken place which had turned the city into a 'problem' and which implied that in order to understand 'the other population' or populations an effort of exploration within the city was necessary; an effort as great as that entailed in exploring foreign lands. 'A hovel in one of the suburbs which they know least would be as strange to most Londoners as a village in the African forests.'[17] The simile recurs relentlessly. Much modern sociology had its origins in this setting.

The contemporary 'problem' is more complex given that there now are 'professionals' as well as explorers, and given, too, that social and fiscal policies designed to protect the privileged or to assist the deprived – usually there are combinations of both – raise sharp differences between groups, some of which express themselves in civic disturbance. The appearance of cities has changed drastically also with sharp and often deliberate breaks in continuity. Susanne Langer's ship constantly changing its location may be more of a place with perceived identity than a constantly changing city located in one place. There are some historians who have doubted whether great cities with historic names, as they exist today, can be treated 'merely, or even primarily, as the descendants of the earlier ones'.[18] 'Particularity' itself is in question.

Obviously, where the question of 'particularity' now stands – or where we think it stands – influences our view about where it once stood. Almost all books on *the city* now begin with twentieth-century 'placelessness'. Here are several examples of recent comment on it. 'Mobility, communication and the broadly distributed fruits of rising productivity are generating a society disperse and heterogeneous, organised by functional relations rather than by proximity.'[19] The crime of subtopia is that it blurs the distinction between places.'[20] 'We reach for some vague concept of metropolis to describe the release of urban potential from its recognised ambit.'[21] 'Oakland: when you get there, there is no there, there,' so Gertrude Stein is reputed to have said.[22] And in these judgements threatened Nature comes into the reckoning as well as the man-fashioned environment.

The richly varied places of the natural world are structured in an ordered relationship that is yet full, for people of drama and surprise. They are

rapidly being obliterated under a meaningless pattern of building, mono-
tonous and chaotic. The new structures will fall down one day but the
obliteration of the natural order is permanent. We are in urgent need of
understanding *places* before we lose them, of learning how to see them and
to take possession of them.[23]

The so-called twentieth-century shift from 'place' to 'placelessness',
like all such so-called shifts, is feared by some, welcomed by others,
both sides sharing strong feelings and powerful language; and often it
can be exaggerated like Mumford's nineteenth-century uniformities.
To most writers it is a *fait accompli*, as the industrial revolution once
was: 'spatial dispersion' and all that seems to go with it is treated as 'a
built-in feature of the future'.[24] To many others it is also a source of
melancholy and nostalgia. 'The great positive values' of an urban
civilisation stem from its 'togetherness', it is said, 'from the concentrated variety that a Manhattan typifies, not from the endless, mono-
tonous homogeneity which middle-class suburban dispersion has
produced.'[25] An English writer, with Richard Hoggart's picture of
recent English social history in the back of the mind,[26] would bring in
working-class suburban dispersion also and might look back with
nostalgia to the cramped and crowded community values of Bethnal
Green.[27]

Other writers, however, salute the emergence of the new, seeing in it
not environmental chaos but the birth pangs of a newly-forming order
with complexity as one of its main characteristics. They have even
found pleasure in seeing the distinctive landmarks disappear. As one
English reviewer put it cryptically in 1966, 'One of the most priceless
boons our civilisation has to offer is the realisation that we do not
know where we are, provided we know where we are going.'[28] American writing is more positive and warm. In one of Ada Louise Huxtable's
illuminating pieces on American architecture which combine excitement in the new and concern for the old she has sympathetically
described Houston, Texas as 'a continuous series of cultural shocks'
where 'no one seems to feel the need for the public vision that older
cities have of a hierarchy of places and buildings, an organized
conception of function and form'. 'New values and new dimensions in
time and space' are being erected in an 'expanding, mobile city' dealing
in distance and discontinuity and continuously measuring its returns
on its commercial investments. It is 'devoted to moon shots, not
moonviewing' and 'substitutes fantasy for history'.[29]

To a historian, much of this contemporary writing, whatever its
angle, cryptic or downright, seems to contain an element of exaggeration which is very familiar throughout the long-running debate
about cities, a debate which can be traced back before the advent of

industrialisation in the late eighteenth and nineteenth centuries. In fact, the contrast between past and present may not be quite as sharp as it is often claimed to be. Cities, however strong their sense of identity, have never been quite the autonomous self-contained places clear to those who draw sharp contrasts. It has never been possible to view them in isolation – either socially or culturally (usually not even visually) – from the countryside or the society in which they sprang up. 'If you think of the city as a fixed place, fixed people, everything else just fits', a historian of medieval cities has written, 'whereas there has always been flow in and flow out. In the Greek *polis* and in every other kind of city people live in the city only because they can get out of it. Even the high Renaissance Italians spent the summer in the country and they found the city liveable only for this reason.'[30] In eighteenth-century England the pattern was systematised and established. Of course, it related then – as it still does – only to those favoured individuals and groups who could make private decisions for themselves about their environment, and the flow did not involve perpetual disturbance to the appearance of the environment. Moreover, some buildings, like churches, which often changed their appearance, were built to last. Most city-dwellers had a sense of place which owed much to such symbols and little or nothing directly to any feeling either of contrast or of interdependence between city and country.

Likewise, while travellers' tales are full of comparisons and contrasts between cities – like early emigrants' letters – most city-dwellers had little experience of travel to other cities which would have afforded them alternative sources of contrast between their own cities and other 'places'. Now a far greater number of them have, even though packaged travel in particular often leads not to the recognising of different places as other places but to the superimposing on them of institutions and patterns of life with which the travellers are already familiar. As long ago as 1887, Frederic Harrison complained of a tendency among travellers to make places abroad as much as possible like places 'at home'. 'In things spiritual and temporal alike', he wrote, 'our modern mania abroad is to carry with us our own life, instead of accepting that which we find on the spot. The generation which planted London-on-the-Sea is succeeded by the generation which has planted Paris-on-the-Alps, Paris-on-the-Riviera, and Paris-on-the-Bay-of-Naples ... *Coelum non vitam mutant qui trans mare currunt.* We go abroad but we travel no longer.'[31] We lose the sense of place in the process as we have lost it increasingly around the Mediterranean coast, but fortunately not in the hinterland.

Travellers through time have not made the recent history of 'place' and 'placelessness' any more clear than most travellers through space. When Lewis Mumford, in my view quite wrongly, argued that 'placelessness' was a by-product of the industrial revolution, he was already within a tradition, although he sharpened it when he wrote that in the wake of coal and steam the same kind of urban industrial community proliferated all over the world – Dickens' 'Coketown', alias Smokeover, Mechanicsville, Manchester, Birmingham, Essen, Elberfield, Lille, Roubaix, Newark, Pittsburgh, or Youngstown, the same place with different aliases.[32] In fact, as we now see at a greater distance, the industrial revolution during its early stages encouraged many new aspects of urban differentiation – in social and economic structure, even in buildings – sharpening the distinction between Birmingham and Manchester, for example, and directing public attention not to what they had in common but to their differences. There was no period of urban history when more attention was devoted to the 'identity' of particular places. At the same time, Nature was seen in different perspective – with a special sense of 'place' here also (as, for instance, in the 'discovery' of the Lake District or later of the Alps) – while the 'special' distinctiveness of the older historic places of the past was emphasised. Few of these cities, indeed, were swallowed up in industrialisation, and it is fair to say that Florence, Venice and Athens – to take three only of the great cities of the past – were rediscovered in detail as 'places'[33] by outsiders during this period.

Travellers were particularly sensitive to identity in this age of exploration, not least in America, where the differentiation of American cities had been stressed by many travellers long before Lord Bryce made his well-known complaint that all American cities were alike, except that some were built in stone and some in brick. Charles Dickens' *American Notes* of 1842 deserve to be set alongside Henry James' *Notebooks*, brilliant in their pictures of London and Paris, for sensitive, highly individualised comment on cities. 'Every thoroughfare' in Boston, according to Dickens, 'looked exactly like a scene in a pantomime ... I never turned a corner without looking for a clown or a pantaloon, who, I had no doubt, were hiding in a door way or behind some pillar close at hand.' Philadelphia was handsome, but 'distinctly regular. After walking about it in an hour or two, I felt that I would have given all the world for a crooked street.' Washington was the city not of 'magnificent distances', as it claimed, but of 'magnificent intentions'. 'To the admirers of cities it is like a Barmecide Feast: a pleasant field for the imagination to rove in ... Such as it is, it is likely to remain.'

Dickens is well-known for his 'symbolic' picture of Coketown, taken over by Mumford, and for his imaginative insight into the rich street life of Victorian London, well noted by Rasmussen. His verbal pictures of London were never 'photographs'; they always related appearance to mood and sometimes to the mood of a whole society, as at the beginning of *Bleak House* (1852-3) or as in an article of 1854 in *Household Words*, where he described the railway terminus works between Camden Town and Bloomsbury as 'a picture of our moral state'. 'They look confused and giddy', he went on, 'with an air as if they were always up all night and always giddy.' 'We are, mind and body, an unsettled neighbourhood,' he concluded. 'We are demoralized by the contemplation of luggage in perpetual motion.'[34] His impressions of American and Italian cities should be set alongside such writing about England.

When searching for city 'identity' there is much to be said for turning to those books which provide evidence of a very special kind of distinctive personal experience and express it in such memorable form that the verbal statement in itself conveys the 'mood' of the city as well as the mood of the artist to people who have never even seen a picture of the place. I am in complete harmony with Professor Leo Marx in his emphasis on the role of the writer and the artist[35] (much more could be said of the latter) and more recently of the film-maker in forging the sense of place, adding that it may be very particular as well as typal.

Verbal as well as visual accounts are usually far more relevant than architects' photographs or planners' models, which not only leave out but often misrepresent. As V. S. Naipaul has put it in his fascinating book on India, 'No city or landscape is truly rich unless it has been given the quality of myth by writer, painter or by its association with great events.'[36] The 'great events', however, are not strictly necessary. The sense of place, indeed, as expressed in words and pictures encompasses feelings that particular places are nasty as well as beautiful, hateful as well as lovable. One of the most remarkable documents of the British industrial revolution is called *A Gazeteer of Disgusting Places*, published in 1843. In contemporary settings, there is sometimes a twist as far as the 'nasty' is concerned. Twentieth-century travellers from Europe – in certain moods, at least – have often felt a sense of exhilaration in moving rapidly through the 'placeless', brightly-lit, super-highway, motel, gas-station, used-car fringe of the United States. They have caught a sense of the United States as a different 'place', even when the local environment is most 'placeless' and even when the generalised features of areas of sprawl and blight have rightly been condemned by all writers, American and foreign, on the quality of environment. This 'liberating' effect is doubtless associated with an escape from the 'rootedness' of familiar places, the kind of rootedness which made Tennyson write that 'a known landscape is to me like an old friend that continually talks to me of my own youth and half-forgotten things'.[37]

A basic distinction must always have been drawn between impressions of the identity of places as set out in travellers' tales and the sense of identity felt by those who live in an environment and experience it directly and continuously. The problem of city identity can be fully understood, therefore, only if we pass from artistic expressions of highly distinctive experience (often shot through with myth and symbol) to manifestations of common experience – to the identification of people with their environment and to the processes by which they become so identified or fail to become identified. Some people, whether or not they live in suburbs, have always been more interested in their own homes as 'places' than in the cities in which their homes are situated. Others, however, including those who have had little chance to shape their private environment, have treated either their own 'neighbourhood' environment or the city as a whole as the focal 'place'. They have enjoyed the 'contagion of numbers', the bright lights, the noise and the bustle, in the same way as Charles Booth's East End Londoners, who had a very strong sense of 'place', enjoyed the East End.[38] Booth himself described how each district in his survey had 'its character, its own particular flavour. One seems to be conscious of it in the streets. It may be in the faces of the people.' Some cities, including the great capital cities, have always had a 'lure' as 'places', and a sense of attraction has been converted into a sense of belonging.

There have been times in history, moreover, when for most of its inhabitants the sense of the city has seemed to be stronger than the sense of class (if not usually of ethnic division). At such times civic pride, on the one hand, and civic challenge to solve urgent 'problems', on the other hand, have inspired large-scale environmental change, sometimes promoting a sense of civic gospel.[39] Behind such a strong sense of the city there has often been not only a feeling of caring but a strong element of rivalry, of competitiveness with other 'places'. 'The true grandeur and prosperity of our town', wrote one Birmingham man comprehensively in 1881, 'is such as no competition can diminish, no jealousy malign, and no lapse of time make dim.' Even when the suppositions of civic loyalty have not been stated so explicitly, they have often been felt strongly: they are in line with medieval 'celebration'.

We know very little in detail of the phenomenon of civic pride – less, indeed, than we know of city conflicts and of the urges, democratic or autocratic, to solve civic problems. It is obvious enough, however, first, that to 'outsiders' civic pride, whether expressed in buildings or happenings, often seems disproportionate and ill-founded. (There is often an immense consequential credibility gap which affects even historians.) Second, it is equally obvious that civic pride can be manipulated and exploited by 'booster' interests. Nonetheless, while nineteenth-century 'monumentalism' in architecture – as expressed, for example, in town halls – often contributed to civic pride in collective possession, there was pride also in drains and sewers; in what was hidden beneath the ground as well as what was displayed above it. Since the quality of environment in terms of basic health indices improved in some places while it was not improving or actually deteriorating in others, there was scope to express local pride in terms of the 'Sanitary Idea'.[40]

How effective civic pride was in influencing the attitudes of those who were 'not protected from the welfare impulses of others' – to employ a useful phrase of Professor Burger[41] – can only be examined in relation to particular cases. Yet when civic pride is absent, attempts to replace it by national programmes of urban development – either from above or from below – often lose not only in lack of grasp of 'local place' but in strength of feeling. This is one reason why nineteenth-century experience is seriously misjudged if all industrial cities are thought of as being 'the same', just as twentieth-century experience is also misjudged if all suburbs are thought of as being the same, a tepid compromise between metropolitan convenience and pastoral peace. In both cases varieties of economic and social structure have to be taken into the reckoning along with cultural differences associated with them. The sense of place, indeed, is not necessarily destroyed in suburbia even when suburbs look alike: in some cases it may even be enhanced in twentieth-century versions of individual or collective pride which may be as disproportionate as older forms of civic pride.

III

Against this historical background, what have been the changes which have influenced modern attitudes toward the distinctiveness of places? 'Looking alike' is certainly part of the story, in so far as it has diminished visual variety, the variety of 'features', and in so far as it has registered 'feeling alike'.[42]

There has also been a tendency within architecture itself to search for what C.W. Moore has called 'general' solutions as distinct from 'specific' solutions which start with particular places. 'The general solution whether curvily sculptured or puritanically cubed, is the diagram of an independent idea, conceived in isolation' or in creative fantasy or in somebody's – not necessarily the architect's – Utopia.[43] In addition, there has been a displacement of local materials in building and an exploitation of universal materials, a long-term shift which had its origins in the healthy desire to experiment as much as in the need to cut costs.[44] Historians of architecture can doubtless point to other factors which have influenced this story, particularly the education both of architects and planners and their sense of their own role. Fortunately there have been changes recently as a 'new wave' of architects has come out of the schools 'with a sense of context' so that as the American architect, E. L. Barnes, has put it optimistically, it may be the case again in the future that 'the cities are going to have the concern that you see in a place like Florence ... some sense of continuity even with changing styles.'[45]

The social forces, however, have been complex. First, local initiative has been limited not only by lack of imagination but by the increasing power of central government. This power has often been expressed bureaucratically in terms of standard setting, usually with the help of quantitative formulas, the standard turning into the norm. Care for 'place' was little considered between 1945 and 1970, other national social goals being treated as primary. The post-Second World War public housing programme in France, for example, led to standardised building of identical large blocks of (ugly) flats on the outskirts of provincial cities which until then had survived as visually and socially distinct and integrated 'places'. Likewise, as London grew and when the plain quantitative question was put 'How can we get land for our surplus population?', planners often answered it by riding roughshod over local issues associated with 'place' and high rise ruined scale.

Second, much that is 'distinctive' in individual buildings and – more important – in whole *milieux*, has been destroyed not only through the pressure of market-forces but through public action. Thus, in Britain, for example, the historic city of Worcester was massacred after 1945, with acres of medieval streets near the cathedral razed. Market-forces were responsible not only for the often crude transformation of inner-cities but for the proliferation of subtopia, but those who wish to 'control' them in the latter situation were usually more concerned to 'preserve' rural amenities than to maintain the sense of place. Ian Nairn, for example, having argued that 'the crime of subtopia is that it blurs the distinction between places', goes on to state that it does so 'by smoothing down the difference between types of environment – town and country, suburb and wild – rather than directly between one town and another'. His sharp formal distinction between metropolis, town, arcadia, country, and wilderness leads him to advocate not means of directly maintaining the particular sense of place but rather of channeling 'the existing mess into these legitimate environments'.[46]

Third, changes in the scale of business organisation have led to a multiplication of the same kind of institutions everywhere – hotels, shops, banks, insurance offices – with far less 'local' variety in typal form than there can be seen, for instance, in the typal forms of parish churches, medieval and modern. Very little local initiative has been left to the architects of most of these buildings and, at most, concessions have been made to 'local flavour', as in the case of some of the biggest chains of international hotels. Fourth, however, it is not simply 'organisation man' who is to be 'blamed' for what has happened. Consumers' expectations – their sense of 'urban amenities' – have become increasingly set in a national or international matrix.[47] Urban response has become generalised in quite different local environments. What is *wanted* is not to be different but to be the same.

Fifth, the modern communications system, physical and cultural, registers all this even when it does not add new elements of its own. The automobile obviously changes the dimensions of 'place', but as long ago as 1836 Emerson foretold a future when 'regions' would become 'neighbourhoods', and 'roads' 'streets'. Before the building of great highways tore into the heart of cities and introduced a new 'placeless' geography, the railways were often accused – even though they led directly from one 'place' to another – of destroying the sense of 'place'. Now Colin Buchanan has written eloquently and forcefully of 'the conflict between towns and traffic' in such distinctive places as Bath.[48]

Where the sense of place has survived, it has been for deliberate reasons of history or for historical reasons which are concealed from view. Warsaw was rebuilt as it had been in 1939 – a triumph of historical feeling not only for place but for the particular visual forms associated with that place – because its rebuilding was a magnificent gesture of pride and hope. Other smaller 'places' in the world which have retained their visual identity in the twentieth century and are now treasured for their distinctiveness, are places, like my own town of Lewes, which escaped some of the social processes I have been talking about because they were 'off the map'. Because they were 'undeveloped' in the past, particularly in the busy nineteenth century, they have a special interest as 'places' now. Other 'places' have gained (paradoxically, it may seem) from the care of commuters to protect environments in which they first acquired a private stake and then went on to develop a public concern. A sense of identity of this kind has been reinforced even within cities themselves – in Foggy Bottom and Georgetown, in Washington, DC, for instance, or in Islington, London – as interest in the part has been extended to commitment to the whole.

IV

What more can policy do in the light of study? First, a strong imaginative sense of particular urban possibilities, based on an appreciation of the complex relationships between social facts and urban forms, needs to be an ingredient in all plans for environmental change. As Geddes put it, 'in every city there is much of beauty and more of possibility'.[49] Plans couched in quantitative terms do no more than set frames, and they contain no kind of guarantees. When London looks for overspill solutions in old places like Bury St Edmunds or Kings Lynn, the problems posed need imaginative answers sensitively worked out in terms of place. The South-East plan of 1964, which was set out in purely quantitative terms concerning population trends and employment growth rates, demanded 'centres of growth alternative to London', but it touched on none of these major issues. Such statements as 'a great deal depends [in plotting expansion] on the size and economic potential of the town itself and on its character' leave to the developer and to the detailed town-planner an enormous responsibility, for which he may not always be prepared, as to identifying what 'character' means. Urban designers have not 'succeeded to the autocratic position of earlier planners': the content of their education and the range and depth of their experience inevitably become matters of public concern. So, too, does environmental education for all, particularly now that it is rooted in visual education and overlaps with heritage education.

Second, there are very special problems, when, as is often the case in Europe, historical residues constitute the very core of the modern urban community. In 1964 the Council of British Archaeology produced a list of historic town centres which it believed were threatened from different quarters. This marked an important shift of emphasis from concern for individual buildings to concern for total environments. Hitherto the English Town and Country Planning Act provided only for the protection of individual buildings: the demand now was for the designation of whole areas of historic interest, the conservation areas identified in the aftermath of the Civic Amenities Act of 1967. The emphasis here was placed on local action. By contrast, in France the scheduling of monuments and the designation of protected areas were administered by central government; and it was national politicians rather than bodies like the Civic Trust in Britain (and the growing network of civic societies) which took the initiative. In the second case, too, the results could be striking. Thus, in Paris, where the forms of the outer suburbs – far more than Haussman's nineteenth-century boulevards – mark a sharp and disturbing break with the very characteristic, traditional Parisian sense of place, André Malraux did an immense amount (with great imagination) to restore (the words 'protect' or 'preserve' in this context convey far too negative an impression) the old historic right-bank district of the Marais in the name of *'sauvegarde et mise en valeur du Paris historique'*. Battles were in progress also throughout the 1970s about the future of Venice and the question as to whether its distinctive visual 'identity' as a unique city could be maintained.

In all these cases, opinions and interests clashed and there was need not only for expert guidance but for enlightened general argument. Answers were seldom simple, although it was clear first that the sense of beauty itself was often at stake, and second, that something more than preservation was needed: the *mise en valeur* of whole areas was the key phrase. Yet the conservation (and equally important, the adaptation of the old) in the interest of 'place' did not mean refusal to contemplate the new. Frederick Gutheim's excellent phrase 'to be in the grain of a city' does not 'mean that there can be no innovation, that design merely projects what has been. On the contrary, the best design is frequently a reaction to historic trends rather than a continuation of them.'[50]

Third, given changes in scale – and bearing in mind also that there is an element of myth in the notion of the contained city of the past – there is a need in the future to think of 'place' in a far wider setting than the small local community. We can no longer say of any place like Bath what was said of it in 1793:

Bath may be said to afford a universal scope for everything that is desirable. The man of pleasure may be satisfied with amusement, the philosopher may analyse its salubrious springs, the antiquarian may pursue his researches till he wearies himself with conjecture, the man of letters will find ample repositories of genius, the poet endless subjects to exercise his wit: the painter may delineate the features of beauty; and last of all the dejected invalid may restore the shattered system of a broken constitution.[51]

Bath now needs its Buchanan and an infusion of national aid. It is significant in this connection that the Council of British Archaeology and other bodies it mobilised saw no answer to their problem of relating present to past – either economic or cultural – in purely local public action. Intense 'localism', indeed, apparently paradoxically, may be an enemy to the continuing sense of place as it is expressed in distinctive form. Extending the argument into the future, since there is no point in merely complaining about scale, it may well be that the sense of place will best be strengthened in modern conditions in areas that are big enough to devise and implement policies to ensure drive, variety, visual contrast, interplay of sub-cultures, coexistence of old and new, and access to the best planning abilities. Within such areas there will continue to be changes. Many of the unplanned changes will be at least as compulsive as the planned ones – throwing up new modes and nuclei, new 'places' within developing networks of transportation and communication.

Fourth, where we are free to create afresh within the spatial, economic, and cultural frameworks of our own societies, attention should be paid to the making of places, places with people. As one American architect has put it, 'When we are at a place we know it. If our image or perception of a specific environmental order is confused or unclear then there is no place. We don't know when we are there; we don't know where we are.'[52] Or as William Blake put it less gently, 'to generalise is to be an idiot; to particularise is the lone distinction of merit'.

At this point value-judgements obtrude. They can never be left out. They are part of the very texture of argument and feeling: not a kind of superimposition on technology or on the politics of adjustment. They were just as plain in the garden-city movement (which had little to do with the sense of particular 'place') or in the 'new towns' development in post-1945 Britain (which in one case, at least, Cumbernauld, has produced a new town with a strong sense of place) as they are in Philip Johnson's passionate plea for monumentalism (which has much to do with the sense of place). Most recently in Britain they have been expressed explicitly by Sir Donald Gibson, Director-General of Research and Development at the British Ministry of Public Building and Works, in his demand for the building in Britain not of new towns but of new cities. Some of these would be deliberately located not on 'neutral' sites, but in 'interesting places', where topographical and visual distinctiveness would be the first component in a new sense of identity, as it has been so often in city-making in the past.[53] Considerations of this kind need to be extended from topography to sociology. The same extension is needed in the United States, where schemes for urban renewal have sometimes meant the neglect of the interests of large numbers of displaced people, and where within most cities it is clear that the sense of the city as a particular 'place' means little to large numbers of alienated people.

Fifth, when we turn from debate to action, the institutional framework within which decisions are taken and the procedures for consultation, survey, planning, and administration need constant review. There is no finality in either framework or procedures. The issues involved in this context are primarily sociopolitical and they cannot be baulked. They could provide ample material for another symposium of greater length and greater intensity in which experience could be pooled and social and administrative responses compared. I myself believe that in a democracy the sociopolitical issues cannot be delegated either to experts or to well-endowed agencies. 'It is only in our mathematical century', Camille Sitte wrote in 1889, perhaps some years too soon, 'that the process of enlarging and laying out cities has become an almost purely technical concern.'[54] When we talk about places, we are talking about life, and we should never try to delegate that.

NOTES

1   The Colombo Plan was one of two Geddes plans in 1921. The first was a Patiala plan in which, turning to what was happening from below, Geddes noted 'the objection of the people to improvements ... the "obstinate prejudices" with which they cling to their old stones'. See J. Tyrwhitt (ed.), *Patrick Geddes in India* (1947).

2   See M. Drabble, *A Writer's Britain, Landscape in Literature* (1980), and G. Grigson (ed.), *Poems and Places* (1980).

3   Yi-Fu Tuan, *Space and Place* (1977), p. 136, p. 6. See also his *Topophilia* (1972).

4   T. Carlstein, D. Parkes and N. Thrift (eds), *Timing Space and Spacing Time*, 3 vols (1978).

5   D. Canter, *The Psychology of Place* (1977). For psychological attitudes to spatial orientation, see also L. Wingo, *Cities and Space* (1963), and two simulating books by P. F. Smith, *The Dynamics of Urbanism* (1966) and *Architecture and the Human Dimension* (1979).

6   He wrote an essay 'Who is Patrick Geddes?'. See A. D. Defries, *The Interpreter Geddes* (1928), p. 5, and M. Stalley, *Patrick Geddes, Spokesman and Man for the Environment* (1972), pp. 95-6.

7   See the pioneering study by K. Lynch, *The Image of the City* (1960).

8   V. S. Pritchett, *London Perceived* (1962), p. 4, and *New York Proclaimed* (1964), p. 13.

9   See A. Briggs, *Victorian Cities* (1963), p. 81. For differing contemporary views of New York, see Bayard Still, *Mirror for Gotham* (1956).

10   Cyril Connolly, 'One of my Londons', in *Encounter*, January 1955, described the different Londons he knew, including the one he liked best and which he could find 'embalmed in books ... between 1760 and 1840, the dandies still outnumbering the slums and the fog as yet barely invented'.

11   S. E. Rasmussen, *Experiencing Architecture* (1959), p. 16.

12   Quoted in W. Bagehot, *Literary Essays* (1966 edn), vol. I, p. 174.

13   Architects themselves have long recognised that within cities – or buildings – there are 'places' with a strong identity which were not planned. 'Users' made them such.

14   See P. F. Smith, *The Syntax of Cities* (1977).

15   S. K. Langer, *Feeling and Form* (1953).

16   See J. Jacobs, *The Death and Life of Great American Cities* (1963), p. 143.

17   See *Victorian Cities*, p. 62.

18   See O. Handlin and J. Burchard, *The Historian and the City* (1960), p. 123.

19 Wingo, *op. cit.*, p. 19.

20 I. Nairn, *Counter Attack Against Subtopia* (1957), p. 355.

21 Handlin and Burchard, *op. cit.*, p. 1.

22 Quoted in S. Chermayoff and C. Alexander, *Community and Privacy* (1966), p. 50.

23 C. W. Moore *et al.*, 'Towards Making Places', in *Landscape*, Autumn 1962.

24 M. M. Webber in Wingo, *op. cit.*, p. 23. This book includes some fascinating differences of opinion.

25 S. Tankel, ibid., p. 57.

26 R. Hoggart, *The Uses of Literacy* (1957), Part I.

27 See the classic study by M. Young and P. Willmott, *Family and Kinship in East London* (1957), esp. Chapter VII, 'Kinship and Community', which deals with home and street, *'localism'* within the villages of the borough', and 'the link through history'. See also R. Roberts on northern Salford, in *The Classic Slum* (1971).

28 S. Mullin, reviewing Chermayoff and Alexander's book in *New Society*, 29 December 1966.

29 A. L. Huxtable, *Kicked a Building Lately?* (1974), p. 148.

30 S. Thrupp, in Handlin and Burchard, *op. cit.*, p. 255.

31 F. Harrison, *Memoirs and Thoughts* (1887), pp. 248-9.

32 L. Mumford, *The Culture of Cities* (1938), p. 196, and *The City in History* (1961), pp. 469 ff. He touched on this theme, indeed, as early as 1922 in his interesting and important essay, 'The City', reprinted in *City Development, Studies in Disintegration and Renewal* (1945).

33 See John Julius Norwich, *Venice, The Greatness and the Fall* (1981).

34 'An Unsettled Neighbourhood', reprinted in *Collected Papers* (1937), vol. I, p. 519. See also A. Welsh, *The City of Dickens* (1971).

35 L. Marx, 'Pastoral Ideals and City Troubles', in the *Smithsonian Annual II* (1968), *The Fitness of Man's Environment*.

36 V. S. Naipaul, *An Area of Darkness* (1964), p. 205.

37 Quoted in Grigson, *op. cit.*, p. 31.

38 C. Booth, *Life and Labour of the People in London*, vol. I (1902 edn), p. 66.

39 See D. C. Hammack, 'Problems in the Historical Study of Power in the Cities and Towns of the United States', in the *American Historical Review*, vol. 83, no. 2, April 1978.

40 See below, vol. II, pp. 134-5.

41 B. M. Burger, in S. M. Warner (ed.), *Planning for a Nation of Cities* (1966), p. 158. See also N. E. Long, 'Political Science and the City', in L. F. Schnore and H. Fagin (eds.), *Urban Research and Policy Planning* (1967); R. C. Hill, 'Separate and Unequal: Governmental Inequality in the Metropolis', in the *American Political Science Review*, vol. LXVIII (1974); and G. Lenski, *Power and Privilege* (1966). For a Marxist analysis of such issues, see M. Castells, *City, Class and Power*, English translation, 1978, of a book which first appeared six years earlier.

42 Naming alike is another interesting nineteenth-century phenomenon. By the end of the nineteenth century there was a large Birmingham in

America as well as in England. 'What the name stood for in England', proclaimed one of its pioneers, 'would be a promise of what the new Birmingham would stand for in America.' (M. P. Crane, *The Life of James R. Powell* (1930), p. 21.) There were also at least fifty-three places in the world called Brighton.

43   C. W. Moore *et al.*, *op. cit.*
44   For attitudes towards materials, see, *inter alia*, N. Pevsner, *Pioneers of the Modern Movement* (1936), and *Pioneers of Modern Design* (1970).
45   Quoted in B. Diamenstein, *American Architecture Now* (1980), p. 21.
46   Nairn, *op. cit.*, p. 356.
47   J. Gottman, 'The Rising Demand for Urban Amenities', in Warner (ed.), *op. cit.*
48   C. Buchanan, *Traffic in Towns* (Penguin edn, 1966), p. 38.
49   P. Geddes, *Patiola Plan* (1921).
50   F. Gutheim, 'Urban Space and Urban Design', in Wingo (ed.), *op. cit.*, p. 107.
51   J. Clarke, *A Tour through the South of England* (1793), pp. 135 ff.
52   S. van der Ryn, in *Landscape*, *op. cit.*
53   In his first University of Leeds Lecture as Hoffman Wood Professor of Architecture, reported in the *Yorkshire Post*, 27 January 1967.
54   C. Sitte, *City Planning according to Artistic Principles* (1965 edn), p. 4.

5   Press and Public in Early Nineteenth-Century Birmingham

There are many legends relating to nineteenth-century history, which have been spun and embroidered in the eventful years which separate the age of Victoria from our own. One of the most important is Lewis Mumford's legend of 'the insensate industrial town'. According to the tale, a handful of mechanical inventors, industrialists, and bankers created almost two centuries ago a new sort of city fashioned after their own image, a city which was not only ugly and formless in its physical appearance, dominated by the grey walls of the factory and the narrow streets of the slum, but was equally ugly and formless in its social life. The iron which had become the master material of the economy had penetrated men's souls as well. Old ties had dissolved, new ones had not been discovered. The gaunt untrammelled individual reigned supreme over a city which had become a 'mere man-heap', and remained such until the grim dramas of the factory struggle and the concomitant battles for political power stirred it for the first time into mass activity.[1]

The legend is a familiar one, and the people who first started to tell it were our respectable grandparents. A genuine revulsion against the horrors of early industrialisation made them look back with a shocked distaste at the worst conditions in the towns and cities of their own youth. Novelists, writers and historians often drew first on their own recollections, while politicians and philanthropists reviewed retrospectively the long hours in the factory; the inadequate facilities for education, sanitation, food and leisure; the exploitation of the work of women and children. Since such critics made their first assessment, we, too, have added our own burden of complaint, pointing to the absence of social control in building or designing; the absence of a social policy in caring for the poor, the unemployed, or the sick; the absence of expert or professional counsel; and the wide gaps in the administration and activity of both local and central government.

I

Like all legends, the story of the insensate industrial town has its significant element of truth. Yet legend it is. To try to show that it is a

106

legend and not a sober piece of historical analysis, I want to take you back to Birmingham of the troubled years between the end of the Napoleonic Wars in 1815 and the passing of the Great Reform Bill in 1832, years when, as George Eliot reminds us, 'there were pocket boroughs, a Birmingham unrepresented in Parliament and compelled to make strong representations out of it, unrepealed corn laws, three and six-penny letters, a brawny and many-breeding pauperism, and other departed evils'.[2] There is a certain ambivalence in George Eliot's own approach to the past, a mixture of approval and disapproval, a sense that all had not got better as optimists claimed. She had no desire, however, to fashion or to reinforce legends. She wished to get at the truth. She also understood the mainsprings of provincial life.

I would not try to claim myself that the turbulent, ever-expanding city of Birmingham, which grew in numbers from about 86,000 in 1811 to nearly 147,000 in 1831, was a model of town planning and tasteful building, but then contemporaries themselves were among the most vigorous critics. The *Birmingham Spectator* of 1824 offered a few polite hints to the Commissioners of Street Acts:

> This town of Birmingham is in a state of most woeful improvement... An atmosphere of dust and *damns* fills our streets. All visible trace of anything like a comprehensive plan or prospective arrangement is lost; and utter discomfort unabated by any attempt at alleviation, seems to have fixed his throne among us for the season. Surely, paying as we do, for the scavenging of our streets, their present state is misery unmerited.[3]

Dust and *damns* might fill the streets, but, as the word *damns* suggests, there was nothing insensate about the response to them. Indeed, the following week, the rival of the *Spectator*, the *Birmingham Review*, was proclaiming that it felt it 'a duty to congratulate our townsmen on the spirit of improvement, which has manifested itself for the last year or two, and still seems to be on the increase in this town' and was praising the efforts 'to place it in the rank and situation it ought to hold among the largest and most opulent towns in the Empire'.[4] It set out this proclamation and tribute in no mood of quiet self-satisfaction, since it went on to attack local nuisances while encouraging local improvements. It made careful suggestions also for a new large public building which would serve for the transaction of public business. The cry was to be taken up repeatedly before the Commissioners of the Street Acts proposed to erect a town hall in 1828 and Barry exhibited his design at the Royal Academy in 1832.[5]

The zeal for improvement was a characteristic feature of Birmingham in the 1820s, the most awkward years of transition in the history of the city and perhaps in the history of the country. The local environment was still not entirely industrial. Within a short walk of Smithfield Market you could discover an excellent garden 'completely stocked with choice fruit trees, strawberry plantations ... very superior asparagus bed, large brick-built summer house, with sash windows ... commanding a pleasant and extensive view, the whole very securely fenced and completely retired'.[6] Such gardens still remained near the centre of Birmingham in the 1870s, when Joseph Chamberlain cleared away the squalid and insanitary property in the neighbourhood of the present Corporation Street. Walter Barrow in 1911 recalled a garden in Bull Street, which belonged to his father, where there was a poplar tree that was green in springtime, and a summerhouse at the end where he used to play as a child.[7]

There is no alias here. Birmingham was Birmingham, and nowhere else. The proof could be demonstrated in many ways – architecturally, politically, economically. Let me prove it by unearthing examples of the intense local pride which stirred Birmingham men and Birmingham periodicals in the 1820s. 'Birmingham is not attractive for its venerable ruins and cathedral', the *Commercial Directory* of 1822 began, 'but the traveller who delights in seeing the human race profitably employed to their own and to their country's advantage will disregard the smoke which sometimes envelops the town and will discern through the veil the bright beams of industry enlightening vast piles of riches.'[8]

It was not only vast piles of riches which were hidden behind the veil. Theatre critics and men of letters shared Birmingham pride with politicians and businessmen. The *Comet Magazine* of 1820 boasted, for example, in its first number that it was 'not inferior to London publications', and in 1823 the editor of the *Birmingham Reporter* was claiming that 'here we have, I may say truly, as good judges of the Drama as preside over the fate of Metropolitan debutantes; – here, though forbearance is used, and direct condemnation is withheld, the sense of merit and imperfection is the same as that which urges the uncharitable decisions of the gods and ultra-gods of London'.[9] Usually London was brought into comparisons. Thus, when Thomas Attwood led a deputation of Birmingham men to London in 1812 to protest against the Orders-in-Council, he could not resist writing back to his wife: 'such a foolish set of mortals as the members of both Houses are, I did never expect to meet with in this world. The best among them are scarce equal to the worst in Birmingham.'[10] This was the same mainspring of local pride which made Joseph Chamberlain write to John Morley decades later in 1883 that 'unless I can secure for the nation the results similar to these which have followed the adoption of my policy in Birmingham, it will have been a sorry exchange to give up the Town Council for the Cabinet.'[11]

The sense of local pride was not, of course, a new phenomenon of the nineteenth century, but it helped to shape the character of men and the moulding of an environment. Perhaps the chief agency in developing and deepening it was the local Press, 'the mighty engine' as one well-known Birmingham personality put it in 1825, 'which has abolished the bars to the Temple of Knowledge'.[12] Yet the local press by itself could not create from the void the colourful town life of the 1820s. My study must begin with the Press, but it must end with the public. The Press influenced the public, but it also mirrored the public. To read through the forgotten magazines and newspapers of the early nineteenth century is to recapture a lost world, to meet unfamiliar people, to penetrate old issues.[13] Occasionally, great landmarks are exposed in new perspectives, like the Reform struggle of 1830 to 1832, when, because of the laws forbidding correspondence between different political societies, the press became the 'means of communication' between Birmingham reformers and reformers elsewhere.[14] At other times, we merely find that the periodicals and newspapers embalm for us 'traits of local life and manners unnoticed in more serious and enduring works'.[15] Significant or insignificant though the details may be, we are left at the end with the whole – a whole which once had the unity of life – and not with a sociological abstraction derived from a set of general principles. 'The insensate industrial town' will fade into the grey shadows, and old Birmingham will live.

II

In 1830, at the beginning of the struggle for parliamentary reform, Birmingham had two newspapers – *Aris's Birmingham Gazette* and the *Birmingham Journal*. One was old, going back to 1741, when Thomas Aris decided, during a visit to Birmingham, to take up residence there and establish a newspaper. It was not the first journalistic venture in the town. There is one surviving copy in the Birmingham Collection of a *Birmingham Journal*, founded in November 1732;[16] and from 1737 to 1741 Robert Walker was printing and publishing in Fleet Street, London, a paper called the *Warwickshire and Staffordshire Journal.*[17] By the time that Aris arrived in Birmingham, Walker also had moved there. Aris, the stronger of the two rivals, at least locally, incorporated Walker's paper in his own, and went on publishing what remained the only newspaper in Birmingham until 1769.

During the eighteenth century *Aris's Gazette* was one of the most lucrative and important provincial papers, ranking with the *Liverpool Mercury* and the *Edinburgh Courant*. Its main strength lay in its advertisements rather than in its news. 'As a source of profit', wrote one of its rivals somewhat petulantly, 'it was considered to hold its head very lofty above its provincial compeers. As an organ of political opinion, it never was esteemed. It felt that its strength lay in its profits, and it did not spare a line which could be devoted to the service of its "advertising friends". It was always anything but a paper of news.'[18] During the nineteenth century the same taunt persisted. The *Spectator* in 1824 bemoaned the fact that 'one of the wealthiest and largest towns in the Empire is furnished with 'a newspaper, as it is called, but whose more appropriate name may be a register of sales or a brokers' guide'.[19] The *Theatrical John Bull* confirmed the opinion that it was 'a vehicle of advertisements and not of news'.[20] The *Argus* always referred to it as 'My Grandmother',[21] and dubbed it 'the most contemptible newspaper in England, the most base in principle, and the most talentless in management'.[22]

This abuse sprang from two main causes – first, the jealousy of the unsuccessful in the face of an established rival which could not be dislodged, and second, the distrust of its political neutrality, of its perpetual sitting on the fence. Such sitting on the fence – 'how to praise all and please all'[23] – was conscious policy. Thomas Knott, who became editor in 1814, believed 'that it had been contrary to the plan of the paper to bias its readers by any leading article; it was preferred rather to give with fairness information on both sides of disputed questions. In the contentions which formerly divided Whig and Tory, the Editor has known no difference.' The emergence of the Political Union in 1829 changed its policy:

> It was only when a power arose in this town, which, from its mode of action, threatened to overturn all social order among us, and to interfere in an unconstitutional manner with the settled institutions of the country, that we at all swerved from the course so long pursued. We then felt it imperatively our duty to oppose ourselves to so dangerous and disorganising a compact, and by perseveringly correcting the daring misrepresentations of its prompters, we endeavoured to prevent the kingdom at large being misled or intimidated by their inflammatory effusions and boastings. We reflect with satisfaction on the stand we made against this body, fully convinced that in so doing we performed a becoming duty to our country, and carried with us the approbation of the moderate and reflecting of all parties.[24]

The strength of the *Gazette* lay precisely in its appeal to the moderate elements in Birmingham. It was always disliked by extremists, and was frequently challenged by rival publications.[25] Myles Swinney's *Birmingham and Stafford Chronicle*, first published with that name in 1773, survived the Napoleonic Wars, while a paper under the same name sponsored by Wrightson, the printer, was published in the 1820s, and disappeared in 1827. It received little praise from its contemporaries. 'Twenty-four columns of dullness', wrote the *Reporter*:[26] 'a milk and water chicken meat publication', proclaimed the *Spectator*:[27] 'hurt-nobody, please-everybody', said the *Theatrical John Bull*.[28] The ending of the venture in 1827 added a few new readers to the *Birmingham Journal*, which was itself at that time according to one commentator half-way between life and death.[29]

This was probably an unfair statement. The *Birmingham Journal*, which had begun in 1825, became the most celebrated of Birmingham newspapers during the fierce political debates which raged around the Great Reform Bill of 1832 and the People's Charter.[30] Originally a 'Tory' paper, it had more than a local significance. Because it printed in full the news of big political meetings and demonstrations, it became a widely known source of information. R. K. Douglas, the famous editor who took over in 1833, and who acted as first Chairman of the Chartist Convention and Secretary of the revived Political Union, was responsible not only for drawing up the magnificently written National Petition of 1838 with its biblical cadences and its eloquent simplicity, but also for turning the *Journal* into a political clarion. An official investigator of 1839 found seventy-one weekly copies of the paper as far away as Dunfermline.[31]

This widespread Radical popularity would have seemed strange to the first founders of the *Birmingham Journal*. The first number saw the light in June 1825 and professed high Tory principles. Indeed, it was projected by local Tories, who were annoyed by a recent article about Birmingham Toryism which had appeared in *The Times*. According to one story,[32] so incensed were the local Tories that *The Times* had disgraced itself and insulted Birmingham, that they solemnly burnt the copy of the paper containing the offensive leader at the Minerva in Peck Lane. An iron dealer took up 'the doomed newspaper with a pair of tongs, placed it on the sheets of iron, and, taking a "spill" between the claws of the tongs, lighted it at the fire of the room, and ignited the ill-fated paper, which, amid the groans and hisses of the assembled patriots burned to ashes'. Having finished this destructive side of their work, the patriots went on to discuss how desirable it was for the party to have an organ in the town, and started a subscription on the spot. The first printer was Hodgetts and the first editor Bakewell, 'a very good reporter, but one of the most milk-and-watery scribes the world ever saw'.[33] In June 1827 Hodgetts paid out the other subscribers and became sole proprietor.[34] The editorship changed in 1828,[35] and for about a year, until November 1829, Mackenzie ran the paper on ultra-Tory lines, bitterly and successfully attacking Catholic Emancipation to such an extent that the finances of the paper revived, thereby in the words of a sympathetic commentator showing how the 'difference between a Socinian and a Protestant Editor was very perceptible'.[36]

The paper was soon to demonstrate the even bigger difference between a Tory editor and a Radical editor. Jonathan Crowther, who came to Birmingham from the *Manchester Advertiser*,[37] led the *Journal* from Toryism (albeit Toryism turning to Attwood) to Radicalism. During the debates on the Great Reform Bill and the most glorious days of the Political Union, the *Journal* printed complete accounts of the proceedings. There was a very close liaison between the *Journal* and the Council of the Union, which had recognised the value of the Press as an ally from the start of its campaign. The sixth article of the list of duties of members of the Council was 'to consider the means of organising a system of operations, whereby the PUBLIC PRESS may be influenced to act generally in support of the PUBLIC INTERESTS'.[38] This was an important development in the organisation of political propaganda in England, and it was widely imitated. The Town Meeting of October 1831 for the purpose of petitioning the House of Lords to pass the Reform Bill resolved that the decisions of the meeting were to be communicated to *The Times*, the *Morning Chronicle*, the *Morning Herald*, the *Globe*, the *Courier*, the *Sun*, and all the Birmingham papers.[39] The *Journal* had by this time become in the words of the *Argus* 'the HACK of the Union'.[40]

Its management had changed. In February 1832, according to the *Argus*, it had become the property of Joseph Parkes, the Unitarian and Utilitarian Radical, who was already influencing its reports, Joshua Schofield, a key figure in Political Union strategy, and along with Attwood one of the first Members of Parliament for Birmingham, and William Redfern. Lewis had replaced Crowther as editor, who now left the editorial snuggery to become 'a mere editor's devil'.[41] Parkes was undoubtedly an important background figure in the *Journal* before he became editor. According to his own manuscript account,[42] the reports of Union proceedings were first taken by *Journal* reporters, and then checked and corrected by him. 'In a very few instances only', he says, 'I erased any seditious words used by the speakers. After publication of the *Journal*, the types were used for the wealth of quarto publication – distributed in large numbers usually throughout the provinces of the United Kingdom.' Parkes was not only responsible for the *Journal* reports. 'Most of *The Times* reports were made up by me from the same slips and usually expressed to Printing House Square, except when in 1832, *The Times* sent down its own reporters. I also throughout the three years supplied Mr Black of the *Morning Chronicle*.' Even newspapers which did not favour the Political Union used Union-supplied reports.

The fact that Parkes contributed to *The Times* was one of the many reasons why the *Birmingham Argus* hated him. For *The Times* the

Argus had a sovereign contempt which it frequently expressed in its pages. 'The old weathercock *Times*' lacked 'the halo of respectable dignity which had once shone round it'. 'Well may the Editor of the *Allgemeine Zeitung* say that the leading articles in the *Times* "are only calculated to impose on the ignorant part of the English public" – *they can deceive nobody else.*'[43] *The Argus* had little to say about the fact that of the London weeklies only the *Spectator* and the *Examiner* supported the Political Union and the *Standard* was bitterly hostile, claiming that the Union was usurping the tasks of government.[44]

The Birmingham Political Union was never completely dependent either on the goodwill of the national press or on the control of the local *Journal*. For a time it had its own *Political Union Monthly Register*, a monthly selling at 6d a copy.[45] The venture did not last. Later it was supported by the *Midland Representative and Birmingham Herald*, which is best remembered because for a time it had as its editor Bronterre O'Brien, who was to play such an important part later on in the history of the Chartist movement.[46] The motto of the paper was 'the Greatest Happiness of the Greatest Number for the Greatest Length of Time', and although this Benthamite slogan appears at first sight as a most innocuous general formula, it was indeed the battle-cry of some of the more extreme among the members of the Political Union.

There were other battle-cries too. The *Herald* was widely read by the Cooperators, who were for the first time beginning to play an important part in local politics under the leadership of William Pare. They had their own journal too – the *Birmingham Cooperative Herald*, which first appeared in 1829,[47] and bore the motto 'Power directed by knowledge'. All these ventures in newfangled ideas were greeted with scorn by the *Argus*. As far as it was concerned (and we must look at it later), the word *revolution* was best anagrammed to read 'to love ruin',[48] Pare was 'the most contemptible of humbugs',[49] and the *Midland Representative* 'mental poison under the guise of patriotism'.[50]

It is possible to penetrate the colourful language of the newspapers in abusing one another to catch a glimpse of the business side of circulation and of the character of the reading public. Newspapers had been taxed since 1712. In 1789 the tax was 2d, and a levy of 3s was made on advertisements. In 1797 the stamp duty went up to $3\frac{1}{2}$d, and in 1815 to 4d, the duty on advertisements rising by another 6d. In practice, on most newspapers some discount was allowed, 20 per cent being offered to any publisher who promptly paid £10 or more, and did not charge more than 7d a copy.[51] In 1819, by one of the Six Acts, the definition of a newspaper was widened to cover 'any pamphlets or papers printed periodically, or in parts or numbers, at intervals not exceeding twenty-six days between the publication of any two such pamphlets or papers, parts or numbers, where any of the said pamphlets or papers, parts or numbers respectively shall not exceed two sheets or shall be published for sale at a sum less than sixpence', exclusive of duty. To enforce the law, what was called a 'security system' was established. Under a penalty of £20, it was forbidden to print or publish newspapers or pamphlets 'which shall not exceed two sheets, or which shall be published for sale at a price less than sixpence, without first executing a bond to his Majesty, together with two or three sufficient sureties conditional that such printer or publisher shall pay any fine which may at any time be imposed on him for any blasphemous or seditious libel'.[52]

It is not difficult to trace the effects of taxation and control on the Birmingham press. Taxation was the most important element in the final price of newspapers. As early as 1743, the editor of *Aris's Gazette* had to apologise for raising the price of his newspaper from 1½d to 2d.

> Gentlemen – I am very sensible, [he told his readers], that to raise the price of any commodity is always both unpopular and hazardous ... and yet I flatter myself that no gentleman would take it amiss if I can't continue it at a price which, instead of serving, can only injure me ... Out of every paper, one halfpenny goes to the stamp office, and another to the person who sells it ... the paper it is printed on costs a farthing ... and consequently no more than a farthing remains to defray the charges of composing, printing, London newspapers, and meeting, as far as Daventry, the Post, which last article is very expensive, not to mention the expense of our London correspondence.[53]

By 1804 Aris's generosity had been forgotten. The paper cost 6d, and bore a 1½d stamp. In 1830 7d was a standard price, and in addition to the stamp tax, by then 4d, there was a duty on paper of 3d a lb, paid at the mills.[54]

The newspaper taxes were highly unpopular. Indeed the *Midland Representative* bore the caption 'price 3½d, taxes to suppress knowledge 4d'.[55] Twelve years earlier George Edmonds had called his *Weekly Recorder* a pamphlet in order to avoid the 3½d tax. He succeeded in evading the tax but had more difficulty in evading a sentence for libel.[56] The *Argus*, which acquired a considerable notoriety in libel actions, was always shrewd in its manoeuvres to avoid tax. In November 1829 the Solicitor of Stamps wrote to say that it was a newspaper 'by reason of its containing articles of news or intelligence'. The editor wisely turned it into a monthly magazine and substituted for news what was euphemistically called 'a brief chronicle of the times'.[57]

Taxation was sometimes less burdensome than a first glance might suggest. Cobbett used to boast that 'the stamp *gives wings* to the *Register*: it makes it fly by the regular channels of the Post Office'.[58] By publishing it in an open, unfolded edition as a 2d 'pamphlet' in 1816 Cobbett had paid only nominal tax, but after 1819 he had to issue both stamped and unstamped editions. Even where no flying had to be done, as in Birmingham, it was possible to collect readers together in reading parties to share what would otherwise have been a most expensive newspaper. Local reading-rooms satisfied a growing demand. The Mechanics' Institute, set up in 1825, had a Library of Reference and a reading-room. In the same year a news room was built, 'a handsome edifice ... ornamented with lofty pillars of the Ionic order'.[59] The *Westminster Review* wrote later that it was organised 'upon a very extensive scale'.[60]

It was not only high taxation which held back general circulation and kept the market for metropolitan newspapers stationary per head of population between 1815 and 1835.[61] Large numbers of people could not read, and newspapers were always backed up by posters, handbills and ballads.[62] 'I know the lamentable state of ignorance in those districts in 1830,' wrote Guest. 'I have entered a room in which twenty men, all black from the pits, were drinking beer, and asked if they wanted a newspaper at only 1d or 2d? and the answer was "*Noa*, I can't read, I wish I kud."'[63] It has been estimated for the United Kingdom as a whole that as late as 1845, 33 per cent of the males and 49 per cent of the females were illiterate.[64]

To get round the difficulties both of high taxation and of illiteracy, the Birmingham Political Union began the practice of having newspapers read aloud at public meetings, and during the struggle for the Reform Bill of 1832 large numbers of people used to meet in their dinner hour and in the evenings to hear the news of the day.[65] As late as 1839, during the Chartist agitation, 80,000 people met in the Bull Ring and 'paid very polite attention to a person reading a newspaper'. On this particular famous occasion more than reading a newspaper was involved. The police attacked with their truncheons and the meeting was broken up.[66]

As a result of the fiscal policy of the government, a popular untaxed press came into existence – what Fonblanque called 'a contraband trade' – whereby 'a cheap illicit spirit, ten times above proof, has been hawked among the working classes'. 'The cheap publications, of whose inflammatory tendency so much is made, are the offspring of the stamp duties.'[67] James Guest, who organised a 'Cheap Book Repository', claimed that he was the first person in Birmingham to sell such unstamped papers. 'I sent parcels to Walsall, Coventry, Stratford on Avon, Stafford, Northampton, Dudley, &c, about thirty parcels

per week in all,' he wrote.[68] The first occasion on which he sold the
unstamped papers was characteristically at a Political Union meeting
in October 1830 in Beardsworth's Repository, the biggest coach
repository in Britain, 320 feet long, where the Union held many of its
meetings: on that occasion he quickly got rid of 300 copies of
Carpenter's Political Letters and Pamphlets.[69] Guest's trade expanded,
and from his shop in Steelhouse Lane he dispatched copies of papers
like Hetherington's *Poor Man's Guardian*, and Cleave's *Gazette*.
Meanwhile John Beardsworth had added to his popularity in 1830
when his horse, Birmingham, won the St Leger at 40-1.

It is clear that Guest was not the only vendor of cheap publications
in Birmingham. He was certainly not the pioneer. Thirteen years
earlier, Joseph Russell, a secularist, was under prosecution for selling
Hone's parodies, and he was tried and convicted at Quarter Sessions in
the summer of 1819. He was further convicted for the second offence
of selling the *Republican*. (In 1830 he was publishing handbills and
ballads.) Various other Birmingham men were prosecuted and sentenced – Ragg, the printer of the first *Birmingham Argus* and Vice-
President of the Radical Union Society, for selling the *Black Book* and
the *Republican*, and Whitworth, Brandes and Lewis for other political
offences.[70] The story of events of 1819 provides the prelude to the
history of Birmingham Radicalism. There was resistance, of course,
but when a landlord and his wife burnt the *Black Dwarf* Radicals
withdrew their custom.[71]

From the point of view of the authorities, the unstamped papers
were a far greater danger to the morale of the public than were the
stamped ones. The stamped papers would be read in the news-room or
in the public house: the unstamped papers, which could be bought in
beer shops and barbers' shops as well as from Radical booksellers,[72]
would often be read at home. 'We go to the public house to read the
sevenpenny paper, but only for the News,' an intelligent mechanic
stated to Edward Lytton Bulwer in 1832; 'it is the cheap penny paper
that the working man can take home and read at spare moments, which
he has by him to take up, and read over and over again whenever he has
leisure, that forms his opinions.'[73] This probably applied to those who
had both 'the appetite for political information' and the ability to
read. Edward Baines, MP, speaking to the House of Commons in
1861, said that Guest had informed him that in 1830 'the daily and
weekly papers were taken almost entirely at public houses, where the
working man took in his news, and left on an average one third of his
wages'.

The Political Union did most to break this monopoly of information, but its leaders were uneasy about supporting 'illicit' publications like Russell's parodies or *Carpenter's Political Letters and*

Pamphlets. There was considerable controversy about 'Victim Funds' for working-class editors.[74] Certainly, the men who spread information often did so at considerable risk. In 1833, for instance, William Cooper, a Birmingham printer, was convicted by the Birmingham magistrates under the Six Acts for selling an anonymous pamphlet with more than one leaf, which reported a Birmingham meeting, without giving the printer's name and address. He was fined £20, although this was subsequently mitigated to £5. Quarter Sessions quashed the conviction, and Martin, the informer, was ordered to return to Cooper the £5 9s 6d paid under the conviction. That was not the end of the story. At Michaelmas Sessions, 1833, the conviction was confirmed and Martin received from Cooper £18 17s 0d[75] costs.

The story shows that Birmingham printers and publishers suffered in the same way as did the London printers and publishers. Although it was working-class elements in the Political Union which took the initiative in pressing for repeal of the Stamp Acts as 'acts of positive despotism', Thomas Attwood himself played an active part thereafter in supporting the repeal of the Radical press which increased in Birmingham during the mid-1830s before and after the revival of the Political Union. Circulation of illegal papers is said to have increased by one-third in 1835, and it could even be boasted (with little evidence) that 'a stamped paper' was regarded as a curiosity in Birmingham as in other large places.[76] Certainly the battle against the stamp was waged just as fiercely in Birmingham as in any other provincial community. The first success came in 1836, when the duty was reduced to 1d, and in 1855 it was abolished altogether. Advertisement duties were more than halved in 1833 and abolished twenty years later. The paper duty was repealed in 1861. By that time there were more than 300 newsvendors in Birmingham, twenty-four booksellers, and over 83,000 papers circulating each week.[77]

This weekly sale marked a striking advance on all earlier figures. Guest estimated that the sale of newspapers and periodicals of all kinds in Birmingham in 1831 was about 7000 a week, 'immoral and objectionable publications forming a very large proportion of this number'.[78] It is possible to break down Guest's total. A sworn affidavit in 1830 revealed that 1812 copies of the *Birmingham Journal* had been sold on Saturday 29 May of that year.[79] It has been calculated that at this time, on an average, each London newspaper was read by thirty people and a provincial newspaper by anything from eight to thirty people.[80] On the basis of twenty persons reading each copy of the *Birmingham Journal*, this would mean that more than one in four in Birmingham could be counted among its readers.

The 1812 was a high figure. When Mackenzie became editor in 1828 there were scarcely 750 readers. By the time that he had left the numbers had gone up to 1250, and he claimed that the average for the twelve months, 1829 to 1830, was about 1000, 'a circulation exceeded by very few provincial papers in the Kingdom'.[81] For the increased circulation during the years 1830-2 the Political Union was largely responsible. According to Mackenzie, 'the Political Council generally order 200 *Journals*, whenever their proceedings are there recorded or any advertisement of theirs inserted'.[82]

The circulation of the *Birmingham Journal* at this time was probably no higher and possibly a good deal less than the circulation of *Aris's Gazette* during the early 1820s,[83] yet with characteristic truculence the *Argus* claimed in July 1829 that it, too, had equalled 'My Grandmother' in sales. This was vain boasting. A rival of the *Argus* went so far to the other extreme as to say that its sales were only about 400 a month. 'I had it from the lips of its present printer, "we print about 400 every month".' This critic was fear nearer the truth when he pointed out that although the *Argus* boasted of its wide circulation, no copy of it had been seen or even heard of in London.[84] With the exception of the *Argus*, 400 was a high circulation to attain. When the *Birmingham Free Press* disappeared in 1830, it had a circulation of about 400 which was said to be well above the safety line.[85] In 1827 the *Birmingham Independent* had claimed that if it could secure a guaranteed circle of 250 subscribing readers it would be able to maintain publication. This it failed to do. The editor had warned readers that if they wanted to have a liberal independent publication, he would 'as far as his limited means would allow, volunteer to serve the Public Cause, but this must mainly depend on the extent of the support that may be extended by subscribers to the Prospectus, previous to the appearance of the contemplated publication'.[86]

The Select Committee appointed to inquire into 'the Present State and Operation of the Law Relative to Newspaper Stamps' set out some interesting comparative statistics for a slightly later period. Here are some some of the trends:

Annual Number of Issued Newspaper Stamps

	1837	1841	1843	1845	1850
Birmingham Journal	131,000	106,000	90,000	218,000	390,000
Birmingham Gazette	154,000	140,000	132,000	108,000	120,000
Birmingham Herald	233,000	140,000	132,000	108,000	120,000
Birmingham Advertiser	54,000	55,000	61,000	49,000	120,000
Birmingham Mercury	54,000	55,000	61,000	49,000	150,000

Our epilogue is the prologue to a different story. The first Birmingham daily newspaper was *The Birmingham Daily Press*, founded in

1855, published by Williams Harris: it was issued on five days a week
with a weekly edition on Saturdays. The brief duel between it and the
Birmingham Post, a daily paper founded in 1857 by John Frederick
Feeney with the full backing of the *Birmingham Journal* (which was
to be incorporated with the *Birmingham Weekly Post* in 1869), en-
livened Birmingham at a time when politics, local and national, had
passed into an entirely new phase. The *Daily Press*, which lost the
struggle, noted in its last editorial in 1858:

> We were fully convinced that it would be a life and death struggle in which
> one or the other must give way ... Birmingham is from more than one
> cause at present unable to support two daily papers, and we have the full
> persuasion that the *Daily Press* will long remain in the memory of those
> who have been for the last three years in the habit of deriving their
> knowledge of public affairs from its pages.

Memories are not long in journalism. Nor was the eloquent statement entirely true to the facts. The main cause why the *Daily Press*
failed was lack of capital. When in 1862 the long established *Birmingham Gazette* – with all its accumulated resources – became a daily,
there was rich and effective rivalry once more.

III

A study of the newspapers suggests that the Birmingham of the early
nineteenth century was a city where politics at least were taken
seriously. As early as 1804, Morfitt had noted that 'the manufactories
have their politicians and republicans as well as the barber's shop and
the ale house'.[87] By 1823 the *London Gazette* was informing its readers
that everywhere in Birmingham there was 'a voluntary disposition
among the inhabitants to the investigations of the maxims of Government and the conduct of their rulers; and many a *lean unwashed
artisan* will discourse upon these topics quite as rationally as some of
the theorists in higher places'.[88] By 1829 the *Argus* contended that
'there is not a city or town in Britain where blind party rage is carried
to so great an extent as in the far-famed manufacturing town of
Birmingham'.[89]

This emphasis on politics was directed and encouraged not only by
newspapers, but also by the wide range of periodicals of various kinds,
which flourished at this time. Birmingham can never have had so many
of them. There still exist copies of thirty different periodicals published between 1815 and 1832. In many cases they had a life of only a

few weeks. The periodical was at best a 'half hardy annual, profuse in its upspringing, but requiring constant care and attention; apt to be nipped in its springtide by the cold breezes of indifference; fickle and unsatisfactory in its blossoming and tolerably sure of entire extinction within a few months from the first sowing of the seed'.[90] This was the metaphor chosen by H. S. Pearson in an article written more than a hundred years ago. It appeared in a magazine called *Mid-England*, which was itself no exception to the general rule. The first number appeared in December 1879 and the last in November 1880. There were twelve numbers in all.

The names of the long list of successful and unsuccessful ventures, many forgotten, are printed in the appendix to this paper. The most famous of them all was Joseph Allday's *Argus*, founded in 1828, surely one of the most extraordinary publications which has ever appeared in any city at any time. It attained the respectable age of about six years, and disappeared not as most of its rivals did because it had ceased to interest or even to pay, but because it had managed 'to set every man's hand against itself'.

Earlier periodicals like the *Birmingham Spectator* of 1824 had fought a continual up-hill battle to rally their apathetic readers. There is something pathetic in the last words of the *Spectator*, when it closed down with the end of the theatre season in 1824: 'Our efforts have not met with that reward which we had hoped for, and we must conclude that our disappointment is the result of our demerit ... We have always endeavoured to make our selection of matter interesting and amusing; and to preserve inviolate the characteristics of courtesy and good breeding.'[91] The *Argus* tried to preserve neither and succeeded where the *Spectator* had failed. It anticipated the popular appeal of late nineteenth-century sensationalism within the framework of local scandal and gossip:

> Yes I am proud – I must be proud to see
> Men not afraid of God, afraid of me –[92]

and its second volume began with the bold words, 'It is generally admitted that we have since the commencement of our "bantling" done more *real* good in Birmingham than all the newspapers and periodicals that ever appeared therein'.[93] Not everyone agreed. For one critic it was 'the most base and profligate production that ever appeared'. Instead of 'forming and instructing the mind', it 'contaminated and vitiated it'.[94]

Tory-Radical in politics, vigorously anti-Catholic and anti-Dissent in religion, the *Argus* revelled in vituperation. 'The canting cry of modern evangelism – the mock humanity of modern philanthropists –

the folly, absurdity, and imposition of our modern political economists – it is our bounden duty to LASH AND EXPOSE.'[95] Anything
liberal, utilitarian, humanitarian, 'hireling Tory', or free trade it cast
into the dust, and thereby with furious zeal tilted against all the most
important forces in the making of nineteenth-century England. This
was its recipe for making a Liberal: 'Take out his brains if he have any,
and wash them well in milk and water; clear the inside of the head of
everything that may have gathered there in consequence of *education*;
and when you have completely emptied the skull (which you will find a
very easy matter) rub it over with a handful of *democratic sage*, well
beaten into dust, &c.'[96] The support of the *Argus* for the Political
Union in 1829 was based on its editor's assessment of Attwood – a fair
one – as 'a bold, independent, talented and a truly patriotic individual'.[97]

Such praise was rare, as rare as the circumstances which generated
the coalition of the Political Union. More frequently the *Argus* talked
not only political scandal but also personal scandal; and it sailed so
close to the wind throughout its whole career that its legal existence
was frequently in jeopardy. The pages of personal scandal do at least
show what a tightly knit-together community Birmingham was at the
time, and not only Birmingham but the Black Country round about.
People knew each other well enough to follow whole chains of initials
and innuendoes which would be incomprehensible in a city as large as
Birmingham today. Joseph Allday, the editor, 'mighty and omnis-
cient', who was to have an extraordinary political career later in the
century as the leader of Birmingham's 'economy party',[98] never actually revealed his identity until 1834 and tried at all times to
hide behind his contributors, but in the long run the periodical
offended so many people that it had to succumb to a series of libel
actions, in which Joseph Parkes played the most prominent part.
Parkes, who had been frequently attacked, expressed as great a relief
when the publication came to an end, as an anonymous pamphleteer
had expressed indignation a few months before. 'To form and instruct
the mind is the first principle of a public writer, not to contaminate
and vitiate it. The art of printing ... in the hands of such unprincipled
and ignorant wretches ... would become the greatest curse that ever
afflicted the human race.'[99]

It is only too easy to see why such indignation was aroused by a
reading of the scurrilous pages of the *Argus*, yet nonetheless when all
the scurrility has been discounted,[100] we are left with a remarkably full
picture of a lively city passing through years of change. Although the
picture is made brighter and clearer by a reading of other periodicals,
the *Argus* undoubtedly provides the best, if the most dangerous,
source. Allday's parting words were 'The present *Argus* is the last of its

race.'[101] But there were many more papers of the same race still to come.

The picture as it emerges from the *Argus* is not only a picture of political strife conditioned by local problems and needs. It is a picture of an active social life, which centred on church and chapel, theatre and ring, platform and home. To relate each of these social institutions to the newspapers and periodicals of the day would be to write a full-scale social history of early nineteenth-century Birmingham. In the context of this discussion, however, all that it is necessary to underline is how important some of these institutions were, and to pay particular attention to one of them – the stage. The theatre of the early nineteenth century is forgotten today, yet it played a most important part in stimulating criticism and encouraging the setting-up of periodicals.

The first performances in Birmingham had been given by groups of strolling players in a shed in the fields, which later became Temple Street: by 1730 they were performing in a stable in Castle Street. In 1740 a theatre was erected in Moor Street, which lasted until 1752 when it became a Methodist meeting house. King Street Theatre was built in the same year and extended in 1774. In the same year an additional theatre was built in New Street and a magnificent portico was added to it six years later. In 1792 there was a disastrous fire there, maliciously planned and apparently well premeditated, since *Aris's Gazette* began its account of the incident by asserting that 'many malicious attempts have been made for some months past to set fire to our Theatre; but at length the wicked villains have succeeded in their execrable designs'.[102] The building was restored, extended, and re-opened by 1796, so that it could now hold 2000 people. This time it had a twenty-four-year life ahead of it, for in 1820 it again caught fire, this time accidentally, yet by a coincidence at exactly the same hour on the same day of the week as the earlier fire, and taking exactly the same time – three hours – to be destroyed.[103] Sculpted heads of Garrick and Shakespeare survived both fires.

The building of a new theatre in 1820 marked the beginning of a new period in Birmingham social history: it took seven months to build and was said to be 'scarcely equalled out of London, either for accommodation or elegance'.[104] In the first place, the new building – The Theatre Royal – was itself a dramatic triumph. 'The form of the Theatre is that of a Lyre ... the ceiling is a stellar dome, supported by Greek pillars ... the decorations of the three tiers of boxes are perfectly classical, being selected and adapted from the antique Temples of Greece', and then to blend old and new, 'over each column protrudes a burnished gold bracket, supporting a rich cut-glass chandelier; and the burner of each light is encircled in a globe ... The chandeliers are manufactured by Messrs. Hawkes of Dudley.' 'The establishment, in the opinion of every person who is able to judge on the subject, may vie with any in Great Britain.'[105] In the second place, the manager, Alfred Bunn (1796-1860), who was to move from theatre in Birmingham to opera in London and frequently to be satirised in the pages of *Punch*, went out of his way to build up a local company worthy of the dazzling interior. In the third place, an attempt was made to win the support of a cross-section of Birmingham's population. Gallery places cost 1s, pit places 2s 6d, and box seats, which accounted for more than half the theatre's revenue, 3s 6d or 4s.[106]

It was the impact of the theatre on Birmingham life which gave the biggest fillip to the publication of periodicals. Many of the periodicals were specially designed to cover the theatrical season, which lasted from June to September. The first was the *Theatrical Looker On* which first saw the light in May 1822. Despite early criticisms that it was subsidised by Alfred Bunn,[107] it soon established its position. Once there was one theatrical periodical, others followed. In 1823 the 2d *Birmingham Reporter and Theatrical Review* was beyond any doubt a local product. It had as its sub-title 'the Opinions, Doubts, and Perplexities of Humphrey Digbeth, Manufacturer and Others' and it criticised acting performances with a homely vigour.[108] 'The Monarch blushed like a rubicund coal from the Wednesbury Iron Works' was a characteristic verdict.[109] It was fittingly proud of its own achievements. 'We are no longer shackled with the opinions of a venal Press. We are no longer under the old régime of newspaper puffs, the olden time, when we believed all that *Aris's Gazette* and the play bills said.'[110]

Despite this liveliness, the *Reporter* disappeared in the year of its inception. The *Looker On* referred to a libel action, which brought about its demise, and generously characterised it as a 'work distinguished only by rancorous defamation'.[111] This standard of unfriendliness was to persist in the relations between periodicals throughout the whole of the 1820s. There was a running fight between different editors, who never attempted to restrain either the violence of their language or the scandalmongering of their articles. This weekly or monthly battle must have given the reading public a good deal to argue about. In 1823 they could study the *Looker On* and the *Reporter*; in 1824 the *Theatrical John Bull* and the *Birmingham Spectator* or the *Theatrical Note Book*,[112] the *Birmingham Review* and the *Mouse Trap*. The *Mouse Trap* put forward as its main purpose the exploration of other people's mistakes. 'Both its title and its quality are catching.'[113] 'Our hitherto peaceful town is at present inundated with a mass of discussion, to which its projectors have had the impudence to affix the term "literary", and it is therefore our duty to ascertain the correctness of the said term.' Literary discussions grew up round the theatre and were persisting even in the hectic year of 1830, when to counterbalance the political excitement of the Political Union, the *Theatrical Tattler*, the *Theatrical Observer*, and the *Theatrical Argus and Stage Reporter* were arguing about the merits of local performances and the relation of literature to stagecraft.

The discussions about the theatre were important, not only because they gave rise to a spate of new periodicals, but also because they launched many local writers into pamphleteering and newspaper work for the first time. Allday, son of a Digbeth butcher,[114] and later editor of the *Argus*, began his career with the *Theatrical John Bull* in 1824. More important still, Joseph Parkes made his literary debut in 1825 with a pamphlet called the *Plagiary Warned, a Vindication of the Drama, the Stage and Public Morals*, which was printed as an anonymous counterblast to two published sermons by John Angell James,[115] minister of Carr's Lane Chapel, protesting against the immorality and danger of visiting the theatre.[116] The fierce controversy which raged round the two eloquent sermons by James, *Youth Warned* and *The Scoffer Admonished*, and his book *A Christian Father's Present to His Children*, provoked more local interest and attention than any other topic until Catholic Emancipation.[117] The controversy was accentuated by some of the remarks made by James about the local Press, which he described as 'the contemptible dwarfs which infest our town'. 'It is to this Press', claimed the *Theatrical John Bull* in 1824, 'that he owes his existence as a minister of the gospel ... It is to this Press that we owe a great part of our pre-eminence over surrounding nations; for it gave to us that bold and independent method of thinking, which leads us to know our principles and guard our rights.'

So important were religious attitudes and loyalties in the town that they touched both politics and literature at every point. Thus, the *Theatrical John Bull*, which had as its motto 'take up arms in defence of the stage', warned that a Birmingham cabal 'not content with political liberty' was now 'looking after political power'.[118] A detailed study of the Birmingham public in the early nineteenth century cannot go very far without an investigation of the organisation and relations of the different religious groups.

Among the most interesting pieces of source material for such a study would be the curious pages of a little magazine called *Jenkinson's Scholastic Tickler* which was first published in March 1829. It had as its motto 'RELIGION is the *sail* and RADICAL REFORM the *rudder*, by which we expect safely to harbour in your *good opinion*'. It obviously appealed to the working people of Birmingham, and reflected many of the contradictions of thought and deep-set prejudices which determined conduct. 'We see one side of the body politic, the rich, totally unconnected with the other, the poor, either in feeling or interest.'[119]

In this remark of schoolmaster Jenkinson we almost return to the generalisations of sociologist Mumford – almost, but not quite, for the *Scholastic Tickler* goes on in a later number to focus its readers' attention to the wide and challenging possibilities of local improvement.

> There is much to reform in our own town without interference in distant climes [it urges]. We intend to show to the Chamber of Commerce, that the Insolvent Laws are radically bad: that the Bankruptcy Laws admit of gross frauds in the working of Commissions. To the Street Act Improvement Commissioners we shall show that the public money may be better employed than in such works as flagging the parade in Paradise Street. A few lessons we shall give to the Guardians of the Poor on the application of the Parish Funds. Frequently shall we visit the Court of Requests to see Justice in Equity administered etc.[120]

It is on Jenkinson's 'etc.' that I propose to end this paper. It was the vigorous refreshing etc. which showed that Birmingham was a thriving local community, and that there was ample recognition that there was still plenty of communal work to be done.

APPENDIX

List of Birmingham newspapers and periodicals (1800-35)

(Newspapers and periodicals marked with an asterisk are listed in *The Times Tercentenary Handlist of English and Welsh Newspapers, Magazines, and Reviews* (1920).)

*1 *The Birmingham Commercial Herald and General Advertiser,* 1804-20.
This paper was first printed by Wilks, Grafton and Riddell. In 1806 it was acquired by Richard Jabet, an active and prominent local figure. 'As the printer of some handbills obnoxious to the poorer classes, he became unpopular, and his house was attacked and destroyed, and his shop windows broken' in 1816.[121]

2 *The Midland Chronicle,* 1811-14.
This independent Whig-Radical paper, costing 6½d, 'the slaves of no

party', was controlled by J. Orton Smith and W. Hawkes Smith. The latter engaged in many political publishing ventures, presenting to Birmingham readers the full Whig-Radical case for the rights of the Press. 'The Press, under Providence, is the mighty engine which has demolished the opposing bars to the Temple of Knowledge.'[122] Hawkes Smith had little regard for inquiries after truth in the fashion of *The Searcher*. 'The search of such an enquirer,' he wrote, 'is like that of the vermin-killer; truth may be the object of his pursuit, but his aim is to extirpate her as an enemy, wherever he finds her.' Jabet's main weapon, in Smith's eyes, was falsehood, his argument assertion, and his 'rock of defence' the Gagging Bills.[123]

3   *The Birmingham Inspector*, 1817, 'a periodical work on liberal principles, printed and published by W. Hawkes Smith.

*4   *The Searcher or An Enquiry After Truth*, 1817, published by Richard Jabet, a counterblast to the *Inspector*.

5   *The Birmingham Argus*, 1818-19.
This paper does not appear in the Birmingham Collection. It was a Radical paper, and has been quoted in secondary authorities, e.g. the Webbs in their *The Parish and the County*. Its printer, George Ragg, was prosecuted in 1819 and sentenced to twelve months in Middlesex House of Correction.[124]

6   *Edmonds' Weekly Recorder and Saturday Advertiser*, 1819 (-23?)
This paper, which was called a pamphlet, was printed by T. J. Vale.

7   *Edmonds's Weekly Register*, 1819, published on Saturdays.

8   *Edmonds's Birmingham Gazette*, 1819-20.

9   *The Selector or Political Bouquet*, 1819.
This reformist paper was also printed by T. J. Vale, price 3d. It attacked the exorbitant newspaper tax, imposed 'for the apparent purpose of keeping the public ignorant on political affairs'.

10   *The Comet Magazine or Literary Wanderer*, 1820.
This magazine, printed by T. Bloomer and published by H. Chambers,

was in the tradition of the non-political, eighteenth-century periodicals, the first (?) of which was *The Birmingham Register or Enter-
taining Museum* of 1764.

11   *The Birmingham Mercury and Warwickshire and Staffordshire
     Advertiser*, 1820.
This paper was begun by James Amphlett of the *Lichfield Mercury*
with the support of Thomas Attwood, Joshua Scholefield, and a
committee of local people. The *Argus*, ten years later, described it as
the 'most sapient of all newsless newspapers'.[125] The name *Mercury*
was revived in 1848.

*12   *The Hazlewood Magazine*, 1822-4. *New Series*, 1827-30.

*13   *The Theatrical Looker On*, 1822-3, printed by James Drake and
covering the theatrical season from May to November.[126]

14   *The Birmingham Reporter and Theatrical Review*, 1823, printed
by Charles Buckton.

15   *The Bazaar or Literary and Scientific Repository*, 1823-5.
This magazine, printed by Ward and Price and published by
W. Cooper, was professedly non-political and non-religious. Litera-
ture and art were its themes.

16   *The Birmingham Chronical and General Advertiser of the Midland
     Counties*, 1823-5.
Myles Swinney's *Birmingham and Stafford Chronicle* had circulated
under various titles between 1773 and the end of the Napoleonic Wars.
Swinney himself died in 1812.[127] Wrightson ran the later *Chronicle*, the
history of which is obscure. In 1823 it was described as 'twenty-four
columns of dullness'.[128]

17   *The Birmingham Spectator*, 1824.
This magazine, published by J. Drake and edited by W. Hawkes
Smith, was the successor to the *Looker On*, though it extended the
interests of its predecessor. 'We will be a Committee of Taste for the
edification of Birmingham citizens.'

*18   *The Theatrical John Bull*, 1824.
Published by W. Cooper, this was the first editorial venture of Joseph

Allday. Part of the interest of the paper lies in its anticipations of the style and outlook of the *Argus*. It lasted throughout the theatrical season, but it was not content with theatrical criticism. It attacked Dissenters. 'Not content with religious liberty, they are longing after political power.'[130] It queried the march of technical progress, which it associated with 'knives and forks, buckles and belts, nut crackers, bottle stands, and Jews' harps.'

19   *The Theatrical Note Book*, 1824, printed by J. Drake, a rival to *The Theatrical John Bull* and disappearing at the same time, 'a little paper of playful badinage'.

20   *The Mouse Trap*, 1824, printed by T. Dewson.

21   *The Birmingham Review*, 1824, published by Butterworth, 'open to all parties, influenced by none'. It wished to see Birmingham *'dulce et utile'*.

*22   *The Birmingham Journal*, 1825 (became the *Birmingham Daily Post*, in 1859).
Its circulation was about 750 in 1828, and had risen to 1800 by 1830, the same circulation as the *Birmingham Gazette*. By the late 1830s it had reached 2500.

23   *The Birmingham Independent*, 1827-8, 'a monthly publication on Parochial and other local subjects', published by Joseph Russell, described in the first number (4 August 1827) as 'a channel of communication to the public mind'. The last number (July 1828) suggested that 'to look into the concerns of the town' required 'a greater degree of information and ability' than had been available.

24   *The Birmingham Magazine or Literary, Scientific, and Theological Repository*, 1827-8.
This 'very respectable magazine' was edited by the Rev. Hugh Hutton, and although J. Drake was a part-publisher, it was probably printed in London. It aimed at 'calm and temperate controversy', and came to an end not because it had failed to fulfil the 'reasonable expectations' of the editor, but because he had had insufficient time to work on it.

25   *The Oscotian*, 1827-9.

*26 *The Birmingham Argus and Public Censor*, 1828-34.

The story of the *Argus*, 'a running commentary on men and things as they are' (January 1831) has been outlined above. Its first printer was J. Webster, who found it expedient to deny that he had been dismissed from the job.[131] Webster was succeeded by Broomhall, and Broomhall by Ford (October 1828). It became a monthly in January 1829, and a new series, beginning August 1829, was printed by Chidlow, who subsequently shared in all the vicissitudes of the paper. He had more than his fair share, indeed, because Allday persisted in denying that he himself was the editor, thus leaving Chidlow to bear the brunt of the frequent attacks launched against the paper. Allday's object, wrote one of his enemies, 'was to screen himself, let the consequences be what they might to others'.[132] In July 1829 Allday was examined for bankruptcy and denied that he was the proprietor of the *Argus*, and a few months later Chidlow was ordered to pay £150 damages for libelling Gibbens, a local banker. A libel in 1831, which led to the April issue being seized, caused the trial of Allday and Chidlow at Warwick. In 1834 the *Argus* at last came to an end. 'A conspiracy of vipers alone could effect by instrumentality of the atrocious law of libel, what public opposition could not attain. The vindictive power of my malignant enemies has triumphed' (July 1834).

27 *The Birmingham Co-operative Herald*, 1829-30.

Photostat copies of this local paper, printed by W. Pastans and run by the followers of William Pare, are available in the Birmingham Collection: it professed to deal with 'social affairs of mankind'.

28 *Jenkinson's Scholastic Tickler*, 1829-30.

29 *The Theatrical Tattler*, 1830 (printed by Drake).

30 *The Literary Phoenix*, 1829-30.

This magazine, published by J. Belcher, proclaimed that the editor aimed at 'the total exclusion of theology and politics. It is to a higher tribunal that he appeals.' It was Tory in outlook and opposed to the 'prostituted *Journal*'.

31 *The Iris*, 1830 ('a magazine of literature and local intelligence' printed and published by W. Cooper), which drew attention in its first number to 'the fate of the several periodicals which have risen like mushrooms, and like them disappeared from time to time'. Ten years later there was a new Tory *Iris* edited and published by T. J. Ousley.

*32 *The Birmingham and Coventry Free Press*, 1830.
This Radical paper, run by Joseph Russell, the well-known Birmingham Radical of the left, lasted for six weeks, only. The *Argus* asked:

> 'What was I begun for
> To be so soon done for?'

'The very name of Russell', it added, 'would be enough to damn any publication of the kind.'

33 *The Theatrical Argus and Stage Reporter*, 1830 (printed by Chidlow).

34 *The Catholic Magazine and Review*, 1831-5.

*35 *The Midland Representative and Birmingham Herald*, 1831.
Edited by Bronterre O'Brien, published by J. Powell, and costing 7d, this paper was subsequently incorporated in the *Birmingham Journal*. Allday attacked it as 'mental poison under the guise of patriotism'.

36 *The Political Union Register*, 1832, a monthly edited by M. P. Haynes.

37 *The Political Unionist*, a weekly, 1832, also edited by Haynes.

38 *The Wasp*, 1832 (printed by Richard Jenkinson for Joseph Allday).

39 *The Tocsin*, 1833.
This was another Allday publication. It disappeared with the *Argus*. 'We might have disposed of both the *Argus* and the *Tocsin* in the "market"', wrote Allday, 'but we neither started nor carried on either of these publications for *gain* – or *filthy lucre* – and we will not *sell* them. We *fall* and THEY die!'

40 *The Midland Chronicle and Beacon for the Working Man*, 1833 (published by Hudson).

*41 *The Birmingham Advertiser*, 1833-47, (printed by William Hodgetts). Its motto was conservative: 'It is good not to try experiments in states except the necessity be urgent or the utility evident and well to beware that it be the reformation that dreweth on the change and not the desire of change that pretendeth the reformation.' Its circulation, about 500 in 1835, doubled during the next two years.

42 *The Pioneer; or Trade Union Magazine*, 1833-40.
This Midlands organ of the Operative Builders' Union, established in September 1833, claimed to have a weekly circulation of up to 20,000. It was edited by James Morrison.

43 *The Birmingham Labour Exchange Gazette*, 1833 (edited by William Pare). This paper cost 1d and was devoted solely to 'cooperative knowledge'.

44 *The Reformer*, 1835 (a liberal weekly owned by the Quaker Joseph Sturge and published by Benjamin Hudson), renamed *The Philanthropist* in the same year. Its motto was 'the greatest possible good of the greatest possible number of mankind' and its main purpose was to advocate emancipation.

45 *The Scourge*, 1835.

46 *The Watchman*, 1835 (edited by Joseph Allday, a self-professed 'tired man', with the motto 'Be Just. Fear Not').

This list of forty-six publications obviously leaves out some periodicals which have disappeared without a trace. References are found to others, including an earlier *Tocsin*. Joseph Allday apparently began his career with a paper called *The Critic*, 'which he devoted to the glorious deeds of prize fighting'. It was a small weekly publication which failed. Walter Showell in his *Dictionary of Birmingham* (1883) referred also to *The Tattler* (1817), 'a two-penny-worth of hotch-potch, principally scandal'. The list also does not include *Aris's Gazette*, which preceded and survived the period, or other pre-1800 ventures. One year after the terminal date the *Birmingham Herald* appeared: it was delivered *gratis* to 5000 businessmen and paid for out of advertising revenue. A contemporary said of its contents: 'news, but no politics'.

NOTES

1 Lewis Mumford, *The Culture of Cities* (1938), Chapter III. See also above p. 88.
2 George Eliot, Preface to *Felix Holt* (1866). See also below, vol. II, p. 50.

3 *The Birmingham Spectator*, no. X, 31 July 1824.
4 ibid., no. I, 7 August 1824.
5 See J. A. Langford, *A Century of Birmingham Life* (2nd edn, 1871), vol. II, pp. 443-4, 550-1. The attention of the Commissioners was first drawn to the plan of a town hall by the Musical Committee of the General Hospital. Barry's plan was not chosen, that of Hansom and Welsh being accepted instead.
6 *Aris's Gazette*, 28 May 1827.
7 Walter Barrow, 'The Town and its Industries', in *Birmingham Institutions* (1911), J. H. Muirhead (ed.), p. 51. See further George Jacob Holyoake, *Sixty Years of an Agitator's Life* (1892), vol. I, Chapter V.
8 Pigott and Company, *Commercial Directory* (1822), p. 1.
9 *The Comet Magazine or Literary Wanderer*, 1 January 1820; *The Birmingham Reporter*, 4 September 1823.
10 Letter from Thomas Attwood to Mrs Attwood, 30 April 1812, quoted in C. M. Wakefield, *The Life of Thomas Attwood* (1885), p. 24. See also below pp. 144-5.
11 J. L. Garvin, *The Life of Joseph Chamberlain*, vol. 1 (1932), p. 385.
12 Letter of W. Hawkes Smith, in the *Birmingham Journal*, 9 November 1829.
13 See, *inter alia*, G. A. Cranfield, *The Development of the Provincial Newspaper* (1962), and D. Read, *Press and People, 1790-1850* (1961).
14 *Place Papers* BM, Add. MSS., 27, 795, f. 160. Place believed that the cause of Reform was probably thereby 'better served than it would have been had the freest communication been permitted'.
15 H. S. Pearson, in *Mid-England*, February 1880: 'Birmingham Periodical Literature Half a Century Ago'.
16 J. Hill, *The Bookmakers of Old Birmingham* (1907), p. 41.
17 *The Birmingham Gazette*, 9 January 1837. In this number the editor gave a brief but interesting history of the *Gazette*. See also Cranfield, *op. cit.*, pp. 51-6. The owners were always cost-conscious and keen on systematic accounting.
18 *The Birmingham Monthly Argus and Public Censor*, June 1830. The article described the *Liverpool Mercury* as 'the provincial *Times*'.
19 *The Birmingham Spectator*, 7 August 1824.
20 *The Theatrical John Bull*, 16 October 1824.
21 The use of nicknames to describe newspapers was not confined to Birmingham. *The Times* was frequently called the 'Thunderer', the *Morning Post* was called 'Jeames', the *Morning Herald* and the *Standard* were known as 'Mrs Harris' and 'Sairy Gamp'. See L. M. Salmon, *The Newspaper and the Historian* (1923), p. 50.
22 *The Birmingham Monthly Argus and Public Censor*, August 1829.
23 ibid., December 1829.
24 *The Birmingham Gazette*, 9 January 1837.
25 J. Hill, *op cit.*, pp. 73-9.
26 *The Birmingham Reporter*, 28 August 1823.
27 *The Birmingham Spectator*, 7 August 1824.
28 *The Theatrical John Bull*, 11 September 1824. Cp. 29 May 1824. 'It

hopes this, and trusts the other – speak out Man! Is it always policy to
steer the milk and water course?'

29   *The Birmingham Monthly Argus and Public Censor*, June 1830.
30   See below, p. 229.
31   Parliamentary Papers, 1839, vol. XLIII, p. 203, quoted by S. Maccoby,
     English Radicalism (1832-1852) (1935), p. 167.
32   E. Edwards, *Personal Recollections of Birmingham and Birmingham
     Men* (1877), p. 6.
33   *The Birmingham Monthly Argus and Public Censor*, June 1830.
34   According to the *Argus*, he paid £400 for it at this time. He had sub-
     scribed £50 in 1825 to the original fund.
35   Bakewell bought a paper in Somerset, giving his opinion that 'DEATH'
     was the inevitable fate of the *Birmingham Journal* (*Argus, loc. cit.*).
36   ibid.
37   There was considerable movement at this time in local newspaper
     editorships. Crowther came from Manchester, Bakewell went to
     Somerset, and MacKenzie to Carlisle to edit the *Carlisle Patriot*. The
     editor of the *Carlisle Patriot* went to the *Leeds Intelligencer*. Mackenzie
     returned again to Birmingham in 1830 to edit for six weeks the
     Birmingham Free Press. The *Argus* described Crowther as 'a penny-a-
     line man' (June 1830).
38   *Report of the Proceedings at the Meeting of the Inhabitants of Birming-
     ham ... for the establishment of a GENERAL POLITICAL UNION*. 25
     January 1830 (printed by Hodgetts).
39   *Report on the Town Meeting*, 20 October 1831.
40   *The Birmingham Monthly Argus and Public Censor*, June 1832.
     According to this account, which is repeated in Edwards, *op. cit.*, p. 7,
     the paper was bought out in February and delivered in March. The
     sum involved was £2000.
41   ibid., June 1832.
42   *Birmingham Collection* 442, 194. 'A Complete Set of the Press Reports
     of the Public Meetings of the Birmingham Political Union', MS. Note
     by Parkes.
43   *The Birmingham Argus*, July 1829.
44   *The Standard*, 6 October, 14 November 1831.
45   *The Birmingham Argus and Public Censor*, June 1832. The two papers
     were edited by a Roman Catholic, M. P. Haynes, and both faced
     financial difficulties (see the *Political Union Register*, March 1832).
46   O'Brien was one of the most important political journalists of his day.
     After editing the *Midland Representative*, he went on to edit the *Poor
     Man's Guardian* (1832-5). See G. H. D. Cole, *Chartist Portraits* (1941),
     pp. 243-7, A. Plummer, *Bronterre* (1971), A. Briggs, 'Feargus O'Connor
     and Bronterre O'Brien' in J. W. Boyle (ed.), *Leaders and Workers*
     (1968).
47   The details of this and other co-operative ventures are given in E. W.
     Hampton, *Early Co-operation in Birmingham and District* (1928).
48   *The Birmingham Argus and Public Censor*, June 1832. *Radical Reform*
     became *Rare Mad Frolic* and *Annual Parliament, I am an Unreal Plant*.

The Political Union became 'Miss Polly Union'.

49 ibid., February 1830.

50 ibid., September 1831.

51 See C. D. Collet, *History of the Taxes on Knowledge* (1899); W. H. Wickwar, *The Struggle for the Freedom of the Press* (1928); J. H. Wiener, *The War of the Unstamped* (1969); and P. Hollis, *The Pauper Press* (1970).

52 60 George III, c. 9 sec. 1.

53 *Aris's Gazette*, 9 January 1837.

54 James Guest, 'A Free Press and How it Became Free', in W. Hutton, *The History of Birmingham*, 6th edn (1860), p. 507. It is possible to trace price changes for other Birmingham newspapers. The *Birmingham Chronicle* cost 3½d in 1769, 4d in 1792, 6d in 1800, 6½d in 1809, and 7d in 1814.

55 It was a similar caption on the *Examiner* in 1830 – 'Paper and Print 3½d, Taxes on Knowledge 3½d, price 7d', which inspired John Francis to begin his struggle 'to accelerate the extinction of the malevolent imposts upon Intelligence' (G. J. Holyoake's Introduction to Collet).

56 He was in fact sentenced to nine months' imprisonment for conspiracy.

57 *Birmingham Monthly Argus and Public Censor*, January 1829. It then cost a shilling. In January 1831 it claimed again that it was 'not a newspaper', but a 'running commentary on men and things just as they are'.

58 *Weekly Political Register*, 29 December 1827.

59 Hutton, *op. cit.*, p. 386.

60 *Westminster Review*, January 1830, quoted by A. Aspinall, 'The Circulation of English Newspapers in the Early Nineteenth Century', in the *Review of English Studies*, January 1946.

61 A. Aspinall, 'Statistical Accounts of the London Newspapers, 1800-1836', in the *English Historical Review*, vol. LXV (1950), pp. 222-3. See also his *Politics and the Press* (1949), p. 23.

62 HO/40/29. There was a long tradition here which went back to Knott and Lloyd's *Warning Drum* at the beginning of the century: *An Address to the People to resist Invasion*. There were *graffiti* too. In 1805 Bisset (*Recollections*, Birmingham Reference Library) noted 'No badgers', 'No War', and 'No King, Lords and Commons'. In 1791 he wrote, 'Church and King' was to be seen everywhere.

63 Guest, *op. cit.*, p. 386.

64 E. E. Kellett, 'The Press', in *Early Victorian England* (1934) vol. II, p. 3.

65 Frederick Hill, one of the Hills of Hazelwood School, was the main reader, although there were other readers in coffee shops, public houses and other centres.

66 W. Lovett, *Life and Struggles*, vol. I, p. 222. See further G. J. Holyoake, *op. cit.*, vol. I, Chapter XLVI, and Edwards, *op. cit.*, pp. 19-37.

67 Quoted from *The Examiner*, by E. E. Kellett, *op. cit.*, p. 7.

68 Guest, *op. cit.*, p. 493.

69 William Carpenter reported in April 1831 that about 900 copies of

his *Political Letter* and pamphlets were being disseminated weekly in Birmingham. (*Ballot*, 4 December 1831.)

70 Joseph Russell, *Trial* (Birmingham, 1822). See also the *Birmingham Chronicle*, 10 August 1820. The opponents of the Radicals were well organised in Birmingham at this time into a Loyal Association for the Suppression and Refutation of Blasphemy and Sedition. See Wickwar, *op. cit.*, pp. 107-10.

71 *Black Dwarf*, 29 September 1869.

72 *London Despatch*, 4 December 1836, quoted in Hollis, *op. cit.*, p. 113.

73 Quoted from *The Examiner* by F. Knight Hunt, *The Fourth Estate* (1850), vol. II, pp. 72-3.

74 Wiener, *op. cit.*, pp. 88-90; *Midland Representative*, 20 August 1831.

75 Attwood presented a Wallsall petition in April 1833 and a Norwich petition in 1835. He also joined a deputation supporting total repeal in February 1836.

76 *Weekly Herald*, 3 July 1836.

77 Guest, *op. cit.*, p. 508.

78 ibid., p. 503.

79 *The Birmingham Journal*, June 1830.

80 *Westminster Review*, April 1829. Quoted by Aspinall, *op. cit.*

81 *The Birmingham Argus and Public Censor*, July 1830.

82 Letter from Mackenzie to the *Argus*, 5 June 1830. He claimed that during his editorship the average number of advertisements increased from twenty-six to fifty-four.

83 According to the *Argus* of November 1829, the *Gazette* had a circulation of 4000 during the mid-1820s.

84 *Jenkinson's Scholastic Tickler*, October 1829.

85 *The Birmingham Argus and Public Censor*, July 1830.

86 *The Birmingham Independent*, 28 July 1828.

87 Quoted J. A. Langford, *op. cit.*, vol. II, p. 283.

88 *The Bazaar* or *Literary and Scientific Repository*, 21 July 1823.

89 *The Birmingham Argus and Public Censor*, July 1829.

90 H. S. Pearson, *op. cit.* For Holyoake's comments on the mixed fortunes of periodicals, see J. McCabe, *Life and Letters of George Joseph Holyoake* (18XX), vol. I, p. 160.

91 *The Birmingham Spectator*, 16 October 1824.

92 *The Birmingham Argus and Public Censor*, January 1829.

93 ibid., October 1828.

94 *The Birmingham Monthly Argus Exposed* (1831).

95 *The Birmingham Argus and Public Censor*, December 1829.

96 ibid., December 1829.

97 ibid., July 1829.

98 For a sketch of him, see E. Edwards, *op. cit.*, p. 70. See also *Birmingham Morning News*, 6 May 1878.

99 *The Birmingham Monthly Argus exposed by a Person fully acquainted with the Whole Machinery (Public and Private) of that Base Publication* (printed and published by R. Ellis, 118 Snow Hill, 1834?).

100 It is important to remember, as Allday points out (the *Argus*, May

1831), 'The law of libel is undefined; the nature of a libel has not yet been exactly ascertained; it is one of those things which gives the law its "most glorious uncertainty".'

101 *The Parting Words of Joseph Allday* (1834), written in Warwick Gaol.

102 *Aris's Gazette*, 20 August 1792. See Hutton, *op. cit.*, p. 287. 'The probability is, that happening so soon after the riots, this supposition was circulated without any foundation.'

103 Langford, *op. cit.*, p. 397. See further *The Bazaar*, 10 July 1823.

104 Hutton, *op. cit.*, p. 288.

105 *Aris's Gazette*, 7 August 1820.

106 J. Drake, *The Picture of Birmingham* (1825), p. 36.

107 *The Theatrical Looker On*, June 1822.

108 *The Birmingham Reporter*, 3 July 1823.

109 ibid., 19 June 1823.

110 ibid., 28 August 1823.

111 *The Theatrical Looker On*, 17 October 1823. *The Mouse Trap*, no. 1, 13 September 1824, called Francis Lloyd, the editor, 'as contemptible a booby as ever had existence'.

112 28 June 1824. This publication proclaimed the most grandiloquent purpose – 'the patronage of the Drama in this town, the enlargement of the worthy people's understanding, and the general benefit of mankind'.

113 *The Mouse Trap*, 13 September 1824.

114 'This theatrical butcher, whose element is slander, and whose most delicious food is human flesh', *The Mouse Trap*, *op. cit.*

115 '*Why* ANGEL *we know not*', *The Theatrical John Bull*, 29 May 1824.

116 *The Christian Father's Present to His Children* included the famous words 'the theatre is one of the broadest avenues, which lead to destruction'. Alfred Bunn replied in *A Letter to the Rev. J. A. James*. See *The Birmingham Spectator*, 7 August 1824.

117 *Theatrical John Bull*, 28 August 1824.

118 ibid., 29 May 1824. The paper questioned some of the recent encomia on James Watt. 'How ridiculous ... to talk about Naval and Military Commanders and James Watt in the same breath.'

119 *Jenkinson's Scholastic Tickler*, June 1829.

120 ibid., October 1829.

121 Hill, *op. cit.*, p. 77.

122 Letter from W. Hawkes Smith, dated 9 November 1825, in the *Birmingham Journal*, 12 November 1825.

123 *The Birmingham Inspector*, 10 May 1817.

124 See Wickwar, *op. cit.*, pp. 108-9; A. Bain, *James Mill*, p. 439.

125 *The Birmingham Argus and Public Censor*, June 1831.

126 James Drake, a leading stationer, published a well-known *Picture of Birmingham* in 1824.

127 Hill, *op. cit.*, p. 79.

128 *The Birmingham Reporter*, 20 August 1823.

129 *The Birmingham Spectator*, 31 July 1824.

130 *The Theatrical John Bull*, 29 May 1824.

131 *Aris's Gazette*, 6 October 1828. Webster, Broomhall, and Ford 'soon found reason to decline doing business with the "responsible editor in the background",' *The Birmingham Monthly Argus Exposed* (R. Ellis).
132 ibid.

6 Thomas Attwood and the Economic Background of the Birmingham Political Union

At a meeting of the Birmingham Political Union in May 1833 the principal guest, Daniel O'Connell, congratulated his audience on having carried the Reform Bill through to success, for, he went on, 'it was not Grey and Althorp who carried it, but the brave and determined men of Birmingham'.[1] In the heat of the struggle, even some of the Whig ministers were willing to admit in the famous words of Russell that 'it is impossible that the whisper of a faction should prevail against the voice of a nation'. One of them told Thomas Attwood in May 1832 that 'we owe our situation entirely to you'.[2] Lord Durham maintained that 'the country owed Reform to Birmingham, and its salvation from revolution'.[3] Earl Grey himself, after the safe passing of the Bill, thanked Attwood for all that he had done 'to maintain popular support for the measure outside the House of Commons'.[4]

The origins of the Birmingham Political Union are embedded in Birmingham economic history from 1812 to 1832; it is necessary, therefore, to explore the background of that Union – how it emerged and how it was organised – relating its history to local pressures and to local interests. There was a direct connection between the economic structure and development of Birmingham and the politics of the city; and this connection was analysed and exploited by Thomas Attwood, who played the leading part in the setting-up of the Political Union. Born in 1783, the son of a banker and the nephew of an ironmaster, Attwood, who became a country banker, married a Tory and sometimes considered himself a Tory even after he had taken up parliamentary reform. By January 1830 his position in the movement for parliamentary reform was so important that Francis Place considered him 'the most influential man in England'.[5]

Attwood has often been dismissed as a currency fanatic, 'a provincial banker labouring under a financial monomania',[6] and Radicals and Tories alike were often contemptuous of his currency projects.

138

Cobbett, whose views on the currency were diametrically opposed to Attwood's, commiserated with the audiences who had to listen to him speak for four hours or more;[7] O'Brien thought him 'a paper-money schemer';[8] O'Connor called his financial scheme 'rag botheration';[9] John Stuart Mill argued that in face of Attwood's currency proposals even 'a Radical Reformer can, without deserting a higher trust, allow himself to assume, in the main, the garb and attitude of a conservative'.[10]

Despised as they often were, Attwood's currency schemes were the link between his economics and his politics, for the currency question was 'the central pivot upon which the whole of his life turned'. Even the reform of Parliament was, to him, but a secondary question in comparison, and if he could have prevailed upon any government to adopt his monetary views, 'he would never have joined the ranks of the reformers.'[11] During the hectic struggles for the Reform Bill – and later for the Charter – Attwood gathered around him and held together in Birmingham a group of active supporters, who shared his conviction that economic reform was the 'end' and political reform the 'means'. Although other groups coalesced with his original supporters in 1830 and 1831 to press for parliamentary reform, the currency group remained the most articulate body of the kind in Birmingham. It provided the kernel of the Birmingham Political Union, thereby differentiating the Union throughout the struggle from most of the other Political Unions,[12] which as far as political tactics was concerned, imitated its example. The group survived 1832, and influenced the beginnings of Chartism.

Attwood's currency thesis represented more than a mere private fad of his own: it had a particular and direct relevance to the problems of Birmingham. It enabled Attwood to mobilise opinion by the exploitation of local grievances, since the economic situation provided material which he had only to model and develop. His use of the currency formula enabled him to unite the opinion of both middle and working classes, and thereby at the same time to preserve social peace. Behind his economic outlines was a whole social philosophy:

> The interests of masters and men are, in fact, one. If the masters flourish, the men are certain to flourish with them; and if the masters suffer difficulties, their difficulties must shortly affect the workmen in a threefold degree. The masters, therefore, ought not to say to the workmen, 'Give us your wages', but take their workmen by the hand, and knock at the gates of the Government and demand the redress of their common grievances. In this way, the Government is made answerable for its own acts at its own doors; and in this way only can the rights and interests of the middle and lower classes be supported.[13]

The social philosophy thus proclaimed gained much of its force and colour from the special characteristics of economic society in Birmingham and the Midlands, just as the underlying economic theory was sorted out from reflections on the challenging experiences of business life in Birmingham in the twenty years before 1832. First stated in Attwood's pamphlets and miscellaneous writings,[14] the social and economic theories became politically important in national as well as local terms only in 1829, when Attwood turned from writing to action, and from backstairs politics to open platform agitation.

Before that important step was taken, it was not only Attwood who had to change: England also had to change with him. In 1825, during a visit to London, he had written to his wife: 'You may be assured that, whatever I do with the Ministers, I shall have no contact with the Radicals, unless things take a strange turn'.[15] Between 1825 and 1829, things did take a strange turn. Catholic Emancipation split the Tory Party, and old Brunswickers became for a brief period new reformers. During the political upheavals of 1829 Birmingham politics were deflected into a new course. Thomas Attwood's philosophies provided the guiding principles of the Political Union.

II

Birmingham in the years 1812 to 1825 was a changing city. In a period of thirty years its population had doubled. The face of the town had completely altered.[16] Each year, local expansion brought within its boundaries open tracts of countryside. Alongside this development, which was already turning Birmingham into a 'city of suburbs', there was a wider development of the Black Country as a whole. 'The neighbouring hamlets are approached by her streets, and ere long will merge in her arms as Deritend, Bordesley, Duddleston and Edgbaston ... the great and multitudinous assemblage of one people – one vast manufacturing community – one Birmingham.'[17] During the eighteenth century the city was already becoming the commercial metropolis of the Midlands, the capital city of an expanding industrial region, based on coal and iron. Distinguished by the diversity of its 'trades', it had earned the title 'toyshop of Europe' and its local smiths had become the centre 'in scarcely more than a hundred years of a web of commercial transactions, which covered the globe'.[18]

Economic differentiation provided an increasing impetus to the demand for representation in Parliament. During the late eighteenth century, when most of the new manufacturers were more interested in applying economic pressures than in seeking political reform,[19] it was recognised that it was an advantage to have a county Member for Warwick, whose especial duty it would be to attend to Birmingham's interests.[20] In 1780 Birmingham manufacturers appealed to the Earl of

Dartmouth, long connected with the county of Warwick, to help them to secure the election of Sir Robert Lawley on the grounds that he was familiar with the industrial and commercial interests of the growing town. 'The various commercial regulations, so frequently made by the Legislature, affect the trade and manufacturers of this city very much', they wrote, 'and render it an object of great importance to its inhabitants that gentlemen may, if possible, be chosen for the county who are connected with the people, and not entirely un-informed of the particulars in which their interests consist.'[21] The sense of 'interests' was strengthened in 1785 when Samuel Garbett played a key part in the setting up of the General Chamber of Manufacturers of Great Britain, with Birmingham as the centre of a national lobby.[22]

When in the early nineteenth century Warwick Members failed to attend to Birmingham interests, the demand for separate represent-ation grew. In 1812, Sir Charles Mordaunt, whose family had close connections with the constituency, was bitterly attacked by a town meeting on the grounds that he had received with indifference a letter from 14,000 Birmingham constituents protesting against the Orders-in-Council, and that he had not attended the examination of evidence in support of the allegations made. While Attwood was the hero of Birmingham in 1812, Mordaunt was the villain.[23]

The growing recognition of the need for separate representation on economic grounds nonetheless took a long time to become effective, although Birmingham had active Whig and Radical groups through-out the whole period, described by their local enemies as early as 1817 as 'the whole tribe of Hampdenites, Spenceans, Universal Suffrage Men, backers for Annual Parliaments, dabblers in disorder, amateurs of Revolution'.[24]

The economic views of such groups were on the whole orthodox in national terms, centring on the demand for 'retrenchment', although one prominent Radical, George Edmonds, favoured 'cheap money in 1820. 'The motto of the community', wrote the *Birmingham Inspector* in the same year, 'must be Economy! Economy! Economy!'[25] There were demands, too, for the repeal of the Corn Laws.[26] Sometimes militant Whiggism or Radicalism and economic defeatism could go together. 'The commercial situation in which this city has placed itself', the *Birmingham Inspector* went on, 'was an artificial one' and 'it is scarcely conceivable that such a pitch should ever again be attained, unless the rest of mankind could forget all that they have learned during the last thirty years.' France had not been eliminated as a competitor, and America was 'fast approaching to rivalry with us in mechanical skill'.[27]

Attwood shared neither such economic defeatism nor the ideology of political reform. As early as 1811, he had put his trust not in retrenchment but in high wages, backed by consumer and investor demand and supported by a managed credit system;[28] and as late as 1817, he was in sympathy with the Tory view that 'Birmingham is a peaceable town and a loyal one', where unfortunately 'a few meddling men have interfered to ... break the harmony of its inhabitants'.[29] Yet he was afraid of the political consequences of distress. There was 'no knowing' what a parcel of hungry Burdettites might 'take into their heads'.[30] Members of Parliament for rotten boroughs were 'just as likely to be honourable, useful and upright Members of Parliament, as those who have been chosen by a large population and who have innumerable interests to attend to, which are often different or hostile to the interests of the country.'[31]

Not surprisingly, Lord Liverpool, the Prime Minster with whom Attwood corresponded, was able to write in a memorandum of 1821 that the most respectable inhabitants of Birmingham were opposed to separate representation.[32] He knew, indeed, that Attwood's Tory country banking partner, Richard Spooner, nominated in 1820 for the Warwickshire seat, had been strongly supported by Peel as well as by the inhabitants of Birmingham, and it was only a second defeat for Spooner in 1822, when a major Birmingham effort was made to secure his election, that it began to seem unlikely that dynamic Birmingham interests could be adequately represented through the county.[33] Yet even five years afterwards, *Aris's Gazette* could still remark complacently that 'we are at present well represented in Parliament by our county members and cannot place ourselves in a better position.'[34] Two years later still, long after Attwood changed his views, the *Birmingham Journal*, not yet launched on its reforming career, was writing that the loss of a Bill introduced in Parliament by Charles Tennyson to transfer the East Retford seat to Birmingham and supported by Attwood – was not to be regretted. 'The advantage of sending representatives is merely theoretical and is surely attended with disorder.'[35] Lord Palmerston was more realistic when he stated that 'to extend the franchise to large towns on such occasions ... was the only mode' by which Parliament could 'avoid the adoption at some time or other of a general plan of reform'.[36]

While both the *Journal* and Palmerston were restating old cases, the more vigorous and more scurrilous Tory-Radical periodical, the *Birmingham Argus*,[37] was writing that 'the very serious losses to which the trade of Birmingham has been exposed ... might have been greatly diminished, if not entirely prevented, had we been so fortunate as to have possessed two FAITHFUL REPRESENTATIVES IN PARLIAMENT during the last thirty or forty years, a defect which we sincerely hope will soon be remedied.'[38]

The same point was to be made just as generally in 1832 by a West Midlands businessman, Richard Fryer, when he told a Wolverhampton Political Union meeting:

Fifty years ago we were not in that need for representatives which we are at present, as we then manufactured nearly exclusively for home consumption, and the commercial and manufacturing districts were then identified with each other; where one flourished, both flourished. But the face of affairs is now widely changed – we now manufacture for the whole world, and if we have not members to promote and extend our commerce, the era of commercial greatness is at an end.[39]

III

Differentiated economic interest was not the only basis of the demand for separate representation. Economic fluctuations and their perceived consequences provided the spur. Indeed, fluctuations were of very great importance not only in stimulating the demand for reform but in determining the timing and character of the political agitation. It was debt and distress, Cobbett exclaimed, that brought Birmingham merchants and manufacturers 'these lords of the anvil', to 'pass resolutions ... such as will make you stare to read'. 'These men know their own affairs at any rate ... For once they have spoke truth.'[40]

Between 1811 and 1830, there were such notable fluctuations in iron prices that Birmingham enjoyed alternating periods of prosperity and depression. Iron prices provided an index of prosperity or distress throughout the whole wide range of Birmingham and West Midlands business. Slumps in these prices pushed both masters and men out of work, while booms generated confidence, which rippled out through all the ancillary metal trades. Fluctuations of a marked and violent character encouraged speculation about economic first causes and inspired Attwood's and other Birmingham theories of income and employment.[41] The theories were, in turn, applied to politics. In 1776, the Birmingham rhymster John Freeth had sung of Birmingham's tranquillity:

> In no place besides that's so populous grown,
> Was ever less noise and disturbance known:
> All hands find employment, and when their work's done,
> Are happy as any souls under the sun.[42]

Freeth was too optimistic. Already in the eighteenth century, Birmingham, with its increasing dependence upon foreign markets, was vulnerable to boom and depression.[43] Four years before Freeth produced his rhapsody, which includes the lines,

The envy and hatred elections bring on
Their hearty intention is always to shun,

Matthew Boulton was writing that 'the trade of Birmingham is so dead at this juncture that the London wagons have to make up their loadings with coal for want of merchandise.'[44] Even during the Napoleonic Wars there were difficult years, like 1795 and 1800, when unemployment and high food prices led to serious disturbances; and in 1810, a year of good trade, troops had to be called out to deal with a market riot over the market price of potatoes.[45]

The depression of 1811 was deeper and more momentous than any before. 'The trade of Birmingham, Sheffield &c. quite at a stand', observed the Commercial Correspondent of the *Monthly Magazine* in January 1811, 'and no orders for execution there, except a few for our home consumption.'[46] The commercial slump was followed by a fall in iron prices, and an industrial recession:

> Even the smelting, that till within these two years, afforded some degree of profit, now affords no profit whatever. The stock of iron has increased; every manufacturer is overburdened with stock, and if he sells his iron, he only sells it at his own loss ... Great numbers of labourers have been dismissed within the last twelve months ... and labourers that twelve months ago could obtain in the iron works 20s. a week, cannot now obtain more than 10s. or 12s., and hundreds of them are to be had at 12s.

At one time in 1811, over 9000 people in Birmingham alone were in receipt of poor relief.[47] The fall in profits and the unemployment of labour led to local disturbances. By 1812, 'a disposition to tumult ... was manifest by the populace, who assembled in large numbers in the Market Place, and proceeded to some acts of violence'.[48]

It was against this troubled background that Attwood was launched into politics. He had been chosen High Bailiff in 1811 at the early age of twenty-eight, and in his official capacity as chairman of Town Meetings, he was soon brought into close touch with local opinion. 'Never in any former instance, or upon any other subject', it was claimed, 'were the genuine feelings of by far the greater majority of the collected inhabitants of the town so strongly excited, or so unequivocally expressed.'[49] By his lively interest and exertions, Attwood cut a popular figure with both businessmen and artisans.

At this time, local distress was explained not by a general theory but by a specific cause, the passing of the Orders-in-Council and the United States Non-Intercourse Act,[50] and it was believed that if the Orders were repealed, trade would revive automatically. Attwood went to London, therefore, as head of a local delegation of merchants and manufacturers to plead the town's case. For his services, which may have been less attentive than he thought,[51] he was thanked both by the businessmen and by the artisans, headed by a 'committee of arrangement', and in 1813 he was presented with a commemoration silver cup worth 200 guineas for services 'without Doubt engraven on the Memory of every Mechanic in the Town'.[52] Among the artisans was George Edmonds, son of a Baptist minister, who was to lead his own Radical movement for reform in 1819[53] and who was to stand firmly behind Attwood for a second time from 1829 to 1832.[54]

If in 1812 people tended to account for 'distress' by alleging the specific effects of special legislation – and the Whig politician Henry Brougham did his best to mobilise threatened interests there and elsewhere[55] – after 1815, when the Birmingham iron trade failed to find peacetime markets and iron prices fell, there was a search for more general explanations, and the search persisted even though there were once more clearly ascertainable special reasons for the slump, a fall in demand for 'particular articles of which the demand for naval and military purposes forms ... a large proportion to the total supply'.[56] As Birmingham was severely hit, it was plausible to write, as did one commentator, that

> No town in the Kingdom is at this time experiencing such difficulty and distress as Birmingham for this obvious reason, that no other place received so much direct employment from Government during the war. This great annual expenditure was suddenly withdrawn, and there are now nearly a fifth part of the population receiving weekly relief, the masters being no longer able to employ the men; very many indeed having been ruined themselves.[57]

The cause, the writer held, was beyond control. 'This is a deplorable state of things', he noted, 'but it has not been occasioned by any misconduct or impolicy; it is the plain unavoidable consequence of events over which no man or body could have any control.' Its worst effects could be overcome by charitable relief.

Attwood was unimpressed by such reasoning, particularly after the post-war crisis had been followed by more ups and downs in iron prices and in the prices of iron products; and when Charles Babbage collected various statistics of hardware prices in Birmingham and the Black Country during the years 1818 to 1832,[58] claiming that they reflected cost reductions associated with the development of new machinery (see Table 1), Attwood and Birmingham writers of his school claimed that most of the articles produced in Birmingham had not been affected by the use of machinery (see Table 1, p. 147). Consequently, therefore, they went on, the figures afforded a proper criterion by which to determine 'the depreciation of labour and capital'. What struck less sophisticated contemporaries was the break with the relatively recent past. Thus, Catherine Hutton pointed out in the fourth edition of William Hutton's *History of Birmingham* that William had never foreseen a time when 'the manufactures and the poor's rates' would not increase and decrease together. The state of Birmingham in the year 1817 could not have been anticipated. 'The poor always found employment.'[59]

Against the background of a general downward price movement, short-run cyclical fluctuations continued. The year 1819, when Edmunds' Radical agitation took place,[60] was, like 1811, the trough year of a trade-cycle, although the price of iron in that year was high, and iron movements did not mirror general movements in a perfectly symmetrical way.[61] The years 1824-5, however, were boom years in both the iron trade and in economic activity as a whole. Indeed, the King's Speech in 1825 proclaimed that there never had been a period in the history of the country when all the great interests of society were at the same time in so thriving a condition. 'During the whole of 1824 and 1825', wrote T. C. Salt, a Birmingham manufacturer, who was later to collaborate closely with Attwood, 'the stock went off so rapidly into consumption that we could hardly keep the shopkeepers supplied fast enough'.[62]

The break, when it came in December 1825, was alarming. 'It would be impossible to give an adequate idea of the panic which prevailed,' the *Morning Chronicle* reported following what seemed unprecedented financial disturbance in the City.[63] Attwood, who later described the panic as 'dreadful',[64] urged the Bank to issue notes, and claimed that it was as a result of this that at a 'lucky moment' a box of pound notes which had been overlooked was discovered in the Bank and issued just at the right time.[65] 'I am not yet a *minister* quite', he told his Tory wife proudly, '*although I may perhaps be called a privy councillor*.'[66]

The aftermath was very different. By October 1826 Peel was questioning Attwood's 'confident Belief that the Prosperity of the Country is quite so dependent on the abundant issue of a Paper Circulation as it appears to you to be', and Attwood was questioning Peel and Liverpool's political capacity to lead the country. 'If I were a demon, I should take a very sincere pleasure in seeing things taking so rapidly the course which I have prophesied for ten years.' 'The positive misery among the lower classes' was becoming 'frightful'.[67] A petition of manufacturers in 1826 commented unhappily on the slackening of demand for Birmingham manufactures and called attention to the dangerous fact that 'in order to meet this state of trade, we have been compelled to dismiss great numbers of our workmen, and have

TABLE 1, *Comparative Prices of Hardware Manufactures in and near Birmingham, 1818-32*

Name of articles	Unit	1818	1824	1828	1830	1832
		s. d.	s. d.	s. d.	s. d.	s. d.
Anvils	Cwt	25.0	20.0	16.0	13.0	12.9
Awls, polished	Gross	2.6	2.0	1.6	1.2	1.0
Bed screws, 6 in.	Gross	18.0	15.0	6.0	5.0	4.9
Bolts for doors, 6 in.	Dozen	6.0	5.0	2.3	1.6	1.6
Braces for carpenters, 12 bits	Set	9.0	6.3	4.2	3.5	2.10
Bits tinned, for bridles	Dozen	5.0	5.0	3.3	2.6	2.3
Buttons for coats	Gross	4.6	6.3	3.0	2.2	–
Buttons small, for waistcoats	Gross	2.0	2.0	1.2	8	7
Currycombs, 6 barred	Dozen	2.9	2.6	1.5	11	11
Candlesticks, 6 in, brass	Pair	2.11	2.0	1.7	1.2	1.2
Commode knobs, brass, 2 in.	Dozen	4.0	3.6	1.6	1.2	1.2
Frying pans	Cwt	25.0	21.0	18.0	16.0	18.0
Hinges, cast butts, 1 in.	Dozen	10	$7\frac{1}{2}$	$3\frac{1}{2}$	$2\frac{1}{4}$	$2\frac{3}{4}$
Shoe hammers	Dozen	6.9	3.9	3.0	2.9	2.9
Latches for doors, bright thumbs	Dozen	2.3	2.2	1.0	9	9
Locks for doors, iron rims, 6 in.	Dozen	38.0	32.0	15.0	13.6	13.6
Locks for guns, single rollers	Each	6.0	5.2	1.10	– 1.6	
Plates for stirrups	Pair	4.6	3.9	1.6	1.1	1.0
Sad irons and other castings	Cwt	22.6	20.0	14.0	11.6	11.0
Shovel and tongs, fire-irons	Pair	1.0	1.0	9	6	5
Tinned table spoons	Gross	17.0	15.0	10.0	7.0	6.9
Trace chains	Cwt	28.0	25.0	19.6	16.6	15.6
Vices for blacksmiths	Cwt	30.0	28.0	22.0	19.6	17.0
Japanned tea-trays, 30 in.	Each	4.6	3.0	2.0	1.5	1.5
Iron wire, no. 6	Bundle	16.0	13.0	9.0	7.0	6.0
Brass wire	lb	1.10	1.4	1.0	9	9

generally placed the remainder of them upon four, three, and even two days' work per week'.[68]

The 'positive misery' increased between 1826 and 1830 while the political situation opened up following the death of Liverpool in February 1827.[69] Attwood welcomed the coming to power of the Duke of Wellington in 1827 – 'we have suffered so much from fools that I should be glad to see men of some sense in the management of affairs'[70] – but his view that they would 'settle the Currency at once'[71] was soon proved erroneous. Wellington believed that the people had enjoyed 'a fictitious wealth' during the wars and that to deal with distress they would need to display 'quiet and sober habits'. Such a diagnosis and suggested treatment were of no interest to Attwood.[72] His correspondence with Peel continued, but there was no meeting of minds in this case either, as the latter refused to admit that there was a 'deficiency of money' and (with an eye on Birmingham) warned that 'the world is glutted ... with British manufactures'.[73]

Peel certainly did not lack local information then or later. Thus, B.W., a Birmingham merchant, wrote to him in October 1830 that 'the articles I sold for 12s., I am now selling for 7s., and a very limited demand at that price ... This is a very fair average reduction of a great variety of goods manufactured in Birmingham and its neighbourhood.'[74] Meanwhile, the cost of materials had fallen between 1825 and 1829 by about 15 per cent, with the rest of the fall reflected in wages and profit reductions. These views of B.W. were shared by the neighbouring Staffordshire ironmasters, who claimed a little later, when the national political situation had further changed, that the price of pig and bar iron had fallen catastrophically during the same period of 'alarming and long-continued depression'. 'We have practised all manner of economy', they went on, 'and have had recourse to every possible improvement in the working of our mines and manufactures. Our workmen's wages have, in many instances, been greatly reduced, and such reductions have been attended with, and affected by, very great suffering and distress – but the royalties, rents, contracts and similar engagements under which we hold our respective works and mines, have scarcely been reduced at all.'[75]

By 1829, Attwood's well-articulated general theory to explain local fluctuations of income and employment, more fully outlined below, already had a growing audience. B.W. shared his sense of apprehension as he continued:

Many goods are now being made at an absolute loss ... Under these appalling circumstances, no-one with feelings of humanity can be surprised that there should be a very general feeling of discontent among the middle and lower classes, and a disposition to attach blame to the Government for the privations they are experiencing ... From my rather intensive inter-course with the small manufacturers and workmen, I am well aware that Societys are now forming for the express purpose of intimidating the Government.

Cobbett would have agreed, for, as he had already told Attwood, whose currency views were so different, the distress was 'like the air itself' and even more vividly that the choice was '*Assignats, Equitable Adjustment or a Blow-up*'.[76] The last of these was, of course, the last thing the ironmasters wanted, and they were soon to press for 'the establishment of some just, adequate and efficient currency which may properly support the trade and commerce of the country, and preserve such a remunerative level of prices as may ensure to the employers of labour the fair and reasonable profit of their capital and industry as well as the means of paying the just and necessary wages to their workmen.'[77]

Attwood also made a strong appeal to disgruntled farmers suffering from the post-war fall in farming prices and profits. He contributed to the *Farmers' Journal* and gave evidence to the Parliamentary Committee on Agricultural Distress in 1821 of which Ricardo was a member. He was in close touch with C. C. Western, a persistent agricultural critic of 1819, and with Tory country gentlemen like Sir Richard Vyvyan.

IV

Middle-class and working-class discontents were moving together in Birmingham in 1828 and 1829. This was one of the most important features of the years which provide the background for the emergence of the Political Union. It was accounted for, however, not only by the fluctuations of the trade-cycle but by the structure of the local economy. Birmingham was a town where, in George Eliot's phrase, 'some slipped a little downward, some got higher footing'. Small masters might fail in their enterprise and become journeymen again. Successful men, employing 'by twenties and thirties instead of by half dozens',[78] might climb high up the social ladder, only to fall again as a result of local fluctuations. 'I could name to you works in the iron trade which literally *lost fortunes* to their old proprietors in the years 1815 and 1818.'[79]

A French visitor, Léon Faucher, comparing Birmingham industry with French agriculture, was to talk of 'social parcellation',[80] while nearly thirty years later Richard Cobden emphasised the healthy political effects of such a social structure. When Bright moved to

Birmingham after being defeated in Manchester in 1857, Cobden
compared Birmingham favourably with the cotton capital. The more
healthy state of Birmingham, he claimed,

> arises from the fact that the industry of the Hardware district is carried on
> by small manufacturers, employing a few men and boys each, sometimes
> with only an apprentice or two, whilst the great capitalists in Manchester
> form an aristocracy, individual members of which wield an influence over
> sometimes two thousand persons. The former state of society is more
> healthy and natural in a moral and political sense. There is a free-er
> intercourse between all classes than in the Lancashire town, where a great
> and impassable gulf separates the workman from his employer ... If Bright
> should be able to lead a party for parliamentary reform, in my opinion,
> Birmingham will be a better home for him than Manchester.'[81]

In a social setting which was perceived to be of this character — and
there were some working men in Birmingham itself who did not
perceive it in that way — it seemed natural that in a time of distress
the discontents of working classes and middle classes should move
together; and B.W. was right to remind Peel that

> the returns of Birm'm and its Neighbourhood bear no proportion to the
> returns of Manchester, Leeds etc. There are thousands of manufacturers in
> Birm'm, who do not return £50 per week (the majority I have no doubt is
> under £20 per week), consequently when profits are so reduced they are
> unable to meet their engagements and support their families.[82]

The small Birmingham manufacturers, tied by heavy fixed charges
for rent and in the iron industry proper for royalties, were facing long-
term commitments which became heavy burdens in periods when
profits were falling. In many sections of the iron industry there was a
high ratio of fixed to circulating capital, and overheads were high. The
natural tendency in lean years was to dismiss labour, and so produce
local unemployment, or to reduce wages. At worst, bankruptcy would
follow. Many disgruntled manufacturers found their way into the
Political Union: indeed, critics of a proposed revival of the Union in
1835 claimed that the old Union had been made up 'in greater part, of
everyone that was in debt, and everyone that was discontented'.[83]

The discontented members of the working classes, who felt the
impact of fluctuations in Birmingham prosperity in the shape of
unemployment, were an unpredictable force. As early as 1804, a local
writer had pointed out the political dangers of idleness, and had
painted a picture of 'the well compacted phalanx of loungers' at street

corners, who discussed the downfall of states, 'the imperfections of thrones and dominions, and the perfectibility of human nature, the bill of rights and the bill of wrongs'.[84] By 1829 there had been sufficient political argument to prepare the way for diverse political ideologies. Yet the lesson, as it was set out by Attwood, remained the same. 'The Jacobins might as well clamour to the winds as to a well-fed and fully employed population.'[85]

The political significance of unemployment had been apparent in 1811; in 1817, when Henry Brougham, active again, presented to Parliament an address and petition from the distressed mechanics of Birmingham, pleading that many of them had been totally unemployed for many months, and that others had been at work for only two or three days a week at reduced wages;[86] and in 1819, when at the meeting at which Wolseley was elected Legislatorial Attorney, large numbers of unemployed workers were present. (*Aris's Gazette* commented on this last occasion that a 'very large proportion of those present would gladly have preferred the pursuit of their usual occupations to an unprofitable attendance of several hours at such a meeting'.)[87] Ten years later, Attwood found unemployed workers sufficiently discontented to make up the mass audiences of his movement, particularly on Mondays, a favourite meeting day, which was generally an idle day with the manufacturers.[88] If this had not been the case, it is hardly likely that crowds, claimed to be as big as 150,000, would have assembled on Newhall Hill. The unemployed elements in Attwood's audiences cannot have been easy to manage, and according to one critic, Attwood himself confessed that they were a 'most unruly flock'.[89]

Unemployment was often deemed to be the cause of the intensity of political agitation in 1830. Thus, a local magnate living in the country near Warwick, wrote to the Home Secretary in 1831 concerning large numbers of unemployed passing to and fro, coming in some cases from regions as far off as Shropshire and Staffordshire:

When they are told that they will be committed as vagabonds, they reply that they wish to be sent to the House, for they cannot be worse off than they are ... When stout and able men demand relief at the doors of houses [he concluded] and declare that they cannot be worse off than they are at present – the consequences are to be dreaded – and if their numbers increase, I do not know how they are to be repelled as they will establish a rallying point for all the idle, dissolute and unemployed men.[90]

The picture of working-class discontent is only complete when a further factor is taken into account – the price of corn. 'A riotous

underground population' only needed famine and privation to goad it
into action. During Birmingham's first crisis in 1811 and 1812, the
price of forge iron was falling, and the price of wheat rising. Wheat
prices began to climb in August 1811 and continued to climb until they
reached their peak just before the harvest of 1812. Similarly, in 1817, a
sharp rise in the price of wheat was accompanied by the first flickers of
post-war Radicalism. From 1818 to 1823, the wheat and iron price
lines followed each other, as shown in Table 2 below. Yet, the sharp
downward movement of iron prices after the peak of 1825 was not
accompanied by a similar downslide in wheat prices. Instead, the price
of wheat rose by six shillings a quarter in 1829 and that of the quartern
loaf by a penny. This rise in wheat prices helped to turn low-paid
workers as well as the unemployed into political malcontents.

TABLE 2, *Iron and wheat prices,* 1810-30

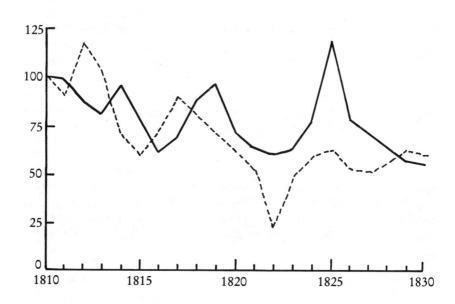

Average prices, 1810 = 100
———— Forge pig iron, £6.6s per ton
- - - - - Wheat, £5.6s per qr

Sources
Iron – S.C. on Manufacturers (1833), Barclay's evidence. Quoted in T. S. Ashton,
op. cit., p. 156.
Wheat – *London Gazette.* Figures quoted by Rostow, *op. cit.,* pp. 123-5.

Looking at the period of falling prices as a whole from 1820 to 1841, the commodities which fell most in price were not those which were consumed by the working classes.[91] Iron prices fell more than the average, and wheat and corn prices less than the average. The relevant data are shown in Table 2.

Carlyle has warned us of tables 'like cobwebs, like the sieve of the Danaides; beautifully reticulated, orderly to look upon, but which will hold no conclusion'. 'Tables', he says, 'are abstractions', and the condition of England question is a most concrete one.[92] It is not difficult, however, to see the very concrete implications of Table 2. In the unincorporated Birmingham of the 1820s and 1830s, the statistical relationship between iron and corn prices leapt to life. Isaac Spooner was merely demonstrating the routine prudence of a magistrate when he wrote to the Home Office in December 1830, from 'this very populous district' of Birmingham, that he was greatly perturbed by the approach of the coming spring. 'The general reports of the harvest lead me to fear a rapid rise in the price of grain about that period. Potatoes are now at a higher price than usual from a deficiency in the crop.' He was speaking from experience when he pointed out that disorders in Birmingham had previously begun 'solely from the high prices of these articles of food'.[93] By the time that he wrote these words, the Birmingham Political Union had already passed through the first period of its history, and an exceptionally cold winter and hectic spring were to lead its agitation forward to a new peak of coordinated effort.

It is now possible to sum up the salient features of Birmingham economic and social life on the eve of the establishment of the Political Union. The foundations of Birmingham politics were laid during the process of increasing economic differentiation. Fluctuations led to inquiry, petitioning and agitation. Lean years, particularly when unemployment coincided with harvest failures, led to short sharp jabs of turbulent pressure. The social cohesion which in times of peace showed itself in the cooperation between master and men, was leading in times of hardship to a joint statement of grievances. Attwood's propaganda filled in any awkward gaps that might have remained. He talked, like Cobbett, of 'Prosperity Restored', the title of a pamphlet of 1817, but he looked more to the potential of the future than the myths of the past. And he believed that it could be realised only through social harmony. 'The interests of masters and men are in fact one ... [By cooperation between them] the Government is made answerable for its own acts at its own doors.'

The social formula which Attwood proclaimed had its roots in Birmingham life. It remains to be shown in more detail first how between 1811 and 1829 his own ideas developed in such a way that he

became the undisputed leader of Birmingham's reform movement, and
secondly how the political events from 1827 to 1830 quickened the
building up of a Political Union.

V

Attwood's approach to local problems was conditioned by his pro-
fession as a country banker.[94] Placed 'in the midst of a great mechanical
population, and deriving in some degree peculiar means of information
from my habits of life',[95] Attwood was naturally interested in the
relationship between the state of local industry and the supply of
money and credit. Economics concerned him as a guide to policy
rather than as a branch of study. 'In no country has political economy
ever been understood', he wrote in 1818, 'the science of wants and
modes and means has been neglected, whilst philosophers have been
penetrating the chemical affinities and measuring the distance of
stars.'[96] On another occasion he called political economy 'a horrid
word and well calculated to alarm and disgust you.'[97]

Great and enlightened minds, 'bursting out from the total darkness
which surrounded them', like the eighteenth-century political economists Hume and Adam Smith, were, he felt, of little practical help in
explaining the economic organisation and fluctuations of Birmingham
industry during the war and in the aftermath of the war. They had
written too early to be aware of the problems of industrialisation.[98]
The 'classical economists' were of no help either: indeed, they were
misleading as guides, for they, too, were ignorant of industry at first
hand. For Ricardo, Malthus and Senior, Attwood never had any
appreciation. While his brother Matthias[99] was attacking them in the
Commons, Thomas attacked them in pamphlets and letters, and while
the government was considering between 1816 and 1819 when to
resume special payments in gold and how to establish a gold standard,
Attwood was laying emphasis on the needs of industry. 'The issue of
money', he believed, '*will* create markets': 'it is upon the abundance or
scarcity of money that the extent of the markets principally depends'.[100]
He was supported in 1817 by another Birmingham voice, that of
Henry James, who urged that 'governments ought to legislate for . . .
the industrious and productive and not . . . for the advantage of those
who have ceased to become so.'[101]

The general relationship between country banking and the policy of
the Bank of England had been discussed on many occasions during the
Napoleonic Wars.[102] It was the post-war deflation, however, which
made the currency question a central issue. Attwood was never a crude
inflationist: indeed, he opposed any 'wild increase of money'.[103] He

tried not only to watch current events but to get back to funda-
mentals, believing that when he had met Ricardo and Huskisson face
to face in 1821 in a House of Commons Committee, he had answered
all their questions most completely 'and evidently to their deep
mortification'.[104] The duel continued after 1832, when Thomas pur-
sued the classical economists relentlessly, if usually ineffectively,
through every debate on the currency inside the House of Commons.

Attwood treated economics as a theory of production and income.
Riches, he maintained, are not to be considered as stores of money, but
as 'stocks of good things' which a nation possesses. They produce
annually a 'whole income or profit of the nation', which provides the
index of its prosperity. Income is absorbed either in consumption or in
'production', and these two lines of economic activity always keep
pace with each other. The unsettling element in the economic system –
and there was an unsettling element which explained not only local
distress in Birmingham but national (including agricultural) distress as
well – was inefficient control of monetary circulation. The amount of
money in circulation depended on the state of the gold stocks of the
Bank of England, when it should have depended on the productive
capacity of the country. The Bank ought to have been compelled, if
need be by a Legislative Commission, to

> regulate the issue of their notes by the *power of labour* in order to prevent
> the possibility of their being induced to withdraw their notes capriciously
> at the one time, and to issue them at another time in greater quantity than
> the full employment of the labourers may require. In the first of these
> contingencies, the nation would be exhausted and destroyed, in the second
> annuitants would be injured, and the depreciation of money would be
> pushed on far more than is necessary for the social welfare.[105]

It is clear from this passage that Attwood was not a crude inflationist. He did not believe that an increase in the supply of money was of
any gain once the conditions of full employment had been reached.
Dismissed by Cobbett as a 'little shilling man',[106] he objected strongly
to 'a wild increase of money',[107] although he did not devote much of his
practical analysis to such a contingency. He could be probing, too, as
in his account of the relationship between restriction of money supply
and the dumping of manufacturers' stocks.[108]

There has been a reaction amongst twentieth-century economists
against the glib dismissal of Attwood as a 'currency monomaniac',[109]
and historians of economic thought have tried to place him in relation
to his contemporaries. The Ricardians, it has been pointed out, tended
to treat the *production* function as fixed, and went on to deduce the

effects on income *distribution* of population changes or of taxation from above.[110] Their main preoccupation was with the partition of the annual increment of wealth among the different classes, and not with production as such.[111] Attwood, by contrast, treated the production function as a controllable variable. Manufacturers could raise it and government could check it. 'The Government have limited our means of producing and consuming: for by limiting the amount of money they have limited our means of exchanging commodities, and this gives the limit to consumption, and the limit to consumption gives the limit to production.'[112] Every 'potential transaction' should be encouraged.[113]

Living up to his theories, Attwood advocated the building of public works at the end of the Napoleonic Wars, to employ not only demobilised soldiers but also the unemployed in general. 'Public depôts of industry' should be set up, where labourers could find employment, and they should be sharply differentiated from 'depôts of charity', houses for the sick, the infirm and the helpless. 'By acting upon this system, we shall obtain a separation between employment and charity.' 'Employment', he went on, 'is a right which a good citizen may claim of his country without any kind of degradation or obligation.' By a system of controlled circulation

> the country might always be preserved in a high degree of prosperity. The prices of bullion would be left to find their own level and would accommodate themselves, like all the other things, to the wants and demands of men ... The fluctuations of prices to which gold, like other things is naturally subject, would act upon insensible masses of metal instead of being forced to act upon life and flesh and blood.[114]

Full employment for the labourer was the corollary of productive prosperity.

> This is the only healthy state of society. The products of labour gradually rise with the increase of demand and consumption ... the demand for labour becomes greater than the supply and the wages of labour rise in the same degree ... the demand for labour is thus always greater than the supply in a healthy state of society. Then the labourer is independent and feels his independence ... he becomes a good citizen and a good subject.[115]

Within this context, Peel's return to gold in 1819 was a policy decision which Attwood was bound to regard as disastrous; and in his economic writings after 1819 he returned to it repeatedly and often highly rhetorically. The Act, he claimed in 1830, richly merited 'the eternal curses of his country', for by means of it, Peel had brought about in England 'more misery, more poverty, more discord, more of everything that was calamitous to the nation, except death, than Attila caused in the Roman Empire'.[116] Almost thirty years after it was passed, he was still complaining of it. 'The branch banks and the joint stock banks proved totally unequal to the duty of supporting the social system under the pressure of the fatal law of 1819.'[117] There had been, indeed, thirty years of 'gross misrepresentation', of 'concealing the truth from the public'.

As many as seventy pamphlets had appeared in 1819, most of them condemning Peel's 'Confiscation Act'.[118] Attwood was not alone in his objections, therefore, but he was exceptionally persistent in reiterating them. One of the reasons why he was increasingly drawn into politics was not only the failure of ministers and politicians in Parliament to listen to him, but the way in which they defended the Act as a symbol of political stability and economic strength. It was Brougham, indeed, through whom he had worked in 1811, who argued that to change the Act of 1819 would be 'to tamper with the public faith'.[119] For Attwood such a defence was intolerable. It was ministers and politicians who had tampered with public faith and forced supporters of the social fabric to seek redress through popular action. If economists have re-examined Attwood's arguments, historians have done little so far to clear away the welter of misconceptions which normally precede any account of his work as a politician.[120]

There was always an element of potential threat in Attwood's message. Economic unrest and unemployment, following bankruptcy, which would shake the middle classes and which was a denial of man's right to work would, in his view, generate political dissension and even anarchy.

Let the tempest of English passions sleep, and English liberties are secure. They will never fall as long as industry is rewarded, as long as food and clothing can be produced without occasioning the ruin of producers. But if the circulating medium is suffered to become insufficient for its purpose, if the lower classes are suffered to remain hungry and unemployed and when they call upon their country for bread their country is to give them a stone, then there is no answer to the extremes to which want and misery and despair may goad alienated and lacerated people.[121]

His brother Matthias drew consistently Tory deductions from this analysis. Indeed, Cobbett in 1818 was accusing him of encouraging the Chancellor of the Exchequer to 'cause bales of paper-money to be poured out as a *remedy* against the workings of the evil-minded and

designing men who were urging the people on for parliamentary
reform'.[122] After the Act of 1819 Cobbett also accused him – and
country bankers in general – of trying to sabotage it;[123] and at the time
of the 'dreadful panic' of 1825, when the Attwoods were pressing the
Bank to issue small notes, was instructing that the public should
press the run on gold.[124]

Although neither Cobbett nor Thomas Attwood changed his views
on the currency between 1825 and 1829, these were years when 'the
strange turn' which Attwood had mentioned to his Tory wife took
place, so that by 1829 the two men eventually found themselves
working together politically.[125] They were still at political loggerheads
in 1828, when Attwood complained of Cobbett's 'bitter hatred of
existing institutions' which rendered him 'a dangerous guide to those
who wish to preserve them'. Attwood's own position on the suffrage,
however, had changed before 1829. As early as 1822 he had recognised
in public that Radical reform might be necessary for the national
welfare;[126] and in 1825 he had supported the foundation of the
Birmingham Mechanics Institute, strongly criticised by the *Birmingham Journal*, and had gone on to serve on the same committee as
Edmonds.[127]In 1827 he approved of the transfer of the East Retford
seat to Birmingham,[128] and he was a member of the Committee of
thirty-one appointed after the failure of the Bill to collect information
and to discuss the registration of future Birmingham electors.[129]

It was during this period that he realised that he could do little to
change things through correspondence first with Liverpool and then
with Wellington. Having warned Liverpool that 'unless some great
public measure is adopted for the purpose of giving temporary
employment to the mechanical and agricultural population, the
system of riot and plunder will inevitably continue and extend', he was
not content to accept Liverpool's reply that he hoped 'that the loyalty
of those of better sense will be sufficient to check and counteract the
designs of such as would inflame rather than soothe the minds of the
suffering poor at such a moment'.[130] He was even less content with the
approach of Wellington, great though his hopes were when the Duke
came into power.[131]

Attwood's last attempt to rely upon persuasion rather than on
agitation came in May 1829, when he took the initiative in calling
together a Birmingham meeting on 8 May to discuss the distressed
state of the country. The High Bailiff took the Chair, and Attwood
made a three-hour speech, in which he summed up the whole of his
currency doctrines, bringing out their local background and their
political implications.[132] He claimed that he was taking the platform
only out of 'an overwhelming sense of public duty to do all in my
power to relieve the present distress and to ward off that far greater

distress which I much fear is approaching', and went on to trace in some detail the story of seven fluctuations in trade within fourteen years. His voice was persuasive, and he won the approval of the meeting for a series of resolutions, most of which had been turned down by the Birmingham Chamber of Commerce ten years before. The most important of them stated that

> the want of employment, the deficiency of wages, and the present and almost unexampled distress of the country are mainly to be attributed to the attempts which the Government is making to restore the ancient and obsolete currency of the country without having previously effected a corresponding reduction in the taxes and moneyed obligations of the country.[133]

In his speech, Attwood gave priority to financial reform. He spoke feelingly on the abolition of small notes and recalled the earlier vacillations of Parliament on the subject,[134] going on to claim that all the difficulties of the times originated 'in the mortal subject' of currency mismanagement. At the same time, he held out a new hope for parliamentary reform. He had hitherto attacked 'Jacobins' and had once written that poor wretches who clamoured for 'Burdett and liberty' were more stupid than Birmingham mobs or men in love.[135] Now he explained that after restoring prosperity, 'if my fellow townsmen desire it, I am ready to co-operate with them heart and hand in every just, legal and constitutional exertion to obtain a radical reform in their Commons House of Parliament.'

The meeting of 8 May passed thirty-one resolutions in all, and drew up a petition with 8000 signatures, which was presented to the Lords by Carnarvon on 26 May, and to the Commons by Brougham – who figured yet again in the Birmingham story – on 4 June. Neither Carnarvon nor Brougham committed himself to Attwood's currency thesis, however, and Brougham went out of his way to reiterate what he had said in 1819 – that he wanted no more 'tampering with the currency'. Matthias was there to support the Birmingham proposals, but they were contemptuously rejected by the Wellington government.

The failure of Wellington to accept the petition or any of the arguments on which it rested led Attwood into more active politics. In August he was planning a Birmingham Reform Association, and dining with men who were later on to play a big part in the Political Union.[136] On 14 December 1829, 'when hundreds of the inhabitants were shivering by their cold firesides'[137] – for two months every canal leading in and out of Birmingham had been frozen – Attwood and fifteen other men met together and founded 'the Political Union for the Protection of Public Rights'. They included Joshua Scholefield, a merchant banker, fifty-six years old, who was to represent Birmingham along with Attwood, after the Reform Bill of 1832; the lamp manufacturer, T. C. Salt; the pearl button manufacturer, Benjamin Hadley; the silversmith, Charles James, who had already written – and was to write far more – on the currency question;[138] and G. F. Muntz, who had sent off a letter to Wellington on the currency question only that day.[139]

On the following Monday, when employment in Birmingham was said to be at a standstill, the rules of the new Union were signed and accepted by twenty-eight people, and it was resolved that they should be submitted for the approbation of the people. The big meeting to secure this approbation was held on 25 January 1830 at Beardsworth's Repository, where 10,000 people or more were present. The Whig High Bailiff had refused to convene the meeting,[140] but Beardsworth had cooperated in allowing the organisers to light five large coke fires inside the Repository to keep the crowd warm. Six hours of speech-making may have had the same effect, as currency reform and parliamentary reform were now mixed together:

The general distress which now afflicts the country, and which has been so severely felt at several periods during the last fifteen years, is entirely to be ascribed to the gross mismanagement of public affairs. Such a mismanagement can only be effectually and permanently remedied by an effectual reform in the Commons' House of Parliament. For the legal accomplishment of this great object, and for the further redress of public wrongs and grievances, it is expedient to form a GENERAL POLITICAL UNION between the Lower and the Middle Classes of the People.[141]

In order to complete the picture of the events of 1829, it is necessary to turn, however briefly, to the national political scene – to the crisis in the Tory Party, brought about by Catholic Emancipation. The split in the ranks of the Tories produced a temporary alignment between Brunswickers and Reformers, which played an important part in the tangled politics of Birmingham in the months before the setting-up of the Political Union, and in the first phases of its activity.

VI

Catholic Emancipation was proposed in the Royal Speech on 5 February 1829. On 5 March, Peel moved that the House of Commons should go into committee on the laws imposing disabilities on the Catholics. A Bill was introduced on 10 March, and on 13 April it received the Royal Assent. There were some Tories who were so disturbed by the new line in Wellington's policy, that they were prepared to recommend parliamentary reform in order to get the measure repealed. Their leading representative was the Marquis of Blandford.

> The Marquis had been a violent opponent of the Catholic Bill. He had seen that Bill carried in defiance of public opinion by a Parliament which changed its sentiments at the nod of the Minister, and from that moment he had become a fiery and reckless reformer, frequently forcing the question against the wishes and advice of its longer tried and more experienced patrons, and never distinguished by moderation in his schemes.[142]

On 2 June, he first raised the question of parliamentary reform in the House of Commons.[143] 'The country expects, I may say demands, some statutory provision for the safety of its interests; the interests of its agriculture; its trade; its manufactures; its finance.' Blandford linked Roman Catholic 'aggrandisement' with national distress as the bases of his practical suggestions, and quoted Burke to justify his view that 'representation is the sovereign remedy for every disorder and the infallible security against popular discontent'.

From this time onwards, Blandford's stand in Parliament was very closely linked with Attwood's increasing political activities in Birmingham. Although the two men did not meet in 1829, they had a mutual friend, described as Scott.[144] Furthermore, Attwood's business partner, Spooner, was married to the sister of Sir Charles Wetherell, a vigorous opponent both of Catholic Emancipation and of parliamentary reform. The most interesting link of all was provided by Cobbett, who sent a copy of Attwood's speech of 8 May to Blandford, 'telling him that that was the pivot on which all must turn'.[145] The advice was taken. On 29 January 1830, Blandford became an honorary member of the newly-founded Birmingham Political Union.[146] While the Political Union was carrying resolutions supporting Blandford's schemes on 25 January 1830,[147] and Attwood was still professing himself a Tory,[148] Blandford was learning and expounding the Attwood currency thesis:

> Recourse has been had either from ignorance or from design to the most monstrous schemes in tampering with the currency or circulating medium of the country; at one time, by greatly diminishing the value of the same, and at another time by greatly augmenting such value, and at each and every of such changes which have been but too often repeated, one class of the community after another has been plunged into poverty, misery and

ruin, while the sufferers, without any fault or folly of their own, have been hardly able to perceive from what hand these calamities have come upon them.[149]

Blandford's alliance with Attwood – which was soon over[150] – should not be regarded as an individual aberration. The 'inflationists' had at least as wide an audience in 1829 as they had in 1819, and many Tories formed part of it. 'Is it not, think you, most strange and ominous', asked one Whig speaker in Birmingham in January 1830, 'that the high Tory party, which for the last sixty years, has so stiffly and invariably opposed reform of Parliament ... should have recently entered throughout the whole kingdom into a league, offensive and defensive, with the liberal currency men?'[151] Others besides Tories were affected. Sir Francis Burdett[152] and Sir James Graham[153] had been and were prominent advocates of currency reform, and Graham was able to say at a Cumberland meeting in February 1830 that Wellington must

> revise those measures relative to the currency which have produced greater changes in property than the Revolution of 1688 or even the great civil wars. The continuance of the Duke's Government rests upon public opinion ... he must be the Minister of the People, or cease to be a Minister at all. His continuance in office depends upon the public voice.[154]

It is fascinating that Cobbett was the most important link between Blandford and Attwood in 1829, but the fact underlines the confusions of politics in that year. When the Birmingham Political Union was set up in December of that year, it could draw on both Radical and Tory support. The odd attitude of Cobbett, who had once dismissed Attwood as 'Little Lord Shilling', is interesting throughout, and of great importance. On 24 June 1829 he had written to Attwood, thanking him and his 'townsmen' for the petition and the speech.[155] On 19 December he announced his intention of visiting Birmingham 'because that town has been distinguished above others by the Petition sent from it during the last session of parliament'.[156] On 6 February 1830, he reprinted in the *Weekly Political Register* the rules and regulations of the new Union, and gave it a wide and favourable publicity.

> This is a very important matter. We see at last the middle classes uniting with the working classes. Everywhere where I have been I have endeavoured to show the necessity of such union. The borough-mongerers have long contrived to divide these two classes for purposes much too obvious to mention. At last the middle class begins to perceive that it must

be totally sacrificed unless it makes a stand, and a stand it cannot make without the support of the lower classes.[157]

Political alignments in 1829-30 were far from simple,[158] and it is essential to go back again from the national to the local problem to see most clearly the temporary importance of the talk of a Radical-Tory alliance.[159] Birmingham Tories were split on Catholic Emancipation. In October 1828, the *Birmingham Argus* was praising the penetrating and patriotic spirit of Wellington. By January 1829, however, it was attributing business depression to the 'errors of government', and by February 1829, it was warning its readers that commercial distress and religious irritation at the government's measures would produce a reaction in Birmingham. 'Thanks to our political constitution, sir', it addressed Peel, 'the power which has crushed the nation cannot stifle its voice. It has a voice, sir, aye and a *speaking trumpet* also.' When the Catholic Emancipation Act was carried, the paper came out with a black border, and an obituary lamenting the death of 'MR CON-STITUTION ... at the House of the Incurables'.

It is no wonder, therefore, that while it attacked 'the modern canting commodity called Liberalism', the *Argus* looked forward to Attwood's meeting of 8 May 'with feelings of unequalled intenseness', that it printed regular panegyrics on Attwood, and that it supported the founding of the Political Union. 'We are confident, if the Radicals go hand in hand with the Tories, in a few months this once mighty, happy and prosperous nation will be relieved of the present Ministry, or their present Measures.' It pledged itself to substantial reform, and while attacking reformers of the Cobbett-Hunt type, it claimed as late as February 1830 that 'the Tories are aware that the surest and best method to relieve the country is to cleanse the "Augean stable" and send those members howling to those constituents who sold them and their 1688 Constitution.'

> If the Radicals join with the Brunswickers ... and fight honestly together, we shall soon have cast in oblivion the free traders, the prowling, grasping monopolizers of wealth, the visionary schemers, the jesters of public and private calamities etc.[160]

It is easy to exaggerate the political importance of the *Birmingham Argus*, but it is true, nonetheless, that it provided an active channel of opinion, which must have interested many of the local politicians, and that it reflected influences which were at work in the first few months of the Union's life. The meeting on 25 January, at which the

Political Union was launched, indulged in much anti-Whig talk, and it is not surprising that two able lawyers, Joseph Parkes, who had been joint Secretary of the Representation Committee to watch the interests of the town in the East Retford case,[161] and William Redfern, who openly opposed Attwood on the currency,[162] were strong but lonely dissentients. Parkes began by regretting that he did not see present at the meeting 'many personal friends, and the more opulent and influential public characters of the town, who usually take part in its public proceedings', and went on to oppose the formation of a Union both on tactical and on ideological grounds. 'It did not require the gift of prophecy to foretell that the projected Political Union would not survive the duration of the present Parliament.' Redfern was more violent and received a very bad hearing, particularly when he said that he suspected the sincerity and zeal of 'the gentlemen who now bring forward these measures of reform'. He claimed that Attwood, who had introduced the principal measure, had favoured them with a small text of Reform but had given them 'a ponderous volume of currency'.[163]

Redfern and Parkes did at least attend the meeting, but most of the Whigs stayed away, and they stayed out of the Union until December 1830.[164] While many of them must have felt that its chief object was 'the extension of the well-known views and opinions of the gentleman whose name appears at the head of the requisition',[165] they could not have been happy either with the passage in the first report of the (very authoritarian) Council of the new Union, proclaiming that 'the King's throne presents a *bulwark*, under which his faithful people may find a shelter from the oppressor's wrong' and suggesting that government and Parliament were merely the King's advisers.[166]

What brought the Whigs into line with the agitation was the fall of the Wellington government in November 1830 and the accession of Grey. 'Within our political recollection', wrote the *Argus*, 'we cannot call to mind a more powerful sensation than was produced in this town on the arrival of the official announcement of the resignation of the Wellington Ministry.' The *Argus* hoped that the new ministry would be 'neither purely Tory or purely Whig'. 'There must be retrenchment and reform – *not* annual parliaments, universal suffrage and vote by ballot.'[167]

There was, of course, to be ample reform – and resistance to it – and continuing argument as to whether the reform went far enough. The struggles for the Reform Bill produced new alignments in Birmingham, during which some of the earlier proceedings were conveniently forgotten.[168] Yet Attwood could refer in public to the critical importance of the early meetings when 'the national mind was asleep'.[169] In private, he was already moving in new and wider political circles on visits to London. As early as June 1830, for example, before the Whigs returned to power, he was dining with Lord Radnor and Burdett on one night, with Hume and O'Connell on another, and with Burdett, Lord John Russell and Hobhouse on a third. He found it more difficult then to meet 'old friends' like C. C. Western. One new person whom he did meet was Lord Dillon, 'who professes great intimacy with Lord Grey and said he wanted to learn from me how to extricate the country in the event of Lord Grey coming into power'.[170]

By November 1830, the Political Union had collected a very varied crowd of supporters, but they were still firmly held together by Attwood's dominating leadership. The language that he spoke was not the language of abstract rights and of political liberties. It had nothing in common with the Whig dogma. It stressed local interests and practical objectives, and capitalised on local hardship and distress. 'The way to radicalize a town', wrote one of the curious local periodicals, 'is to squeeze the people well without regard to age or sex, means or circumstance.'[171] The first public meeting of the Union emphasised the squeezing process. Shaw, a local manufacturer, said that he had had seventy-nine persons applying to him for employment in fifteen hours, while Scholefield stated flatly that 'as I defy any man to deny that the deepest distress imaginable pervades the town, there will be less occasion for argument to support the resolution.'[172] In March 1832, the official organ of the Union stressed that it would have failed had it been launched ten years before. 'There was not then sufficient material of excitement.'[173]

Attwood, after tracing the origins of distress and offering a familiar analysis of its causes, declared that the experience of the last fifteen years 'must certainly have convinced the most incredulous that the rights and interests of the middle and lower classes of the people are not efficiently represented in the Commons House of Parliament'. 'The *Citizens and Burgesses* of the House of Commons should be real *Citizens and Burgesses*, men engaged in trade, and actively concerned in it; and having their fortunes and their prospects in life committed to it.' In order to strive for this great purpose, a Political Union, meeting regularly, should be set up. Through its operations,

the PUBLIC OPINION, instead of being scattered and diffused throughout the country, and concealed within the breasts of individuals, will be collected and concentrated in influential *masses* ... and directed into wholesome and legal operations upon the legislature of the country.[174]

While the *Argus* was drawn to belief in parliamentary reform – and the

Political Union – through opposition to Catholic Emancipation, the organisation of the Union itself was strongly influenced by Daniel O'Connell's Catholic Association which was to set up to secure emancipation.[175] Very soon, indeed, Attwood was to work closely with O'Connell outside and later inside Parliament. Moreover, Birmingham Roman Catholics, including the local priest, Father T. M. McDonnell, were to play an active part in the Union.[176] It was O'Connell who presented the Petition for the Union to Parliament in August 1831.

The Birmingham Political Union thus became a flexible instrument, changing its tactics to meet new twists in the general political situation, but it never forsook what Attwood regarded as its most important objective – financial reform in the interests of both lower and middle classes. Because Attwood was so fixed in his emphasis on currency reform, he could vary his political tactics the more easily. Blandford's Bill was taken up, and dropped[177] in 1830, and in 1832 itself, although he had lost some working-class support,[178] as late as May, when the Whig Bill was in danger for the last time he was able to welcome an infusion of middle-class support hitherto denied him. 'We the undersigned inhabitants of the town who have hitherto refrained from joining the Birmingham Political Union', a number of influential local residents declared, 'deem it our duty to our country at this awful crisis to come forward and join that body, for the purpose of promoting the further union, order and determination of all classes in support of the common cause of parliamentary reform.'[179]

Yet a month later, Attwood was still able to say in June 1832, after the Reform Bill had been passed, that in 1830 Blandford's Bill would have satisfied him 'if it had been granted in honesty and good faith'; and in the same speech, still stressing currency reform, he pointed to the Chartist future: If the Whigs were as inactive as the Tories, they would suffer the same fate, and 'if he should ever be compelled to continue the agitation, nothing less than universal suffrage would satisfy him.'[180] 'Our work is half done,' the Council of the Union addressed their fellow countrymen earlier in the same month. 'We must move nearer the prosperity of the industrious classes.'[181] The same message was repeated the following month by Attwood personally. 'We have obtained a moderate share of reform', he told another meeting in the following month, 'and it is now our duty to obtain a large share of prosperity.'[182]

Within a year of the passing of the Reform Bill, despite a greater measure of prosperity than in the previous few years, the Political Union was passing no-confidence votes in the Grey government,[183] and the fight went on, this time straining more seriously than before those good relations between the classes, which had characterised the agitation of 1829 to 1832. As relations became more and more strained, counter-ideologies were stated and developed in Birmingham to challenge that of Attwood,[184] and the simple remedy for distress, first offered in 1816, was no longer accepted as a nostrum. The currency thesis continued to be argued and was taken sufficiently seriously by *The Times* in 1848 to merit a leader criticising Birmingham ideas. Yet whereas the Reform Bill of 1832, so strongly backed in Birmingham, laid the foundations for subsequent nineteenth-century political history, it was another Peel Act – the Bank Charter Act of 1844, strongly attacked in Birmingham – which formed the foundations of nineteenth- and twentieth-century national monetary orthodoxy.[185]

NOTES

1 *Report of the Proceedings of the Great Public Meeting of the Inhabitants of Birmingham and its Neighbourhood*, 20 May 1833. This and other Reports of town and Union meetings are to be found in the Birmingham Collection in the City of Birmingham Library.

2 C. M. Wakefield, *Life of Thomas Attwood* (1885), p. 277.

3 Mrs H. Grote, *Personal Life of George Grote* (1873), p. 78.

4 Wakefield, *op. cit.*, p. 215.

5 Graham Wallas, *The Life of Francis Place* (1918), p. 251.

6 Benjamin Disraeli, *Runnymede Letter*, 21 January 1836.

7 *Political Register*, 8 September 1832.

8 O'Brien set out his views in the *National Reformer*, 7 January 1837.

9 F. F. Rosenblatt, *The Social and Economic Aspects of the Chartist Movement* (1916), p. 121.

10 J. S. Mill, *The Currency Jungle* (January 1833), reprinted in *Dissertations and Discussions* (1859), vol. I. See also his *Principles of Political Economy* (1857), vol. II, p. 89.

11 Wakefield, *op. cit.*, p. 57.

12 e.g. Place's National Political Union. See Wallas, *op. cit.*, p. 279.

13 *Report of the Proceedings of the Town's Meeting in Support of Parliamentary Reform*, 13 December 1830.

14 The most important were *The Remedy: or Thoughts on the Present Distresses* (1816); *Prosperity Restored: Reflections on the Cause of the Public Distresses* (1817); *Letters to Nicholas Vansittart on the Creation of Money* (1817); *Observations on Currency, Population and Pauperism in Two Letters to Arthur Young* (1818); *Letters to Lord Liverpool* (1819); (with Sir J. Sinclair) *The Late Prosperity and the Present Adversity of the Country Explained* (1826); *The Scotch Banker* (1828). See also F. W.

Fetter, *Selected Economic Writings of Thomas Attwood* (1964) with a useful introduction.

15 Wakefield, *op. cit.*, p. 99.

16 See above, pp. 107-8.

17 L. W. Clarke, *The History of Birmingham* (written 1870, MS. Birmingham Collection: City of Birmingham Library), p. 1. See also above, Chapter 5.

18 W. H. B. Court, *The Rise of the Midland Industries* (1938), p. 147; S. Timmins, *Birmingham and the Midland Hardware District* (1866), p. 216.

19 Witt Bowden, *Industrial Society in England towards the End of the Eighteenth Century* (1925), p. 163.

20 For the relationship between Birmingham and the West Midlands before 1812, see J. Money, *Experience and Identity: Birmingham and the West Midlands, 1760-1800* (1977).

21 E. Porritt, *The Unreformed House of Commons* (1903), vol. I, p. 263.

22 See J. M. Norris, 'Samuel Garbett and the Early Development of Industrial Lobbying in Great Britain', in *Economic History Review*, vol. X (1957-8).

23 *Aris's Gazette*, 7 October 1812. It is fair to say that by 1813 Mordaunt had regained local confidence to a considerable extent, when he was active in opposing a Bill to regulate the business of manufacturers of firearms.

24 *The Searcher*, 4 March 1817.

25 *The Saturday's Register*, 22 January 1820; *The Birmingham Inspector*, 4 January 1817.

26 *The Birmingham Independent*, 3 November 1827, described them as the most injurious part of the oppression by the manufacturing interest. Attwood himself wrote later that he opposed the 'unjust' Corn Laws, but he interpreted them specially as protection against 'the contemplated effects of the Money Laws of 1819'.

27 ibid. There is similar stress on foreign competition in the Tory-Radical *Monthly Argus*, August 1829. 'The Swedish iron merchant is ever competitive in all and every part of the continent. The German wine merchants glut our home and foreign markets .... In France ... they are our rivals in price and quality.'

28 This position was shared by the Tory agricultural interest and continued to win some support. See the *Birmingham Journal*, 9 April 1831, and 23 May 1829, when local 'lords of the soil' were invited to 'receive lessons on the currency question'. Few appeared. The currency thesis was always strongly criticised by Cobbett, who also appealed to the farmers. See below, p. 149.

29 *The Searcher*, 4 March 1817.

30 *Prosperity Restored* (1817), p. 78. For his later attitude to Burdett, see below, p. 165.

31 ibid., p. 120.

32 Liverpool mentioned 'Mr Bolton and Mr Garbett' [*sic*]; 'though neither of them were averse to Parliamentary Reform, they were

decidedly averse to Birmingham sending members to Parliament':
C. D. Yonge, *The Life of Lord Liverpool* (1868), vol. III, pp. 137-8.

33 See Wakefield, *op. cit.*, p. 87. Birmingham electors accounted, as they
had done for decades, for a sixth of the electorate (*The Poll of the
Freeholders of Warwickshire* (1820)). They were active, too, at Warwickshire county meetings: see, for example, *Report of the Warwickshire
County Meeting*, 18 June 1817.

34 *Aris's Birmingham Gazette*, 18 June 1827.

35 *Birmingham Journal*, 31 October 1829. Cp. Liverpool's arguments (*op.
cit.*). Representation of the population of the new manufacturing towns
would be subject 'to a perpetual factious canvas which would divert,
more or less, the people from their industrious habits, and keep alive a
permanent spirit of turbulence and disaffection amongst them'. Mrs
Arbuthnot thought that nothing would exceed the folly of granting
Members to 'these populous towns'. It would cause 'riots' and 'loss of
lives' (F. Bamford and the Duke of Wellington (eds.), *The Journal of
Mrs Arbuthnot*, vol. II (1951), p. 173.) Nonetheless, Tennyson's Bill was
supported by Lawley and Dugdale, the Members for Warwickshire, and
E. J. Littleton, Member for Staffordshire.

36 *Hansard*, vol. IX, col. 1538.

37 See above, pp. 120-2.

38 *The Birmingham Argus and Public Censor*, March 1829. Cp. ibid.,
October 1828: 'With a population of ONE HUNDRED AND FORTY
THOUSAND INHABITANTS: with a manufacture equal in importance
and extent to that of any other town in the Kingdom; and con-
tributing immensely to the support of the government under the
present system of taxation, we ask, is it fair, is it equitable, is it
constitutional to deprive *such a town* of the benefit of representation
in the popular legislative assembly of the country?'

39 *Reports of the Principal Staffordshire Reform Meetings*, 14 May 1832.

40 *Weekly Political Register*, 13 June 1829.

41 For the relationship between Attwood's views and other local currency
theories, see S. G. Checkland, 'The Birmingham Economists, 1815-
1850', in the *Economic History Review*, new series, vol. I (1948).

42 John Freeth, 'Birmingham's Tranquillity' (1776), reprinted in *The
Political Songster* (1783).

43 See Lord Beveridge, 'The Trade Cycle in Britain before 1850', in
Oxford Economic Papers (1940), and W. W. Rostow, *British Economy
of the Nineteenth Century* (1948), especially Chapter II.

44 Quoted in T. S. Ashton, *Iron and Steel in the Industrial Revolution*
(1924), p. 135.

45 Langford, *op. cit.*, vol. II, pp. 240-1.

46 *The Monthly Magazine*, January 1811, 'Monthly Commercial Report'.

47 *Parliamentary Papers, Reports of Committees* (1812), vol. III, p. 27.

48 *Aris's Gazette*, 22 June 1812. See also F. Hill, *Autobiography of Fifty
Years in Times of Reform* (1878), p. 37.

49 *Birmingham Advertiser*, 9 April 1812. See further, *Orders in Council:
a Report of the Proceedings of the Meeting held at the Royal Hotel,*

Birmingham, 31 March 1812. For the vote of the Birmingham Chamber of Commerce, see E. L. Wrighton, *Annals of the Birmingham Chamber of Commerce* (1913).

50 The American market had great importance for Birmingham. See Court, *op. cit.* For the effects of these measures see also below, pp. 217, and for the general background, F. Crouzet, 'L'Économie Britannique et le Blocus Continental' (1958); J. L. Anderson, 'Aspects of the Effect on the British Economy of the Wars against France, 1793-1815', in the *Australian Economic History Review*, vol. XII (1972); and G. Hueckel, 'War and the British Economy, 1793-1815', in *Explorations in Economic History* (1973).

51 *Aris's Gazette*, 22 June 1812; *Midlands Chronicle*, 9 October 1813. The Official *Minutes of Evidence ... on Petitions ... against the Orders in Council* show that Attwood did not escape close and difficult questioning. Some of his questioners felt that he exaggerated the extent of distress in Birmingham: others felt that Birmingham had priced itself out of the international market before 1811.

52 In 1811 about 700 artisans had attended a meeting at the Shakespeare Tavern. See *Report of the Proceedings of the Artisans of Birmingham*.

53 See above, p. 114.

54 For a brief sketch of Edmonds, see E. Edwards, *Personal Recollections of Birmingham and Birmingham Men* (1877), pp. 140-55, and *Birmingham Journal*, 1 July 1868. Edmonds had his own periodical in 1819 – *Edmonds' Weekly Recorder and Saturday Advertiser.* In it he attacked local abuses, like the Court of Requests, as well as the Tory government. See above p. 126. The 1819 agitation culminated in July 1819 with a great meeting on Newhall Hill, at which Major Cartwright was present and at which Sir Charles Wolseley was chosen as 'Legistatorial Attorney and Representative of the City'. For his part in the radical agitation, Edmonds was eventually sentenced to twelve months' imprisonment in Warwick Gaol.

55 See C. W. New, *Life of Henry Brougham*, vol. I (1961), especially Chapter VI. Attwood was also associated with the 1812 and 1813 campaign against the renewal of the East India Company's Charter. 'If the trade to the East were thrown open', he had told a Birmingham meeting in January 1813, 'we should in ten years' time export the present amount, in Birmingham goods alone.'

56 S. Tooke, *A History of Prices and of the State of Circulation from 1793 to 1837* (1838), vol. I, p. 104.

57 *Quarterly Review*, January 1817. See further *Observations on the Manufacture of Firearms for Military Purposes; on the number supplied FROM Birmingham to the British Government during the Late War; ... and upon the Obstacles to Free Export of Arms* (1818).

58 C. Babbage, *On the Economy of Machinery and Manufacture* (1832). The 1832 figures were supplied not by Babbage but by M. P. Haynes, *A Letter to Earl Grey on the Distress which now exists in Birmingham* (July 1832). For Haynes, see above, p. 130. Babbage was at great pains to emphasise the trustworthiness of his sources: 'I have taken some pains

to assure myself of the accuracy of the above table' (p. 117). Haynes declared that Babbage 'in his excellent work, has *proved* that the first three columns are strictly correct'.

59 Footnote to the fourth edition of William Hutton, *History of Birmingham*, first published in 1782.

60 Edmonds had organised a Hampden Club in 1816 and 1817, stressing that it was necessary 'to direct the people's efforts into a legal and a constitutional path' (HO/40/4D; 42/154), *Birmingham Inspector*, 12 April 1817. At an 1819 meeting to protest against Peterloo, there were said to be many armed men.

61 See A. F. Burns and W. C. Mitchell, *Measuring Business Cycles* (1946), pp. 66-71. Offsetting inventory movements led to timing problems, e.g. the effects of the situation outlined on p. 144 above, when in 1811 'every manufacturer was overburdened with stock'.

62 *Committee on Manufacturers* (1833), Q. 4146.

63 *Morning Chronicle*, 15 December 1825.

64 The adjective was used by the *Birmingham Journal* in 1825 itself (17 December 1825).

65 *Birmingham Journal*, 18 March 1856: Wakefield, *op. cit.*, pp. 100-2.

66 Attwood to Mrs Attwood, 17 December 1825 in ibid., p. 99. Cp. Attwood to Mrs Attwood, 18 December 1828 (ibid., p. 115). 'I rather think Mr Peel remembers my services to him during the *late panic*.'. Fetter, *op. cit.*, pp. 114-15 discusses all the available evidence.

67 Peel to Attwood, October 1826 (ibid., p. 104). Liverpool in a letter to Attwood, 2 December 1826 (ibid., p. 106) explained that he was 'truly sensible of the restless and disaffected Spirit which is produced by a period of Distress, and which unfortunately exists in many Places at the present moment'. For Peel, see also C. S. Parker, *Sir Robert Peel*, vol. I (1891), pp. 380-2.

68 The petition is printed in full in Langford, *op. cit.*, vol. II, p. 468.

69 For the general political situation, see A. Briggs, *The Age of Improvement* (1979 edn), pp. 225 ff., and for the issues as seen from the centre, B. Hilton, *Corn, Cash and Commerce* (1973), Chapter 2.

70 Attwood to Mrs Attwood, 18 March 1827 (ibid., p. 109).

71 ibid.

72 *Mirror of Parliament*, no. 40 (1829).

73 Peel to Attwood, 27 December 1828 (Wakefield, *op. cit.*, p. 106).

74 HO/52/11, B.W. to Sir Robert Peel, 21 October 1830.

75 *Memorial of 4 October 1831*. Cp. *Birmingham Journal*, 12 April 1828, which had described 'works *employed* but with no profit to employers'.

76 Cobbett to Attwood, 24 June 1829 (Wakefield, *op. cit.*, pp. 126-7).

77 *Memorial of 4 October 1831*.

78 Clapham, *Economic History of Modern Britain*, p. 176. See below pp. 184-5.

79 Speech of 8 May 1829.

80 L. Faucher, *Études sur l'Angleterre* (1845), vol. II, p. 147. Similar impressions were recorded by other foreign observers like von Raumer, writing in 1835, and Kohl, writing in 1843.

81 Cobden to Parkes, 9 August 1857. Quoted in John Morley, *The Life of Richard Cobden* (1881), vol. II, pp. 198-9.

82 Letter of B.W. to Peel, cited above.

83 *Birmingham Advertiser*, 18 June 1835.

84 Langford, *op. cit.*, vol. II, p. 283.

85 *Observations on Currency, Population and Pauperism* (1818), p. 127. The relation between unemployment and political disturbance was frequently stressed by other writers. At Sheffield, where conditions were somewhat similar to those in Birmingham, Gatty pointed out that 'when the hands of the working classes are completely unemployed, their minds are inclined to become passionately interested in political topics .... So surely as trade fails does the political fervour rise and strengthen.' (Rev. A. Gatty, *History of Sheffield* (1873), pp. 240-1.) The reverse applied in many cases. 'You cannot get them to talk of politics so long as they are well employed,' said William Mathews in 1832. (Evidence given before the Select Committee on Manufactures, Q.9991-3.)

86 The petition is printed in full in A. W. Acworth, *Financial Reconstruction, 1815-22* (1925), Appendix F, pp. 149-51. Details of local unemployment can be collected from many sources. Attwood, in his *Observations*, commented on the large numbers of demobilised soldiers, 'men who have supported the national honour in every quarter of the globe', and who are now 'deserted by their country, when their country no longer requires them, and humbly soliciting material employment, or begging an ignoble bread'. The position in the district around Birmingham was worse in 1817 than Birmingham itself; at Bilston, for example, there were 2000 unemployed. Evidence collected by the Bank of England pointed to large masses of people 'wholly destitute of employment'. (J. H. Clapham, *The Bank of England*, vol. II (1944), p. 59.)

87 *Aris's Gazette*, 19 July 1819. The reporter boasted then that 'not a single individual ... holding a respectable position in society', took a prominent share in the day's proceedings'.

88 HO/51/11, George Nicholls to Sir Robert Peel, 12 October 1830.

89 ibid., Rev. W. R. Bedford (a county magistrate) to Melbourne, 24 December 1830.

90 *op. cit.*, A. J. Likeston to Melbourne, 29 September 1831. Cp. HO/44/19, where an anonymous letter to the Home Secretary mentions 10,000 families in Birmingham without employment.

91 Tooke, *op. cit.*, pp. 209-13. W. T. Layton and G. Crowther, *An Introduction to the Study of Prices* (1938), pp. 64-5.

92 Thomas Carlyle, *Chartism*, Chapter II, 'Statistics'. For statistics, see also above, pp. 57 ff.

93 HO/15/11, Isaac Spooner to Melbourne, 19 December 1830.

94 For the origins and development of country banking, see L. S. Presnell, *Country Banking in the Industrial Revolution* (1956).

95 Wakefield, *op. cit.*, p. 59.

96 *Observations on Currency, Population and Pauperism* (1818).

97   *Report of the Proceedings*, 25 June 1832.

98   See above, p. 24.

99   Matthias Attwood (1779-1851) was a London banker, who first became a Tory Member of Parliament in 1819. He opposed Malthus on the law of diminishing returns (see *Hansard*, vol. VIII, p. 392 ff., and E. Cannan, *A History of the Theories of Production and Distribution* (3rd edn, 1924), p. 167) and Ricardo and Peel on the resumption of cash payments in 1819 (*Hansard*, vol. VII, p. 877). He spoke regularly in the House, and was often praised for his practical knowledge and debating skill. Although Matthias remained a Tory during and after 1832, he continued to share the currency views of his Radical brother. The two brothers are often confused, e.g. in C. Rist, *A History of Monetary and Credit Theory* (1940), p. 183.

100 *A Letter to the Right Honourable Nicholas Vansittart* (1817), p. 5. Vansittart was then Chancellor of the Exchequer.

101 H. James, *Considerations on the Policy or Impolicy of the Further Continuation of the Bank Restriction Act* (1818).

102 See F. W. Fetter, *Development of British Monetary Orthodoxy* (1965).

103 *S.C. on the Bank Charter* (1832), Q.5662. Cp. *A Letter on the Creation of Money* (1817), p. 58: 'Whenever the money of a country is sufficient to call every labourer into action upon the system and trade best suited to his habits and powers, the benefits of increased circulation can go no further.' T. Wilson, in his *Fluctuations in Income and Employment* (1945), p. 31, compares this passage with J. M. Keynes, *General Theory of Employment, Interest and Money* (1936), p. 118. It would be unhistorical to call Attwood's analysis 'quasi-Keynesian', even were the two theories far closer together than they are in fact, but it is interesting to note that there are undoubted similarities of approach.

104 Wakefield, *Attwood*, p. 81. For Ricardo's very different interpretation of the interview, see J. Bonar and J. H. Hollander (eds), *Letters of David Ricardo to Hutches Trower and Others* (1899), p. 149: Mr Attwood, a great publisher of Essays on the currency was called before us ... his claims to infallibility have been sifted by Huskisson and myself, and I believe it will appear that he is no great master of the Science.'

105 *Observations on Currency, Population and Pauperism* (1818).

106 *Political Register*, 7 October 1826. The phrase, originally applied to Henry James, was frequently repeated. Cobbett's suggestion that bills of exchange and notes should be abolished was attacked equally scathingly by Attwood. 'He might as well abolish the plough and the spade.' (*Distressed State of the Country* (1829).)

107 *A Letter on the Creation of Money* (1817), p. 58. For an analysis of his views see S. G. Checkland, *op. cit.*

108 ibid.

109 See R. G. Hawtrey, *Trade and Credit* (1928), Chapter IV, 'Inflationism' (*A Lecture to the Birmingham School of Commerce*, October 1925); L. W. Mints, *A History of Banking Theory in Great Britain and the United States* (1945), pp. 58-9; I. Bowen, 'Banking Controversies in

1825', in *Economic History*, vol. III (1938); R. J. Sayers, *op. cit.*; and, for the background, E. Victor Morgan, *The Theory and Practice of Central Banking* (1943), and Fetter, *op. cit.*, *passim*.

110 A. F. Burns, *Economic Research and the Keynesian Thinking of our Times* (1946), p. 8.

111 J. H. Hollander, *David Ricardo: A Centenary Estimate* (1910), p. 118.

112 *The Remedy or Thoughts on the Present Distress* (1816). Cp. *Letter to Nicholas Vansittart*.

113 *The Scotch Banker* (1828).

114 *Observations on Currency, Population and Pauperism*, pp. 147-8. Cp. *Report of the Political Union*, 3 October 1831: 'every honest labourer in England has as good a right to a reasonable maintenance for his family in exchange for his labour as the King had to a crown on his head.'

115 ibid., p. 92. Cp. W. Beveridge, *Full Employment in a Free Society* (1945), p. 19: 'The full employment that is the aim of this report means more vacant jobs than unemployed men'; and ibid., p. 52, where he outlines the duty of the state to maintain it.

116 *Report of the Proceedings of the Town's Meeting*, 13 December 1830. Cp. Attwood's view (*Hansard*, vol. VII, p. 877). The Act is 'one of the most impolitic and mischievous measures that was ever adopted in this country'.

117 Letter to the *Morning Post*, 1 May 1847. Attwood described himself as an 'old correspondent'.

118 Fetter, *op. cit.*, p. 99. This compared with an annual figure of twenty in 1818 and in 1819.

119 *Hansard*, vol. VI, col. 253.

120 See, for example, the account of Attwood's views, in M. Hovell, *The Chartist Movement* (1925), especially Chapter VI. G. D. H. Cole, in *Chartist Portraits* (1941) set out rather inadequately to redress the balance.

121 *Observations on Currency, Population and Pauperism*.

122 *Political Register*, 23 April 1835.

123 ibid., 8 December 1821.

124 See Fetter, *op. cit.*, p. 112.

125 *The Scotch Banker* (1828), originally in the *Globe*, published between September 1827 and August 1828. Cobbett had strongly attacked Attwood, however, in the *Political Register*, 2 June 1827, and reviewed *The Scotch Banker* in ibid., 24 May 1828.

126 *Report of the Proceedings of the Public Dinner given in Honour of Mr Wooler on his Liberation from Warwick Gaol* (1822), p. 4.

127 *Birmingham Journal*, 8 October, 12 November 1829. 'We object to men taking upon themselves to regulate their own proceedings,' the *Journal* recounted. It also quoted a local description of the Institute as a 'hotbed of sedition'. Brougham was a great advocate of the movement.

128 Addressing a public meeting on 25 June 1827, he went so far as to say that he would support universal suffrage for Birmingham 'if practic-

able', but he made it clear that he did not consider it practicable. Scholefield, Spooner and Timothy Smith also spoke.

129 *Birmingham Independent*, 3 January 1828.
130 Liverpool had at times appeared to be a good learner, but he did not abandon orthodox political economy. In 1826, he blamed the fact that there had been an orgy of over-trading and speculation on the increase in country bank paper circulation (see C. D. Yonge, *Lord Liverpool*, pp. 362-5). The Attwoods hated the phrase 'over-trading'. Matthias was horrified that there were some who considered proposed railway companies, water companies, and gas companies as mere 'bubbles' (*Hansard*, vol. XIV, col. 700). Thomas, in his speech of May 1829, attacked Liverpool for talking of over-trading in 1825. 'Whenever the country prospered, Lord Liverpool thought that there was something wrong in it. Things were never right in *his* eyes, unless the country was at the point of death.' See also Wakefield, *op. cit.*, p. 104.
131 Wakefield, *op. cit.*, p. 109.
132 He liked such summaries, which suggest that he was as much of a historian as a political economist.
133 *Aris's Gazette*, 11 May 1829.
134 The Act of 1819 had contemplated the abolition of small notes in 1822, but in that year, Parliament changed its mind, and the banks were authorised to go on with the issue of £1 notes until 1833. The Bank of England stopped issuing them, but, with or without Attwood's help, conveniently 'found' a supply in 1825 (see above p. 146). In 1826, Parliament passed an Act that no more English notes under £5 were to be stamped, and that none of those already stamped should be issued after 5 April 1829. The date is significant.
135 Wakefield, *op. cit.*, p. 59, p. 66.
136 *Birmingham Argus and Public Censor*, August 1829.
137 J. Jaffray, *Hints for a History of Birmingham* (1857), quoted in Langford, *Centenary of Birmingham Life*, p. 532.
138 See, in particular, his *Plan for Realizing the Perfection of Money* (1832).
139 This was the second of three letters dated 27 April, 14 December 1828 and 8 February 1830. They were published in November 1830. For Muntz's later life as a manufacturer, see an article on him by C. T. Flick, in *Transactions of the Birmingham and Warwickshire Archaeological Society*, vol. LXXXVII (1975).
140 William Chance, High Bailiff, 'To the Gentleman who Signed the Requisition', 18 January 1830 (*Aris's Gazette*, 18 January 1820).
141 'Requisition to the High Bailiff', signed by 200 people.
142 *The Annual Register* (1830), p. 57.
143 *Hansard*, vol. XXI, cols 1672 sqq. The speech was printed in full from the *Morning Chronicle* in Cobbett's *Weekly Political Register*, 13 June 1828.
144 Blandford to Attwood, 29 January 1820, quoted in Wakefield, *op. cit.*, pp. 137-8.
145 ibid., pp. 126-7. Cobbett printed a full report of the meeting of 8 May in his *Weekly Political Register*, 16 May 1829. In ibid., 13 June, he

advised a general reading of Attwood's speech, 'which can leave in the mind of no man of sense a doubt, that convulsion must be the end of the present measures, unless prevented by a reform'.

146   *The Times*, 27 January 1830.

147   *Report of the Proceedings [at the Meeting of the Inhabitants of Birmingham]*, Monday 25 January 1830.

148   ibid. 'The Whigs had done nothing to forward the cause of public liberty. He had never belonged to that party – he was always a Tory, and a real friend to the privileges of the people.'

149   *Annual Register* (1830), pp. 18-19.

150   There is a letter of 20 November 1834 from Blandford to Wellington suggesting that he should be raised to the peerage where 'it will be my Endeavour to give constant support to your Administration'. (Peel Papers, British Museum Add. MSS, 40, 309, f. 289.)

151   *Report of the Proceedings*, 25 January 1930. Redfern was the speaker.

152   *Morning Chronicle*, 25 March 1830. Burdett was the chief guest at the first Annual Meeting of the Birmingham Political Union on 26 July 1830. At a subsequent dinner, he proposed Blandford's health. Cobbett commented petulantly in a letter to Attwood: 'The moment I heard of you having invited the sham king Burdett to Birmingham, I knew you to be a sham yourself' (*Weekly Political Register*, 7 August 1830).

153   Graham followed some of Attwood's views in his *Corn and Currency* (1825). He was active in opposing the abolition of small notes (*Hansard*, vol. XIX, col. 992), and in 1830 sponsored a petition from Cumberland, claiming that 'distress is not confined to one branch of productive industry, but at the same time and with equal pressure, weighs down the landlord and the manufacturer, the shipowner and the miner, the employer and the labourer'. See W. Molesworth, *History of the Reform Bill* (1868), p. 81.

154   *Morning Chronicle*, 1 February 1830.

155   *Political Register*, 29 January 1820. The title had first been bestowed on another Birmingham economist, Henry James.

156   *Weekly Political Register*, vol. 68, no. 25, 19 December 1829. For the local impact of the visit, see the *Birmingham Journal*, 26 December 1829, which in the same number described 'the general languor and depression of our commercial interests'.

157   ibid., 6 February 1830.

158   Blandford wished to dissociate himself from Cobbett. He wrote to the *Standard* (13 June 1829) attacking the ballot and universal suffrage. 'Upon these two points, Messrs Cobbett and Hunt and myself are poles asunder.' Cobbett replied in the *Weekly Political Register*, 25 July 1829. In the meantime, he was engaged in a controversy with Davenport, 'a young man of the collective who has for two or three sessions been racking his inventive powers for the means of talking sense upon the subject of the currency', ibid., 7 November 1829. Davenport, Tory Member for Stafford, was a friend and collaborator of Attwood, and dined with him on 24 October, when the plans for the Political Union were talked over.

159 For the shadow of the Tory-Radical alliance, see Halévy, *Histoire du peuple anglais* (1923), vol. II, pp. 262-5; R. L. Hill, *Toryism and the People* (1929); and below, p. 193.

160 *Birmingham Monthly Argus*, June 1829.

161 There had been a squabble in which Parkes was involved as to whether the expenses of the Representation Committee should be charged to the town. See *Aris's Birmingham Gazette*, 20 July 1829.

162 Redfern wrote a pamphlet in the summer of 1829, attacking Attwood's speech of 8 May 1829.

163 *Report of the Proceedings*, 25 January 1830: *Birmingham Journal*, 30 January 1830.

164 For the so-called Whig 'Cabal' and its influence in the 1820s, see the brief and inadequate account by J. K. Buckley, *Joseph Parkes of Birmingham* (1926). Other members of 'the Cabal' were the Unitarian T. H. Ryland, manufacturer and merchant (see his *Reminiscences* (1904)), and Timothy Smith. The *Journal*, which called them 'liberal illiberals' dealing in 'contumely, abuse and vociferation' (31 January 1829), argued in 1830 (24 June) that the Union had shorn the strength of the 'old oligarchy'.

165 *Aris's Gazette*, 18 January 1830. *The Birmingham Journal*, 30 January 1830, congratulated Parkes and Redfern on coming forward when most of the influential Whig interest was absent. Parkes remained a link between the Union and Whig and dissenting bodies until 1831. The final infusion of strength came as late as May 1832 when some 500 'merchants, bankers, solicitors, surgeons, master manufacturers and other influential men' joined. (Wakefield, *op. cit.*, p. 207.)

166 Quoted in C. T. Flick, *The Birmingham Political Union* (1978), p. 30. This kind of language was significantly extended in Attwood's speech of January 1831. 'The very moment the King commanded them', he told a great dinner, 'they would produce a national guard that would be like a wall of fire around his throne.'

167 *Birmingham Monthly Argus*, December 1830.

168 The *Argus* was beginning to turn against the Union in June 1830. It praised Attwood as a 'wise and prudent leader' and hoped that the members would 'go as far as he does, AND NO FARTHER'. It drew distinctions between members of his Council, 'of various passions, views and interests'. Allday resigned from the Union in January 1831, but he still praised Attwood (see ibid., March 1831), and called him 'the best informed man in England' on the currency question. By June 1831 the *Argus* described the Union as 'a revolutionary club', 'the Town's pest'.

169 *Report of the Proceedings*, 4 July 1831.

170 Attwood to Mrs Attwood, 21 June, 23 June 1830. (Wakefield, *op. cit.*, p. 143). He was still impressed by the fact that Hume was being approached by 'old Tories of Middlesex'. This was one of the 'signs of the times'. Radnor was to make it clear later that he differed from Attwood on currency questions. (Letter to Attwood, 2 June 1831.)

171 *Jenkinson's Scholastic Tickler*, November 1829. See above p. 28.

172 *Birmingham Journal*, 23 January 1830; *The Times*, 20 January 1830.

173 *Political Union Register*, March 1832.

174 *Report of the Proceedings.*

175 W. E. Andrews, *A Letter Addressed to the Members of the Birmingham Political Union* (1830). By September 1830 the *Argus* was describing 'the Catholic Association and this Union' as 'a noble pair of twins sprung from the same parents – Disenchantment and the Love of Self-Aggrandisement'. At the meeting of May 1829, when asked how to achieve currency reform, Attwood replied, 'Union – such as the Irish exhibited.' Attwood also admired O'Connell's emphasis on 'the sinews of the law', and met O'Connell to discuss 'legality' in February 1830. See W. J. Kirkpatrick (ed.), *Correspondence of Daniel O'Connell*, vol. I (1888), p. 199.

176 'As a Politician he is a red-hot liberal,' the *Argus* complained. 'He venerates seditious Daniel O'Connell.' (*Birmingham Monthly Argus*, February 1831.) McDonnell had worked with Attwood on the Mechanics' Institute Committee. O'Connell had visited Birmingham to win support for the Catholic Association in 1825 (Longford, *op. cit.*, vol. II, p. 404), but had been threatened by a 'No Popery' mob on a later visit in April 1829 (ibid., pp. 478-9).

177 In March 1830 the Council of the Union drew up a Declaration supporting Blandford's Bill, presented to the Commons on 18 February. On 17 May an enormous meeting was held to support Blandford. The Council declaration is quite explicit: 'It is not merely the abstract merit of any particular plan which ought to be attended to, but ... its *practicability*.' Attention must be paid 'to the conciliating of all classes of the community, so that it may in fact serve as a common *rallying* point for all'.

178 A Committee of Birmingham Non-Election broke with the Union.

179 Declaration of 10 May 1832.

180 *Report of the Proceedings of the Public Meeting*, 25 June 1832.

181 *Address of the Council of the Birmingham Political Union to their Fellow Countrymen in the United Kingdom*, 12 June 1832.

182 *Report of the Third Annual General Meeting*, 30 July 1832.

183 *Report of the Proceedings of the Public Meeting*, 20 May 1833. O'Connell was one of the chief speakers. Cp. *Birmingham Journal*, 22 April 1833, where Attwood is reported as saying that he had looked round the reformed House of Commons and had almost regretted that 'he had ever lent his humble assistance to the formation of it'.

184 Some of them were being advanced in 1830-2, but they had little effect. The attempts to stir up enthusiasm for the National Union of the Working Classes by Hetherington and his supporters met with little response. The Owenite cooperators, led by Pare, supported the Political Union and Owen himself addressed the Council of the Political Union in November 1832. (See W. E. Hampton, *Early Cooperation in Birmingham and District* (1928).) In April 1831, Bronterre O'Brien became editor of the reforming *Midland Representative*. See above, p. 130.

185   See *The Times*, 4 November 1848. In 1847 Matthias Attwood's *A Letter to Lord Archibald Hamilton on Alterations in the Value of Money* (1823) was reprinted, and a Birmingham delegation headed by G. F. Muntz met Lord John Russell. See also G. F. Muntz, *The True Cause of the Late Sudden Change in the Current Affairs of the Country* (1831) and *The Currency Question;* and *The Gemini Letters* (1843), published anonymously, but claiming to represent the views of 'the most cautious and careful men of business which the town possesses'. See also Checkland, *op. cit.*, and Fetter, *op. cit.*, esp. p. 216, where he attempts a summary.

7 The Background of the Parliamentary Reform Movement in Three English Cities, 1830-1832

Many of the most important political changes of the nineteenth century have been studied exclusively from the standpoint of London. Clear-sighted contemporaries have been long aware of the consequent misrepresentation. 'Londoners are the lapidaries of the nation', wrote Holyoake, 'they polish the diamond found in the counties, and sometimes if no one challenges them, they take credit for the jewel.'[1] Only too often no one has challenged them. The result has been not so much a failure to render credit where credit is due as a failure to understand the mainsprings of national political action. It is only when the local element has obtruded unmistakeably, as in the story of Chartism, that it has been impossible to ignore it. Where it has not obtruded, historians have often been more willing to accept things as they seemed from the standpoint of the capital rather than to investigate them as they arose.

I

The purpose of this article is to investigate some of the local features of the reform agitation of 1830-2, particularly in three large un-represented cities, Birmingham, Manchester and Leeds. 1830 saw the convergence of different local reform movements, each coloured by the social structure and political experience of its area. Between 1831 and 1832 the Whig Reform Bill was considered locally to be not so much an end, as a means to an end; and the objects which it was intended to secure varied in different parts of the country. 'It must be recollected that a Reform in Parliament is only a MEANS to an end', wrote a Newcastle Radical, 'it is a means offered to the people for electing a more free, bold and honest House of Commons ... The ENDS which that House of Commons is to accomplish are yet to be obtained.'[2] When it became clear that the ends were not to be secured as a result of the passing of the Reform Bill, new forms of organisation were evolved to try to secure them afresh, and new alliances and conflicts emerged. Even then, old differences still persisted and undermined the unity of the Chartist movement.[3]

In each of the three cities the most important political problem which emerged was that of reconciling two approaches to reform – the approach of popular Radicals, stirred by distress, whatever their explanation of it, and seeking reform as a cure, and the approach of mercantile manufacturing groups, demanding the representation of local interests. Reconciliation was relatively easy in Birmingham, where social structure and political leadership encouraged co-operation between all reformers.[4] It was more difficult in Manchester and Leeds, where group interests clashed. After the Reform Bill had been secured, Attwood and Scholefield were returned unopposed in triumph as members for Birmingham, while there were bitter election contests in both Manchester and Leeds. The result was that Birmingham secured a position of primacy in the reform struggle, which persisted until the split inside the Political Union in 1838 and the rise of Chartism as a national movement.

The popular Radical approach to reform was well articulated in 1830. It was compounded of three elements – a protest against 'distress', a theory of rights, and a dream, or rather a series of often inconsistent dreams, of 'a different system after the Reform Bill is disposed of'.[5] The theory of rights, inherited from eighteenth-century Radicalism, provided a set of slogans and offered a comprehensive political terminology, though the theory could be related to history or expressed in abstract form. The dreams were as compelling as any theory. 'What did we want the Reform Bill FOR?' Cobbett asked in 1833, providing his own answer – that seemed to him unescapable: 'It certainly was that it might do us some good; that it might better our situation ... this was what *the people* wanted the Reform Bill for, and not for the gratification of any abstract or metaphysical whim.'[6]

When 'distress' reawakened the popular Radicals in 1829 and in 1830, they already had their own traditions upon which to rely. In Manchester, Leeds and Birmingham, there were vivid memories of the post-war agitations, particularly of 1819. In Manchester the memory of Peterloo, 'the field of blood', was kept alive at annual celebrations. In Leeds, at the Radical demonstrations of 1830, the old 1819 banners were carried. In Birmingham, George Edmonds, the Secretary of the Political Union, provided a link between old reformers and new ones.[7] Continuity was never broken. It could have been said of meetings in all three cities in 1830, as it was said of Birmingham, that 'we observed some of our veteran reformers of the ancient days come forth, forgetting their years and their infirmities'.[8]

The approach of mercantile and manufacturing groups to reform was substantially different. In the debates on Grampound, 'the beginning of the end of the old representative system', Lord John Russell underlined the two main reasons for the demand for distinct-ive local representation – first, the increase in the number of questions relating to trade, the Poor Laws, taxation, combinations and other social and economic problems, coming before the House of Commons, and, second, the difference between the station and habits of the county Members and their urban constituents. 'However well in-formed they [the county Members] may be to do their duty to their constituents ... they have not the knowledge requisite to study the grievances and wants of manufacturers.'[9]

It is important not to exaggerate the antiquity of this claim. In the eighteenth century and frequently in the early nineteenth century, manufacturers, while stressing their own local points of view,[10] usually considered their county representatives or representatives of neigh-bouring constituencies as adequate protagonists of their urban interests. In Birmingham strong links were maintained not only with the representatives for the county of Warwick,[11] but also with those of boroughs like Bridgnorth, where the 1826 *Poll Book* listed thirty-one freemen electors from Birmingham, one from West Bromwich and two from Handsworth.[12] In Manchester, considerable reliance was placed on the Members for Lancashire, and in Leeds, particularly after 1820, on the Members for Yorkshire, although as early as 1639 petitioners in Leeds had complained that there were no local burgesses 'to have voice upon any occasions arising touching abuses in the matter of cloathing' or to deal with 'the conveniences or inconveniences of laws relating to cloth'.[13]

When county Members did not prove reliable, there was scope for special economic pressure to be applied,[14] but the political turmoil of elections for a long time seemed more dangerous to local manu-facturers and traders than the advantages of separate representation. As James Ogden wrote of Manchester in 1783,

> nothing could be more fatal to its trading interest than if it should be incorporated and have representation in Parliament, for such is the general course of popular contests that in places where the immediate dependence of the inhabitants is not upon trade, the health and morals of the people are ruined upon these occasions. How much more fatal would the effects be in such a town as this, where to the above evils, there would be added the interruption of trade and the perpetuation of ill-will between masters and workmen.[15]

The same sort of argument was used by Matthew Boulton in Birming-ham, and was quoted by Lord Liverpool and Mrs Arbuthnot in their case against the enfranchisement of the city.[16]

Fear of internal disorder inhibited a whole-hearted acceptance of the need for local representation: it encouraged the perpetuation of theories of virtual representation after they had ceased to retain their force;[17] it drove a wedge between popular radicalism and middle-class reformism. These points were made clear during the Penryn and East Retford debates of 1827 and 1828. In both Manchester and Birmingham the respectable movement for reform was characterised by caution in approach and secrecy in tactics. The *Manchester Guardian*, supporting the introduction of Members of Parliament who would be 'intimately and practically connected with the cotton manufacture',[18] was expressing a relatively liberal point of view when it wrote that 'we would have the franchise on a basis so broad as to secure its being popular, but at the same time, we would subject it to such limitations as might tend to prevent the exercise of a decisive influence on the result of elections by that class which, from want of education, and from penury, is least likely to use it honestly and with independence'.[19] The main purpose of reform, argued speakers at the Town Meeting in May 1827, was to secure representation for an 'acknowledged seat of wealth, industry and commercial enterprise', and to have Members returned 'whose feelings would not particularly incline to the landed interest, but who would be closely connected with the town and well acquainted with its interests'.[20]

These views, parallelled in Birmingham,[21] were out of line with Radical opinion, and the Manchester Representation Committee, working behind closed doors, could urge the high voting qualification of £20.[22] The trouble with the existing franchise, wrote the *Manchester Guardian* with the full support of the Tory *Courier*, was not that 'the lower orders' had no political influence, but that there was no permanent guarantee which would 'prevent those voters who belong to the class in society which is most accessible to bribes from overlaying and rendering of no avail the independent suffrages of people in a superior station'.[23]

In 1827 and 1828 differences between reformers in Manchester were so wide that they were noted in the House of Commons as a serious obstacle to the transfer of the Penryn seat,[24] while the *Birmingham Journal*, urging 'safe and moderate reform', warned sharply in 1828 against 'Parliamentary Reformers, who would involve us in the anomaly of universal suffrage and annual parliaments'.[25] The failure of the attempts to secure piecemeal reform emphasised the necessity for more vigorous political action in the localities, whether the old system were to be modified, or overthrown; and the problem of securing good working relations between all types of reformers was forced even more to the forefront. 'There were materials of discontent enough', Attwood told the first general audience of the Birmingham

Political Union in May 1830; 'the only difficulty was in making them harmonize and unite in some common remedy.'[26]

This paper sets out to examine more closely social relationships and political leadership in Birmingham, Manchester and Leeds, and their effect upon the politics of reform. In each city the central problem was the same, but in each city there were significant and sometimes wide differences in the approach to it. Other cities had different patterns which makes it exceptionally difficult to generalise about the composition and role of the different Political Unions of which there were more than a hundred. Without research, too, it makes it impossible to judge the truth of Attwood's claim that it was places without Political Unions – he mentioned Derby and Nottingham in October 1831 – where there were or would be political disturbances.[27] A Union was founded in Derby, however, one month later, and in Nottingham early in 1832.

II

There were four features of the social structure of Birmingham which made it possible for Attwood to 'harmonize and unite in some common remedy' the diverse elements in local reform circles. The first was the predominance of the small workshop (rather than the factory), where small masters (rather than industrial capitalists) worked in close contact with their skilled artisans. Economic development in Birmingham in the first half of the nineteenth century multiplied the number contact with their skilled artisans. In general, economic development in Birmingham in the first half of the nineteenth century multiplied the number of producing units rather than added to the scale of existing enterprises, although there were some relatively big units, some using steam power. The second was the relative lack of labour-saving machinery to throw workers out of their jobs.

> The operation of mechanism in this town, is to effect that alone, which requires *more force* than the *arm* and the tools of the workman could yield, still leaving his skill and experience of head, hand and eye in full exercise; – so that Birmingham has suffered infinitely less from the introduction of machinery than those towns where it is, in a great degree, an actual *substitute* for human labour.[28]

The third was the marked social mobility, which blurred sharp class distinctions. Small masters might fail in their enterprises and become journeymen again. 'One sees quickly', commented Faucher, 'that the *bourgeoisie*, which is everywhere the base of urban populations, hardly

rises at all in Birmingham over inferior groups in society.'[29] The fourth
was the tendency to regular economic fluctuations, during the worst
years of which the discontents of both middle classes and working
classes, 'the bees of society', moved together.[30] Distress did not
usually divide masters and men in Birmingham; it brought them
together by producing a common statement of grievances.

The propaganda of Thomas Attwood and the Political Union 'of
the Lower and Middle Classes of the People', founded in December
1829, emphasised the necessity for class cooperation. Class co-
operation indeed was the basis of the Union, currency reform the
economic philosophy and the ultimate object of action, and parliamentary reform the means. These three elements were considered
indivisible. Without class cooperation, effective organisation could
not be built up; without parliamentary reform, currency reform could
not be accomplished; without currency reform, class conflicts would
become serious even in Birmingham, and revolution might eventually
break out.[31] The fact that armaments, including small arms, were made
in Birmingham, was often noted.[32] Revolution was the final night-
mare. If great misery had been created by the breaking-up of the French
social system during the Revolution, 'not a tenth part so complicated
as our own social system, what would be the dreadful misery every man
would sustain, be he rich or be he poor, if ever the complicated and
wonderful machinery of English society were suffered to break up?'[33]

If, in the last (and sometimes in the first) resort, Attwood's political
philosophy was conservative,[34] his choice of means and to some extent
his choice of what to him were subordinate targets was essentially
opportunist. He began by supporting the Tory Marquis of Blandford's reform proposals, born in the atmosphere of Protestant
bitterness engendered by the passing of Catholic Emancipation.[35] He
ended his active career by accepting the Six Points of the Charter. At
no stage of his life did he accept the principles of Whiggery, but he was
prepared to work with Whigs[36] and Benthamite Radicals between
1830 and 1832, recognising as did Joseph Parkes, who disagreed with
him profoundly about the currency, 'that the present is the most
eventful political crisis in the history of the country' and that all local
feelings of differences of opinion had to be laid on one side.[37] Between
1830 and 1832, Attwood was careful, however, never to identify
himself too closely with the powerful anti-Whig undercurrent inside
the Union. George Edmonds, who had been involved in Radical
movements more than a decade earlier, and was described by the
Journal as 'the foremost of those to ferment the discontented', talked
of 'patriotic tea-table politicians, who would never do anything except
behind closed doors' and contrasted 'the manly conduct of the Tories
with the insincere dirty conduct of the Whigs.'[38] Muntz dismissed

Whigs as 'always professing to support the interests of the people, but always acting in opposition to their professions'.[39] Attwood, however, always tried hard to maintain the maximum amount of local unity and goodwill. Of Grey, for instance, he later said, 'I looked at his unsullied character with something approaching to reverence'.[40]

The Birmingham Political Union provided a model organisation while the struggle for the Reform Bill went on. From the start Attwood had his opponents, like the artisan James Bibb, who advocated annual parliaments and universal suffrage on lines suggested by Hunt,[41] or Joseph Russell, the freethinking printer, whom Attwood later described as a 'kind of ancient IAGO',[42] but they were usually safely watched inside the Political Union, rather than allowed to organise movements of their own outside it.[43] The one other reform organisation, the Birmingham cell of the National Union of the Working Classes, was not set up until October 1832, after the Reform Bill had passed, and even then it had little influence.[44] It was the Political Union which rallied the survivors of 1819, collected grievances, marshalled arguments and organised crowds. *The Times* called it 'the barometer of the Reform feeling throughout England', and as the impulsive Anglican clergyman Dr Wade, a link with the National Union of the Working Classes,[45] did not fail to point out, it was capable in emergency of becoming a national thermometer too, 'rising to fever heat with rage, indignation and vengeance'.[46]

Attwood's skilled political leadership restrained the over-exuberance of some of his followers. In public he emphasised the lawful character of his organisation; in private, admitting some of its weaknesses, he was proud that he had created a popular instrument to secure well thought-out demands. For him the Political Union was a popular agency, which might secure what he had failed to secure by personal appeals to ministers and men of affairs – curency reform. Whatever abstract difficulties it presented,[47] it was sufficiently interesting to attract an audience of 1300 at the debate on currency questions between Cobbett and Attwood in 1832. A product of Birmingham, it nonetheless allowed for a development of mutual understanding with other groups outside – rural country bankers, disgruntled agriculturalists,[48] ultra-Tories. While the *Manchester Guardian* was beginning to depict the landlord as the villain of society, the Birmingham currency school, advocating high prices[49] and abundant credit, could find strange allies outside. 'You must not think I have no respectable men on my side in politics', Attwood wrote to his Tory wife in the middle of the reform struggle; 'all landowners are with me, although few of them have the courage to own it'.[50]

The question of the Corn Laws was not completely ignored in Birmingham in 1830-2, but it was subordinated to the currency question. In July 1831, Muntz, presiding over the second annual meeting of the Political Union, claimed that there were two possible ways to prosperity after reform itself had been secured – repeal of the Corn Laws or reform of the money laws. He threw all his energies into the latter campaign, he said, for to repeal 'the corn laws *without altering the money laws* would be certain ruin to the landed interest, because they had *upon the average* mortgaged their estates for half their present value'.[51] Attwood hoped that a solution to economic difficulties would be arrived at by which no one would suffer, not even the landed interest, but 'it was the duty of the landed interest to devise the means of supporting the high wages of labour, if they retain a law to support the high value of their produce'.[52] Although he came to support repeal of the Corn Laws, he never indulged in vituperation against the landed interest as such, and was prepared at times to express himself more strongly against the industrial middle classes,[53] and more particularly against 'the monied interest of the City of London'.[54]

In time, Attwood's currency views ceased to appeal to the industrial classes of Birmingham, and the Corn Law repeal formula, imported from Manchester, captured the city just at the same time that it became the central point of orthodox applied economics in the country as a whole, but between 1830 and 1832 Attwood's ideas were dominant, and his organisation supreme. The Political Union, at first 'thought by political men of all parties to be a mere ebullition, which would speedily pass away',[55] had been forged into a powerful instrument at exactly the right time. 'We have reason to know', wrote the *Political Union Register*, 'that Mr Attwood had long had the project in contemplation, and we must admit that the prudence with which he has ever directed the Union, was guaranteed to us by that sagacity which enabled him to select the exact time for the formation of that Union.'[55a]

While the Union set out to rally reformers in all parts of the country[56] and Attwood became in Place's opinion 'the most influential man in England',[57] the way was prepared locally for the great election triumph of Attwood and Scholefield in December 1832. They were both returned unopposed,[58] and toured the streets of the city in an open car drawn by six grey horses amid the cheers of the entire population.[59] The demonstration was a proof of substantial local unity, which would have been impossible in either Manchester or Leeds. The election programme was broad enough to appeal to all – 'to stay the march of Anarchy – to relieve the general Distress – to rectify the general wrongs – to secure a full measure of Justice, Liberty and Prosperity to all, and to unite all classes and all sects of my countrymen in peace, happiness and contentment'.[60]

III

If Birmingham was a city of united opinion and co-operative effort, Manchester was a city of cleavages, of social separation and often of open class antagonism. Its most important economic unit was the factory, for although there were large numbers of non-factory workers, the factory workers were more important than in any other city. The factories themselves were often large – in 1832, average employment in the Manchester spinning mills was over 400, and two large firms employed more than 1000 people.[61] The Manchester factory owner, who insisted that he had made his way forward by thrift and hard work,[62] was already separated by a wide gulf from his workers.[63] In times of bad trade, as in 1829, there was open hostility between spinners and masters. It was in that year that the combination of workers 'assumed a formidable and systematic shape' when John Doherty, who had migrated to Lancashire in 1816, built up the Union of Operative Spinners to fight drastic wage reductions.[64] Doherty, like other spinners before him, although conscious of 'the misrepresentation of the people',[65] was sceptical of reform unless it involved social readjustment, based on the right of workmen to 'the whole produce of their labour'.[66] 'Universal suffrage means nothing more than a power given to every man to protect his own labour from being devoured by others.'[67]

The Manchester spinners were the aristocracy of local labour:[68] alongside them the handloom weavers faced the daily challenge of the machine, their condition growing worse as the factory system developed.[69] They were always a threat to local good order, even when they were not actively engaged in machine-breaking or in political demonstrations. Place noted how there were large sections of working-class opinion in Manchester, concentrated among the handloom weavers, which hoped for revolution rather than reform, 'a revolution in which they might gain, but could not lose'.[70]

If the extremism of considerable numbers of the working classes in Manchester was the first reason why it was impossible for a middle-class leader in that city to manage the reform agitation in the way that Attwood managed the agitation in Birmingham, the second reason was the caution of large numbers of the middle classes themselves in their approach to reform. There was little middle-class interest in large-scale parliamentary reform in Manchester before 1830 except in clearly defined radical circles. As late as June of that year, the *Manchester Guardian* was praising the Wellington regime for doing more 'in the way of adapting our institutions to the change and exigencies of the times, than any which has preceded it, or any which would be likely to be formed in its stead'.[71] Although the Revolution in France quickened interest in reform in Manchester[72] and the formation of the Grey government was applauded locally, there were few demonstrations of enthusiasm among influential manufacturing and merchant groups.

The exception was the small but 'determined band' of middle-class Radicals led by Archibald Prentice, who were shocked by the abuses of the 'old system', particularly by the continued existence of the Corn Laws, and who tried to secure united action in Manchester on the basis of 'cheap bread' and 'thorough reform'. Prentice, like Attwood, believed that middle-class and working-class discontents and grievances moved together. He wrote in 1829:

> The want of a thorough reform in the Commons House of Parliament will be treated as the great source of the poverty, misery and crime that reigns among the labouring classes of the country; of the dreadful prevalence of embarrassment and insolvency among the middle classes, and the shameless, abandoned political profligacy, which has scattered to the winds of heaven the hereditary respect of Englishmen for the aristocracy of their native land.[73]

Unlike Attwood, Prentice found it difficult both to win the support of the middle classes and to secure the confidence of the working classes. Indeed, it was his most bitter complaint that

> the two classes were ranged against each other in a hostility which daily grew more bitter, each taking that antagonistic position to the other that they should have taken against what occasioned the distress of both – ruinous restrictions on trade and a heavy aggravation of the burthen of taxation ... without a corresponding reduction of the public expenditure.[74]

There was no effective theory in Manchester to bring the classes nearer together in the same way that Attwood's currency panaceas did in Birmingham. Sometimes, indeed, the retrenchment and *laissez faire* economic doctrines of local cotton manufacturers widened rather than narrowed the gap between the classes, and even the repeal of the Corn Laws or their modification, which was conceived of by the manufacturers as one of the first fruits of parliamentary reform in the same way that currency reform was in Birmingham, seemed to offer only dubious benefits to factory workers. In 1830-2 the Manchester merchants and manufacturers had not yet discovered their Cobdens and Brights to shape for them a programme, which, even though inadequate in its list of items and appeal, would at least talk of social justice as well as economic expediency.

At first the special interests of the manufacturing classes were stressed at the expense not only of the landlords, but also of the

factory workers.[75] The early advocates of free trade, the Birleys, the
Greens, the Bradshaws and the Hardmans of 1815, 'took the untenable
and unpopular ground that it was necessary to have cheap bread in
order to reduce the English rate of wages to the continental level; and
so long as they persisted in this blunder, the cause of free trade made
little progress'.[76] The Manchester cotton workers looked for other
remedies, although Prentice and the group of Radicals associated with
him, supported by the politically important 'shopocracy' of the town,
tried to widen the basis of anti-Corn Law propaganda by claiming that
the Corn Laws not only penalised the merchant and manufacturer, but
also limited the demand for labour and consequently wages, while at
the same time raising the price of food, and thus forcing down real as
well as money wages for the working classes. In such a situation it was
the duty of masters and men, who had previously contended with one
another, to unite cordially 'to give a decisive blow to the system which
impoverished them both – a system which more than all the tyranny
that employers had ever exercised tended to oppress the people'.[77] A
total repeal of the Corn Laws, a great reduction of taxation, and
parliamentary reform all went together. Reform was only a means.
'The Reform Bill itself has been hastened on mainly by the conviction
that without a great organic change in our representative system, the
landlord's monopoly could not be destroyed.'[78]

Prentice's statement of the case for the repeal of the Corn Laws
aimed at securing widespread working-class support. Although it did
not secure it, it is clear that the emphasis on corn in the reform politics
of Manchester can be related to local social and economic conditions
just as clearly as the emphasis on currency in Birmingham. While the
small Birmingham manufacturers looked to high wages, high profits
and high prices as indices of economic prosperity, the Manchester
manufacturers put their trust in low wages, competitive profits and
cheap prices. While the iron interests of the Midlands were often
insular in outlook, preoccupied with an expansionist credit policy at
home, the Manchester cotton lords were usually internationalist in
outlook, surveying, with eager interest, movements in international
prices and on the exchanges. 'The attention is drawn as naturally to
questions of Custom and Excise, as that of the farm labourer to the
state of the weather in the time of harvest.'[79] In 1830 Manchester
cotton, an imported crop, accounted for more than half the British
export trade in manufactured goods, and the attitude of the mill
owner was summed up by J. Deacon Hume in 1833, as 'I must have the
world for my workshop, and the world for my customer.'[80] Against
such a local background, opposition to the Corn Laws became natural
and inevitable, and the landlord began to appear as the real villain
of society.[81] As early as 1822, when Attwood was pleading on behalf of

the farmers, the *Manchester Guardian* was pointing out that if farmers and landlords had come to depend on high prices, it was because they lived without 'prudent regulation of their personal expenditure, and were too much inclined to rely on the indestructability of their property. Unlike the wise tradesman, they had not learned to save in times of prosperity to sustain the losses and disappointments of inevitable depression.' The basic ideas of the Manchester School were as surely rooted in local soil as were the basic ideas of Attwood and the Birmingham economists. As Dicey pointed out, 'Manchester's political theory was shaped by the practical inferences that it drew from commercial experience.'[82]

In so far as Manchester was interested in currency questions, it was rigidly orthodox. 'We want a regulating medium', said Wood, the Treasurer of the Chamber of Commerce in 1821, 'and there is nothing like gold for that purpose. No circumstance can depreciate its value. Nothing can impair our confidence in it.'[83] There were no country bankers in Manchester to press for an alternative policy; indeed, in the whole of Lancashire there were only three to six banks which issued local notes.[84] In such circumstances there was little scope for an expansionist theory of employment. The financial crisis of 1825 reinforced earlier beliefs in a metallic currency, which would check 'rash adventurers in business'.[85] Three years later, as the time approached for the withdrawal of small notes, while Birmingham was stirred to renewed political pressure to have the withdrawal suspended, Manchester business stood firmly beside Wellington in his decision to maintain his policy unchanged.[86]

The lack of unity of ideas or interests in Manchester was parallelled by a lack of united organisation once the reform campaign had been launched in Birmingham and London. There was no single Political Union to canalise local enthusiasm. In November 1830 a Manchester Political Union was set up with a council composed largely of shopkeepers along with two wealthy members and a few working men,[87] but its influence was restricted to the Prentice group.[88] One of the first acts of its council was to fix a subscription of a shilling a quarter, and to lay down that admission could only be secured with the council's approval and with the written attestation of two householders that the applicant was of good moral character.[89] At its first meeting 'Firebrand Broadhurst', a working-class veteran of 1819, moved the addition of two working men to its council but was defeated.[90]

It was not surprising that a rival working-class body, advocating universal suffrage, the ballot and annual parliaments, was set up early in 1831 with the object of devising the best methods of obtaining the rights of the labouring part of society.[91] It consisted mainly of weavers, and four of its leaders were finally arrested and were sentenced to a year's imprisonment in March 1832. They included Nathan Broadhurst, 'one of the foremost of the red hot radicals . . . and a leader of the gang called the Hunt mob'[92] – he claimed that society would benefit more if the judges were hanged in the Bristol Riots trial rather than the criminals – and Ashmore, who threatened that he and 200 men could shake Manchester Prison. They held their meetings on Sundays, 'because it has been customary for the Master of Factorys to lock up their Bastilles whenever our Public Meetings have taken place'[93] and organised branches or *lodges* in the neighbourhood to spread their propaganda.

Quite distinct from this group, Doherty, while urging that 'operatives should no longer be the slaves of masters and tyrants', was urging in October 1831 that 'the people ought no longer to be shuffled off with a Bill that could do them no good, but ought to take their affairs into their own hands, and by force to compel the Government to do that which was right'.[94] While the Prentice Union supported the Reform Bill and cautious middle-class elements were rallying to its support, all these working-class organisations were pitted against it, although they were sometimes pitted against each other. The more violent their language, the greater was middle-class suspicion of them. Joint action was never possible, not even at crucial moments like October 1831, when the fate of the Reform Bill was in the balance, or in May 1832, after the more violent leaders of the working-class Radicals had been sent to gaol. An abortive attempt at union in May 1832 only led Watkin, a sympathetic middle-class reformer, to write 'no union with such men as the leaders of the existing clubs is possible . . . they seek for confusion and want only the countenance of the wealthy to produce it'.[95]

The open divergences between different local groups were reflected in December 1832 at the first election in Manchester.[96] It was a bitterly fought contest between five candidates – and Melbourne[97] was told by a Manchester magistrate that 'we approach the election with no little ground for apprehension in the midst of such a population as ours'.[98] Yet of the five candidates, only one, Cobbett, was calculated to quicken apprehension into alarm. Philips was a local Liberal cotton merchant, a man of wealth; Samuel Jones Lloyd was a Whig banker who was to take a diametrically opposed attitude to currency questions to that of Attwood; Charles Poulett Thomson, a Radical free-trader and Benthamite, supported by the Prentice groups, was a Radical with ambition; Hope, a Tory churchman, was already a Member of Parliament; and Cobbett had supporters who were accused of threatening 'the voters of other candidates in their progress to the booths'.

Out of this jumble of names, the middle-class *Manchester Guardian* merely wanted a Member with intimate knowledge of the cotton trade, who would understand the 'interests of the community' and save the city the trouble and expense of deputations 'dancing in anxious attendance upon the ministers and public boards'.[99] Cobbett, who was mainly concerned with the parallel election at Oldham, claimed that such narrow vision was justified only if Parliament was merely a Chamber of Commerce,[100] and advocated instead his own social programme, which would prevent the Reform Bill from becoming a 'barren measure'[101] and which would ensure future prosperity, 'better victuals and better clothes'.[102] This practical approach to the fruits of reform was less effective in its appeal than it might have been, because of fierce rivalry between Cobbett and Hunt. It was Hunt who had been the idol of 1819, and Hunt attacked Cobbett furiously in 1832 before Manchester working-class crowds.

The two most important features of the election were a Tory-Radical alliance between the defeated candidates Cobbett and Hope and the emergence of the nucleus of the later Anti-Corn Law League around the sponsors of the successful candidates, Poulett Thomson and Philips.

The Tory-Radical alliance, forecast by the *Manchester Guardian*, before the poll, [103] was not strong enough to emerge victorious, but it was strong enough to reveal a widespread local suspicion of Whiggery, which was considered as a common enemy. Cobbett received most plumpers – 283 – and he shared 302 votes with Hope.[104] Manchester Toryism had not been strong enough before the election to mobilise Radical antagonism against the Whigs, as it did in Leeds, but the 'unholy alliance of tory and radical'[105] was strong enough to continue sporadically in the 1830s, particularly at the time when incorporation and the police question were interesting the public.

It was less effective locally, however, than the holy alliance of nonconformists, shopkeepers, and Radical merchants and manufacturers, which went on to organise the Anti-Corn Law League. Yet this holy alliance, too, was sceptical of traditional Whig principles. At the celebration dinner in December 1832, Philips spoke of the sunset of 'pure Whiggery', and Poulett Thomson looked forward to a 'temperate but searching reform of all our institutions'.[106] These advancing horizons pointed to the new politics of the late 1830s and 1840s, but they did not offer much hope to those left in 1832 outside 'the pale of the constitution'. While Attwood moved ahead in Birmingham from the Reform Bill to the Charter, the Manchester Members made no new points of contact with the unrepresented. To Faucher and Engels, writing in the 1840s, Manchester was more than ever a city of suspicion and antagonism.

There were unexpected later links with the history of Birmingham and the West Midlands. Philips retired in 1847 to an estate in Warwickshire, where he became High Sheriff in 1851, while Lloyd, one of the defeated candidates, who had been raised to the peerage as Lord Overstone a year earlier, was perhaps the most inflexible supporter of the Bank Charter Act of 1844. His ideas were anathema to Attwood.

IV

Leeds differed from Manchester in the relative newness of its more important social and economic changes which had taken place since the turn of the century. In 1796 there had only been six or seven steam-engines working for mills in Leeds, and one for a dyeing house. In 1830 there were 225.[107] The expansion of machinery and the growth of the factory system had revolutionary effects on local social structure. 'The work of men which had been central became auxiliary.'[108] The trend was clear in 1832 when the economic revolution was far from complete, and the woollen industry was still under a 'transitional regime, a halfway house between two rival kinds of industry',[109] hand and power production. Traditional workers were alarmed. 'The operative cloth makers and dressers, heretofore so independent and comfortable ... are now dependent on a very partial and precarious employment.'[110] Fears turned into social complaints. 'The rapid increase of that branch of machines [power looms] which inverts the decrees of Providence', complained a Leeds petition of 1830, 'is an evil of such magnitude as to strike at the very existence of the working classes at no distant date.'[111]

Rapid changes in the social structure of Leeds and its district produced a first generation of discontented and displaced men, some of them former master clothiers, who were forced into employment in subordinate positions in the mills which had helped to supersede them. What was true of the Leeds cloth industry was even more conspicuously true of worsted production, which was centred on Bradford, and which by 1830 was a large-scale factory industry.[112] Indeed, the whole district west of Leeds was an area of contrast and conflict.

In such a setting the opposition between middle-class factory owners and factory operatives was at times as pronounced as it was in Manchester. The working classes were, however, more conservative in Leeds. Less settled within the framework of an industrial society, they found obvious political contrasts and even paradoxes all around them. 'In Lancashire', wrote Faucher, 'traces of historic time have disappeared under the luxuriant vegetation of manufacturing industry. All is recent. In Yorkshire, on the contrary, present is always juxtaposed with past so that they become in a sense contemporaneous.'[113] The operatives could frequently rely for support in their industrial struggles on a Yorkshire squirearchy which was itself unsettled in a new society[114] and on organised Tory groups inside the new industrial towns, which even as early as 1826 were prepared 'in most inflammatory language' to exhort the operatives to rebel against the tyranny of the power loom.[115]

Between 1830 and 1832 the industrial struggle in Leeds centred on the introduction of machinery, and relations between employers and workers dominated all other issues. The result was that while the mill owners and merchants were pressing forward for a plan of political reform, based on support for the Whig government and the rights of the £10 householder, the working classes were being stirred not for parliamentary reform, but for factory reform. Two distinct and competing agitations emerged, each with its own separate chronology.

The character of the two agitations was reflected in the outlook and personalities of the two main antagonists – Edward Baines, who had become editor of the vigorous Whig *Leeds Mercury* in 1801, and Michael Sadler, Tory MP – for a rotten borough – and religious philanthropist. Baines believed in the principles of pure Whiggery, in so far as they could remain pure in a smoky atmosphere. His approach to the Reform Bill was based on considerations of principle. His son wrote how in 1832 Baines had centred his attention on

> the crying abuses of the old system – the represented boroughs without inhabitants, the unrepresented boroughs with a population and wealth like those of capital cities, the extreme and ridiculous inequalities in the extent of the suffrage, the enormous expense and great temptations to corruption and debauchery attendant upon elections of seven to fifteen days' continuance, the inconvenience of having only one polling place for large counties, the heavy cost of out-voters, and other evils which the Reform Bill remedied.

He regarded the passing of the Reform Bill 'as one of those peaceful constitutional victories, which are the glory of England – victories the fruit of extending knowledge ... which speak a national sense of justice ... and which contrast so happily with revolutions of violence and blood'.[116] Approaching the reform question in these terms, it is not surprising that he was active in persuading the Yorkshire Whig electors to choose Brougham as a candidate in 1830,[117] and the Leeds Whig electors to choose Thomas Macaulay in 1832.

Sadler was an old Tory, brought up as a Methodist, and irritated by the advance of industry and any talk of free trade. As Member of Parliament for Newark from 1829 onwards,[118] he went out of his way to stress the positive reforms which he believed would help factory operatives more than the pursuit of any abstract principles. He fought the 1832 election in Leeds on factory questions – thereby inevitably losing the support of some Tory factory owners, like the Gotts – and relied on the upsurge of operative opinion in the Leeds neighbourhood between 1830 and 1832 as a 'sort of antagonist irritation' to the Reform Bill campaign.[119] 'Mr Sadler is an anti-reformer', wrote a hostile pamphleteer in 1832, 'and he hopes by this [Factory] Bill of his to set the master and manufacturers and their men together by the ears, and get quit of the Reform Bill: in this we can tell he will be mistaken. The manufacturers of Lancashire will have a change; they *will* have their own representatives in the national council.'

The upsurge was important, for it broke down many of the conventional barriers of party opinion. At the very moment when Baines raised the parliamentary reform question, Richard Oastler and his supporters were raising the cry of factory reform. The first big parliamentary reform meeting was held in Leeds in March 1830. In September 1830, Oastler's first letter on 'Yorkshire Slavery' appeared in the *Leeds Mercury*. It inevitably accentuated local cleavages. 'Ye are compelled to work as long as the necessity of your needy parents may require', he told the child operatives, 'or the cold-blooded avarice of your worse than barbarian masters may demand.'[120] The controversy issued out into organisation. While in 1831 Baines was building up the Whig Political Union, which held its first meeting in December 1831, and his Association for the Return of Liberal Members to Parliament, Oastler was creating his network of Short Time Committees, consisting almost entirely of operatives in local mills and workshops.

Leeds was a centre of both movements, and the divergence between them was marked from the start. The parliamentary reform issue gained widespread support in February and March 1831, just at a time when a 33-week strike at Gott's works focused attention on working-class questions;[121] and the Union leaders, among them Joshua Bower, a rich glass manufacturer, had a way with the crowd. Yet in April 1831, when Parliament was dissolved and Grey appealed to the country, Oastler, backed by the Tory *Leeds Intelligencer*, used the occasion to issue a *Manifesto to the Working Classes of the West Riding* which made no mention of parliamentary reform at all, but which urged the workers to demand from all candidates at the election a straight pledge in favour of a ten-hour day. In the autumn of 1831, when the reform crisis reached a new peak, Baines stirred up Leeds Whigs and reformers in general to new endeavours,[122] while Oastler, goaded on by the defeat of Hobhouse's Factory Bill in the House of Commons, increased the momentum of the factory agitation. Hobhouse wrote to Oastler that he regretted to perceive that the discussion on the factory system was mixed with party politics in Yorkshire and 'more especially in the town of Leeds',[123] but the letter merely reinforced Oastler's growing sense that he had raised in the factory questions issues not of philanthropy but of political action.[124]

In the light of this divergence between middle-class parliamentary reformers and working-class factory reformers, a key position was obviously held by working-class political reformers in the town. They formed a quite distinct group which had been created between 1819 and 1830, particularly by James Mann, a bookseller who had previously been a cloth-dresser, and whose house as early as 1819 was described as 'the headquarters of sedition in this town'.[125] They supported a political programme based on universal suffrage rather than an economic programme based on machine-breaking or strikes, for, as they put it, to build unions of trades was 'only like lopping the branches of a cornel tree, leaving the corrupting root to strike forth with greater strength than before'.[126]

As late as September 1831 this Radical group was prepared to devote most of its energies to the parliamentary reform question, and even to provide speakers on a common platform with the supporters of Baines. But Baines strongly disliked universal suffrage, the ballot and annual parliaments,[127] which Mann and Foster, the two leading Radicals, put into the forefront of their programme. At the first important meeting of the Radicals on the eve of the crisis in September 1829, Baines, who was present, warned them not to meet in holes and corners, but to unite in a common cause with all other reformers. A few days later he pronounced them 'wholly unfit to take the lead in the promotion of any great national measure'.[128] The operative Radicals were fairly quiet from October 1829 to March 1830,[129] although they maintained their newspaper, the *Leeds Patriot*, with John Foster as editor, and offered long-distance support to the Birmingham Political Union.[130] In February they attacked the limited reform, proposed by Russell, of separate representation for Leeds, Manchester and Birmingham as an attempt 'to divide the reformers generally and confer no benefits on the people at large'. In March they moved amendments at a Whig public meeting, and in May they held a mass rally on Hunslet Moor, and proposed the formation of a Political Union, not on the lines of the Birmingham Political Union, but on those of the Metropolitan Political Union, with an elected council of not more than fifty members.[131] The vicissitudes in the progress of the Reform Bill through Parliament brought them into some sort of rough-and-ready agreement with the Leeds Whigs, and they appeared on the platform at the big Whig rally on 26 September 1831.[132]

This was the last time, however, that they were closely associated with the Whigs. When Hunt visited Leeds on 3 November 1831, he commended Sadler to the political Radicals despite his Toryism, and claimed that 'he would be ten thousand times more disposed to assist the working classes than the briefless barrister Macaulay'.[133] A fortnight later the Radicals set up a distinctive working-class Political Union, and from the moment of its formation they interested themselves as much in the Irish question and the Ten Hours Bill as in parliamentary reform. When the Grey government fell in May 1832, instead of supporting the fallen administration, they attacked it as a coalition to deprive the operative classes of all political influence for ever.[134]

In the meantime, the Leeds Tories more than met the Radicals half-way. As early as March 1831, Baines wrote to his son of Hunt's 'flirtation' with the Tories and his allegation that the working classes had been betrayed by the Reform Bill, and claimed that 'wonderful to be said, the Honourable William Duncombe, one of the [Tory] members for Yorkshire, is of that opinion'.[135] The Tory *Leeds Intelligencer* held out an open hand to the Radicals,[136] and Sadler himself went out of his way to meet them. The *Intelligencer* claimed that 'if a still lower class of voters were admitted under the Bill, Mr Sadler's supporters would be more than proportionately increased'.[137]

The result of these Tory-Radical alignments and the alienation of local operatives from the cause of parliamentary reform was a bitter election contest in Leeds in December 1832. Macaulay and Marshall, the Whig candidates, were as violent in their language as their single Tory opponent, Sadler, whose 'coquetry with the Radicals' did not help him in middle-class circles.[138] If Marshall, the wealthy flax spinner, was attacked as a capitalist, possessed of the 'mechanical power' which 'crushed the operatives, men, women and children to the earth',[139] Sadler was attacked by Macaulay as 'a convenient philanthropist', rather like 'a certain wild beast called the Hyaena who, when it wishes to decoy the unwary into its den, has a singular knack of imitating the cries of little children'.[140]

Despite the noise and bustle of the Tory-Radical alliance in Leeds[141] – and Sadler's personal canvas – the Whig £10 householders triumphed, polling heaviest in the out-townships and saving themselves from becoming the laughing stock of England by giving their votes at their first election to Sadler, 'the man who STROVE TO PREVENT US HAVING ANY VOTES TO GIVE'.[142] Although Sadler received 932 plumpers as against Marshall's twenty and Macaulay's twenty-one, and although he received 44 per cent of the votes cast, he was at the bottom of the poll.[143]

The result of the election was a victory, if not a triumph, for the Whigs, but it provoked interesting Tory reactions. At a dinner the Tories gave on 21 December, Sadler explained the defeat in terms of the narrowness of the new franchise, which still excluded the operatives. 'The people are entirely without representation,' he said. Oastler employed the same theme at Wakefield on 20 December, when he denounced the £10 franchise, and looked forward to a wider suffrage to secure factory reform. He hoped that rejuvenated Toryism would have its part to play in such a movement. 'Now Tories, what say you? Will you join the Whigs against the people? If so, you are a set of unprincipled knaves, and deserve to meet with the first reward of roguery. Will you go forward then with "the people" and thus save the nation from anarchy and blood?'[144] The Reform Bill had settled nothing, but it had provided a challenge. The challenge in his view was not political but social,[145] and the hope for the future lay not in abstractions, but in practical measures to deal with the condition of England.

This should not be the last word on Leeds. The next Tory candidate in 1834, Sir John Beckett, was an impeccable local banker, although he once replied in answer to a question at the hustings, that he would have no difficulty in saying that he did not object to operatives meeting together to prevent wage cuts and to defend social rights.[146] Of the successful candidates in all three constituencies in 1832, only Macaulay could be described as non-provincial, and he resigned in December 1833 when he was offered a post in India. He had shown how representative his Whiggery – or at least his Whig rhetoric – was when he had written in the *Edinburgh Review* in 1829 long before it was certain that the Whigs would return to power, 'Our fervent wish ... is that we may see such a reform of the House of Commons as may render its votes the express image of the opinion of the middle orders of Britain.'[147] His Whig instincts were more clearly demonstrated when he objected to the choice of Edward Baines Senior as his nominated successor: 'he is a highly respectable man – liberal, moderate, honest and intelligent; and these qualities have made him very powerful and useful in his own town. But he has not quite so much polish or literature as the persons among whom he will now be thrown.'[148] The Whigs might flirt with urban 'provincialism', but their own predilections – and anticipations – were different.

V

In each of the three cities discussed in this article, there was a tendency for the local problem to colour the approach to reform politics – in Birmingham, currency; in Manchester, corn; in Leeds, machinery and the length of the working day – and in each of them, too, there was a tendency to find local people to argue the relevant case. The alignments on these issues corresponded closely to the facts of local social structure, but successful change in each case demanded a national rather than a local remedy, and there was no doubt as to whether it would be immediately – or ever – applied. In each city the demand for parliamentary reform was positive, in the sense that men asked clearly and with determination, 'What would parliamentary reform *do*?' As Molesworth pointed out in his *History of the Reform Bill*, written in 1865, 'the clamour for reform sprang not so much from a sense of the theoretical imperfections of the then existing state of things' as from a sense of distress and an expectation of alleviation and improvement.[149]

Attwood expressed the same point of view in 1832 itself.

> It was often said that it was the Duke's declaration against reform which drove him from office, but with this opinion he differed. It was at least the distress of the country which primarily led to the agitation of Reform, and had it not been for that, his Grace's declaration, however abrupt and unjustified, would have had no consequences. Distress was the cause – Reform the effect.[150]

Reform itself needed to be justified by its results. 'The Reform Bill can no more rectify our ills than it can have caused them. It is from a different system after the Reform Bill is disposed of that we are to expect any improvement in our affairs.'[151]

Considered against such a background of reform politics in these cities, the Whig ministers in London appear not as masters of the situation, but merely as the temporary directors of it. They were anxious to acknowledge the place of trade and manufacture in a changing British economy by enfranchising cities and towns which represented new interests,[152] and to attach the middle classes to the established institutions of the country by making them consider the House of Commons as an ultimate tribunal where grievances could be discussed and remedied.[153] When they talked in such terms and not in terms of traditional abstractions, they were nearest to the opinion of the cities,[154] but they were also submitting themselves to a subsequent scrutiny and a possible judgement. 'With the people, the Whigs may continue to rule', was a popular cry, 'without them, they are doomed to destruction.'[155]

This was only one perspective, however. The cities were at one in their provincial pride, but they did not bring any coordinated action to bear on government between 1829 and 1832. Even in Birmingham, which, unlike Manchester or Leeds, acquired a position of primacy at this stage in nineteenth-century political history largely because the Political Union succeeded in becoming 'a great partnership and fraternisation of the class', the Union 'never transcended its provincial character'.[156] Whether or not the currency was deflated, the sense of moral power was often inflated. Thus when Elihu Burritt claimed that 'Birmingham was not merely the accidental scene of one of the greatest political events in English History. It organised the force that produced the event,'[157] he was more of an inflationist than Attwood. During the Reform Bill struggle itself the Union had relatively little contact with other Political Unions except in the West Midlands area. As for the Whigs, they could bring the Political Unions into their political calculations, but they saw the future of politics quite differently and ultimately in a conservative way.[158] By contrast, for the popular Radicals, 1832 could not be a final measure, and optimism was difficult to quench. Within a year of the passing of the Act, while Whigs in London talked of finality, Oastler was able to stir up Yorkshire,[159] Doherty to create a National Regeneration Society,[160] and Attwood, basing his hopes on a million unemployed within the foreseeable future, to dream of vast new changes. Indeed, in 1836, when the succession of good harvests which favoured the Whigs came to an end, Attwood was remarking:

Men do not generally act from abstract principles, but from deep and unrewarded wrongs, injuries and sufferings. The people of England never came forward to advocate the abstract principles of Major Cartwright . . . but when they saw and felt that the yoke of the boroughmongers was laid heavy upon them they very easily and very quickly shook it off. When their employment and wages were gone and the boroughmongers stood convicted before the country, the boroughmongers were very quickly cashiered. Now when the next opportunity comes, a further reform of Parliament will be a much quicker and easier operation.[161]

Time was quickly to prove how wrong he was.

NOTES

1 G. J. Holyoake, *Sixty Years of an Agitator's Life* (1892), p. 42.
2 Newcastle Public Library, *Outlines of a Plan for a Northern Political Union* (1831). The Grand Northern Union was described in a report of the Council of the Birmingham Union as 'the only one to compete with the Birmingham Union in importance'.
3 See A. Briggs (ed.), *Chartist Studies* (1960), and below, p. 229.
4 See above, pp. 165-6.
5 Birmingham Public Library, *Report of the Proceedings (of the Birmingham Political Union)*, 7 May 1832.
6 *The Political Register*, 22 June 1833.
7 *Report of the Proceedings*, 17 May 1830.
8 See above, pp. 164.
9 *Hansard*, vol. XLI, col. 1097. In October 1827 the Members for Warwickshire themselves confessed that while they 'had always endeavoured to do the best in their power to further the interests of Birmingham ... they felt that their knowledge of various subjects connected with the manufactures of the place was defective'. (*Birmingham Independent*, 4 October 1828.)
10 e.g. *The Bradford and Wakefield Chronicle and General Advertiser*, 6 August 1825: 'It would be the very height of absurdity for the representative of such a county as Yorkshire to know nothing of woollen manufacture, to be ignorant of what might augment or what might diminish the staple trade of his constituents; so in a farming district it would be a palpable piece of folly to choose a representative whose knowledge of agriculture was confined to the distinguishing of oats from barley or peas from beans.'
11 As early as 1692, it was because of the action of Newdegate, the Member for Warwick, that Birmingham secured its first big gun contract. For the significance of the 1774 election, see the thorough study by J. Money, *Experience and Identity, Birmingham and the West Midlands, 1760-1800* (1977), esp. Chapter VII. In 1780, the 'Manufacturers of Birmingham, a broader group than the so-called 'Manufacturing Gentry', sent a petition to the Earl of Dartmouth claiming that 'the various commercial regulations, so frequently made by the legislature, affect the trade and manufacturers of this city very much and render it an object of great importance to its inhabitants that gentlemen may, if possible, be chosen for the county who are connected with the people, and not entirely uninformed of the particulars in which their interests consist' (Hist. MSS. Comm. *13th Rep.* Appendix, part I, p. 253; *Victoria County History of Warwickshire*, vol. II, p. 227).
12 In 1818, *The Wolverhampton Chronicle* (10 June 1818) reported a meeting of Bridgnorth electors resident in Birmingham, which recommended the choice of the Tory candidate, 'being persuaded that the interests of the town of Birmingham are materially connected with the

proper representation of the Borough of Bridgnorth from whose members they have for many years received on all occasions, when called for, the most important services'. At the election of 1830, £357 was paid by the two Whitmore candidates for the conveyance of voters from Birmingham to Bridgnorth and their return.

13 H. Heaton, *The Yorkshire Woollen and Worsted Industries* (1920), p. 226.

14 Carefully organised economic pressure was applied in Manchester in 1774 against the fustian tax, and in Manchester and Birmingham in the 1780s. See Witt Bowden, *Industrial Society in England towards the End of the Eighteenth Century* (1925), and A. Redford, *Manchester Merchants and Foreign Trade* (1934). In the 1820s the avowedly non-political Chamber of Commerce in Manchester memorialised the Board of Trade, sent letters to ministers and petitioned Parliament. As markets widened and problems increased in range, such intermittent economic pressure seemed inadequate.

15 James Ogden, *A Description of Manchester by a Native of the Town*, reprinted in *Manchester, A Hundred Years Ago* (1877), p. 93.

16 See above, p. 142.

17 Burke's defence of virtual representation had specifically mentioned Birmingham. 'Is Warwick or Stafford,' he asked in 1782, 'more opulent, happy or free than Newcastle, or than Birmingham?' (*Works*, VI, pp. 149-50). In 1817 a Manchester pamphlet stressed the same line of argument: 'Every Member of Parliament is a Representative of the People at large, and the members of Newton, near Warrington, where there are only 20 electors, as much represent me as the members of Lancashire, where there may be 20,000 electors' (*The Speech of John R., Schoolmaster, residing at a Village near Manchester* (1817) p. 5). Cp. a Birmingham speech by an old inhabitant in 1827: 'as for the representation itself, a greater curse could not be entailed on the town: through the members of the adjacent counties the town was virtually represented' (*Birmingham Journal*, 10 January 1827).

18 *Manchester Guardian*, 19 May 1827.

19 ibid., 27 April 1827.

20 *Wheeler's Manchester Chronicle*, 27 May 1827.

21 *Aris's Birmingham Gazette*, 25 June 1827, advocated reform as a 'boon calculated to confer most important benefits on the town'. Yet later in the year it claimed that 'we are at present well represented in Parliament by our county members .... There were no members in the House of Commons of more independent principles.' (29 October 1827.)

22 Manchester Representation Committee, *Minutes*, 12 November 1827 (*Manchester Central Library*).

23 *Manchester Guardian*, 8 December 1827.

24 *Hansard*, vol. XVIII, col. 684.

25 *Birmingham Journal*, 9 February 1828.

26 *Report of the Proceedings*, 17 May 1830.

27 Letter to Mrs Attwood, 13 October 1831. (Wakefield, *op. cit.*, p. 184.

28 W. Hawkes Smith, *Birmingham and its Vicinity as a Manufacturing and Commercial District* (1836), p. 16.

29 L. Faucher, *Études sur l'Angleterre* (1856 edn), vol. I, p. 495. See also A. Fox, 'Industrial Relations in Nineteenth-Century Birmingham', in *Oxford Economic Papers*, New Series, vol. 7 (1955).

30 See above, p. 154, and below, p. 237.

31 Furthermore, if before 1830 'the rights and interests of the industrious classes in the community had been represented in Parliament ... the cause of the distress would have been ascertained, and the proper remedy would have been applied without delay' (*Report of the Proceedings*, 25 January 1830). This was a very dubious link in Attwood's chain of argument.

32 As early as 1816 Attwood had warned Liverpool of the local dangers being increased because of 'the facility of obtaining firearms and other offensive weapons' (Wakefield, *op. cit.*, pp. 59-60). Cp. HO/43/24/449; 41/1/43. In January 1817 the 5th Dragoons were quartered in the centre of the town.

33 *Report of the Proceedings*, 17 May 1813.

34 During the first phase of the Political Union, he professed himself a Tory as he had done earlier. 'The Whigs had done nothing to forward the cause of public liberty. He had never belonged to that party – he was always a Tory, and a real friend to the privileges of the People' (*Report of the Proceedings*, 25 January 1830). See below, p. 225.

35 See above, pp. 161, 176.

36 Many of the Whigs were lukewarm or even hostile to the Political Union. As late as October 1831 a resolution (at a public meeting) thanking Attwood and the Political Union was withdrawn on the grounds that 'it would create disunion'. (*Report of the Town's Meeting*, 20 October 1831.)

37 *Report of the Proceedings*, 13 December 1830.

38 ibid., 25 January 1830: *Birmingham Journal*, 12 November 1825.

39 ibid., 20 May 1833. Muntz went on to say that 'he detested party men of all kinds; but of the two give him Tories rather than Whigs, not that he should be satisfied with them when he had got them.'

40 *Birmingham Journal*, 10 January 1835.

41 *Report of the Proceedings*, 17 May 1830. Bibb, who for a time sat on the Council of the Birmingham Political Union, was later Treasurer of the West Bromwich Political Union.

42 *The Substance of the Extraordinary Proceedings of the Birmingham Political Council*, 3 July 1832.

43 Edmonds, who might have been a rival to Attwood, did indeed announce in March 1832 that he would stand for Parliament (H.O. 52/20, *The Poor Man's Paper*, printed by J. Russell; *Birmingham Journal*, 28 July, 11 August 1832; *The Wasp*, 14 July 1832; J. Scholefield, *Statement of the Circumstances between Mr. Edmonds and Mr. Scholefield* (1832)).

44 It was set up by extremists who 'are tired of the Council and their leader' (H.O. 52/20, Thomas Lee to Melbourne, 25 October 1832). Disagreement between Attwood and Henry Hunt went back to January 1831 (*Birmingham Argus*, February 1831). Hetherington visited Birmingham on 29 October 1832 and addressed a meeting, where Hunt also was present and Dr Wade was in the Chair. Salt, one of the pioneers of the Political Council, tried to speak, but was howled down by the crowd (Lee to Melbourne, 29 October 1832; *The Poor Man's Guardian*, 29 October, 3 November 1832). Although the new Union was of little importance locally, the Committee of Non-Electors argued forcefully that 'we, the source of all Property, and the greatest in point of number, are by that Bill [the Reform Bill] denied the exercise of our Elective Rights' (*Declaration of the Committee*, August 1832). It pressed for universal suffrage, vote by ballot, annual parliaments, the abolition of property qualifications, and 'the reduction of military power'. It did not mention the currency issue, but it disclaimed any hostility towards the Birmingham Political Union 'to which association many of us belong'.

45 For Wade, see T. H. Lloyd, 'Dr Wade and the Working Class', in *Midland History*, vol. II (1973).

46 *Report of the Proceedings*, 7 May 1832.

47 *The Birmingham Journal* (27 December 1836) admitted of the currency question, 'for its complicated and apparently distant nature, there are hardly ten men in the House that understand and take an interest in its discussion; and to the people it is a sealed book altogether.'

48 See above, p. 166.

49 High prices, according to Charles Jones, one of the leaders of the 'Birmingham School', showed that trade was prosperous, and that production and consumption were keeping pace with each other. Paper currency had maintained prices high until 1820. 'The paper currency has now for years past been perfectly assimilated to the wants of the country and has proved itself a most valuable friend, causing almost all ranks and descriptions of men to flourish, and this it has done during the pressure of wars, taxes and changes unparalleled in the history of this country' (*The Saturday Register*, 19 February 1820). For the views of the *Manchester Guardian* on currency reform, see an article of 20 June 1829 describing as 'objectionable' any attempt by a country to devalue its currency.

50 Attwood's *Observations on Currency, Population and Pauperism* (1817) had been addressed to Arthur Young, and in 1827 he was in correspondence with Sir John Sinclair, former President of the Board of Agriculture; and when he visited London in July 1830 he regretted that he had no time to call on Western 'or any other of my political friends'. From the other side, as late as 1844, Newdegate, the Warwickshire Tory squire, told the Commons that the views of the Birmingham economists were almost identical with his own (*Hansard*, 3rd series, vol. LXXV, col. 830). See also, F. W. Fetter, *The Development of British Monetary Orthodoxy* (1965).

51 *Report of the Proceedings*, 4 July 1831. Muntz did not favour universal suffrage: he believed more could be done for the poor by relieving taxation (*Report of the Proceedings*, 7 May 1832).

52 ibid.

53 He wrote to his wife, 27 April 1820, that they 'were fit for nothing, but *dumb sheep*, to be shorn at the will of their masters'. In 1831, he claimed 'that knowing much of the middle and little of the higher and lower orders of society, the middle was the worst of the three ... as full of vice as the egg is full of meat ... servile to our superiors, arrogant to our inferiors, jealous towards each other, indignant towards all'. (*Report of the Proceedings*, 4 July 1831).

54 'The great limbs and interests of the country ... are *starving* for the want of money, at the very moment that half the circulation of the kingdom is determined in *stagnant masses* into what is called the money market, in order to *gorge* the monied interest.' (ibid.)

55 *Place Papers*, Add MSS 27, 789, f. 75.

55a *The Political Union Register*, March 1832.

56 'All the other unions look to the Birmingham one', wrote J. S. Mill, 'and that looks to its half dozen leaders, who consequently act under the most intense consciousness of moral responsibility' (*Letters of J. S. Mill*, vol. I, p. 7, 20 October 1831). A hostile critic commented, 'England is now actually governed by the Political Unions. The Parliament of Birmingham issues edicts' (*The Bristol Riots*, by a citizen (1832), p. 26).

57 *Place Papers*, Add MSS 27, 789, f. 127.

58 For the abortive effort of Edmonds to secure nomination as an independent reformer, see above, p. 114.

59 *Aris's Gazette*, 24 December 1832. 'Persons of all ranks from the highest to the poorest were to be seen participating in all the delirium of extatic [*sic*] joy' when Attwood returned to Birmingham after the passing of the Reform Bill (*An Account of the Public Entry given by the Inhabitants of Birmingham to Thomas Attwood Esq.*, 28 May 1832). 'The final knell of despotism had tolled.'

60 Attwood's *Address to the Electors*, 29 June 1832.

61 G. R. Porter, *Tables of the Revenue, Population etc. of the United Kingdom* (1836), vol. II, p. 102.

62 'Man', John Davies told the Mechanics' Institution in 1827, 'must be the architect of his own fame' (*Wheeler's Manchester Chronicle*, 20 October 1827).

63 Cp. E. C. Tufnell, (1834), who argued (*Character, Objects and Effects of Trades Unions*) that 'where a large capital is invested in machinery and buildings, the workmen are able to exercise a much greater control over their employers'; and John Doherty's *Address to the Operative Spinners* (1829), where he argued that the owner of a large factory had the power to make large numbers idle.

64 HO/40/27, The Borough Reeve and Constables to the Home Office, 26 May 1830. Doherty later stated that he had been influenced in his dreams of a large-scale trade union organisation by the Catholic

Association (*Select Committee on Combinations*, vol. VIII (1837-8), Q.3446).

65 *The Manchester Guardian*, 17 February 1830.

66 At a meeting in October 1826 a speaker claimed that the purpose of parliamentary reform was 'to secure the labourer the fruits of his own labour ... and to every British subject a full participation in all the privileges and advantages of British citizens' (*Wheeler's Manchester Chronicle*, 28 October 1826).

67 HO/52/18. *A Letter from One of the 3730 Electors of Preston to his Fellow Countrymen*, enclosed in a letter from Lowe to Melbourne, 3 December 1832. See also Doherty's pamphlet, *A Letter to the Members of the National Association for the Protection of Labour* (1831).

68 J. P. Kay, *The Moral and Physical Condition of the Working Classes employed in the Cotton Manufacture of Manchester*, 2nd edn (1832), p. 26, and E. Baines, *The History of the Cotton Manufacture in Great Britain* (1835), p. 446. There is a very full and thorough recent study by R.G. Kirby and A.E. Musson, *The Voice of the People: John Doherty, 1798-1854* (1975). *Wheeler's Manchester Chronicle*, 15 August 1818, stressed that 'no class of people' in the country had enjoyed 'such constant and uniform employment for the last twenty-eight years'.

69 The number of handloom weavers in the cotton industry did not begin to decline until after 1830. Indeed, until that date their numbers probably increased (S.J. Chapman, *The Lancashire Cotton Industry* (1904), p. 28). See also D. Bythell, *The Handloom Weavers* (1969).

70 *Place Papers*, Add MSS 27, 792, f. 15.

71 *Manchester Guardian*, 12 June 1830.

72 A meeting was held in August at which cautious middle-class merchants, like Mark Philips, who later became first Member of Parliament for Manchester, talked for the first time of thoroughly 'purging the House of Commons', and reforming the present system of representation (*Manchester Guardian*, 28 August 1830).

73 *The Manchester Gazette and Times*, 30 May 1829.

74 The group was always active in local politics, urging the need for cheap government, and allying itself with the important 'shopocracy'.

75 For instance, in 1815 the manufacturers opposed the Corn Laws, 'because they believed that raising the price of food would *raise the wages of labour*, and thus prevent their competition with the manufacturers of other countries'. (The same argument was repeated in 1825 by Garnett Prentice, *op. cit.*, pp. 70, 305).

76 W. Cooke Taylor, *Life and Times of Sir Robert Peel* (1842), p. 111.

77 *Cowdray's Manchester Gazette*, 25 January 1826.

78 Prentice, *op. cit.*, p. 352. Later, after Cobden had made a middle-class/working-class alliance seem more effective, the continuity of agitation between 1832 and 1846 was perhaps exaggerated. 'In other places',

wrote J. Reilly in his *History of Manchester* in 1861 (vol. II, p. 343), 'there was a praiseworthy impatience of the absurdity of permitting a mound of earth to send members to Parliament, while great manufacturing and commercial towns, each the centre and market of important districts, sent none; but nowhere more than in Manchester – perhaps nowhere so much – was the attention placed on the end, while endeavouring to obtain the means.'

79   H. Dunckley, *The Charter of the Nations* (1854), p. 13.
80   Letter from J. Deacon Hume to the editor of the *Morning Chronicle*, 12 December 1833.
81   *Manchester Guardian*, 22 January 1822.
82   A. V. Dicey, *Lectures on the Relation between Law and Public Opinion in England during the Nineteenth Century* (2nd edn, 1920), p. 179.
83   *Wheeler's Manchester Chronicle*, 25 August 1821.
84   A. Prentice, *Manchester*, p. 128. When two Manchester banks proposed to issue notes in 1821, a meeting of local manufacturers and merchants pledged itself not to accept local notes under any circumstances (*Manchester Guardian*, 25 April 1821). The local hostility to paper money went back to 1788, when Manchester businessmen suffered heavily as the result of the failure of a Blackburn firm responsible for an enormous note issue. See T. S. Ashton, 'The Bill of Exchange and Private Banks in Lancashire, 1790-1830', in *The Economic History Review*, vol. XV (1945).
85   A petition of the Manchester Chamber of Commerce, setting out the virtues of a metallic currency, can be found in its *Minutes and Proceedings*, vol. II, p. 408, 18 February 1826.
86   *Manchester Guardian*, 20 December 1828. The same paper, 25 April 1829, explained carefully that the depression in trade was unaffected by the currency. Cp. *The Speech of Thomas Attwood on the Distressed State of The Country*, 8 May 1829 (Birmingham, 1829), which explained local depression entirely in terms of the currency. After the *Manchester Guardian* commented unfavourably on this speech (16 May 1829), Attwood wrote to the newspaper stating his views (20 June 1829). The editor commented that an increase in the volume of currency to stimulate 'a return to 1825' could not be achieved without a diminution of its value, a flight of gold overseas, and a financial 'convulsion'.
87   A. Prentice, *op. cit.*, p. 37. It is clear that the Union existed in secret committee before it announced itself to the public, but it resolved not to call a public meeting until 500 members had been enrolled. (*Manchester Guardian*, 21 August 1830). The Whigs did not join the organisation until March 1831, when they were regarded with some suspicion by the more seasoned members.
88   Its activities were ignored by all the Manchester newspapers except the *Manchester Times*, which Prentice himself edited.
89   *Manchester Times*, 4 December 1830.
90   ibid., 27 November 1830. At the same meeting one working-class critic dismissed Prentice as a 'saucy Scotsman'.

91 *The Poor Man's Guardian*, 27 August 1831. It is not clear exactly when this Union was set up, or whether it preceded its London counterpart. Hunt acted as an intermediary in relations between London and Manchester, and visited Lancashire at the invitation of the Working Men's Union in April 1831. His objections to the Reform Bill were echoed by extreme Radicals in Manchester, like the one who wrote to *The Poor Man's Guardian* in April 1832 that the Reform Bill was 'the most illiberal, the most tyrannical, the most hellish measure that ever could or can be proposed' (11 April 1832).

92 HO/52/18, Foster to Melbourne, 22 January 1832. Foster claimed (HO/52/13, 27 November 1831) that the members of the Union were 'men of the lowest description, so much so that the general body of respectable workmen refuse all connection with them'. Yet it had 6000 members at this time, and Foster feared that it would become dangerous if it joined up with Doherty's Union.

93 HO/40/26, Foster to Melbourne, reporting a demonstration at Dukinfield, addressed by Doherty. The tricolour flag, he claimed, was carried, and some of the crowd were 'armed with pistols'. The Whigs were as alarmed by such demonstrations of working-class strength as the Tories had been. See Kirby and Musson, *op. cit.*, pp. 185-6.

94 *Place Papers*, British Museum, Add. MSS 27, 791 f. 242. Doherty launched his *Voice of the People* on 31 December 1830. He was bitterly attacked by Prentice (*Manchester Times and Gazette*, 4 December 1830). He included a considerable amount of political material, and in April 1831 the Cap of Liberty was introduced into the membership card of the National Association for the Protection of Labour.

95 A. Watkin, *Extracts From His Journal*, 1814-56 (ed. A. E. Watkin, 1920), pp. 162-3.

96 For some of the details, see L.S. Marshall, 'The First Parliamentary Election in Manchester', in the *American Historical Review*, April 1942.

97 HO/52/18, Foster to Melbourne, 11 December 1832.

98 ibid.

99 *Manchester Guardian*, 9 June 1832. The *Manchester Guardian* had been recommended by Foster to Melbourne in February 1832. 'I will give directions that you are supplied regularly with the *Manchester Guardian*, being a newspaper in good circulation, and the one in which there is in general the best information' (HO/52/18). By contrast, the Radical *Manchester Advertiser* characterised its rival as 'the common heap in which every purse-proud booby shoots his basket of dirt and falsehood . . . the foul prostitute and dirty parasite of the worst sections of the mill-owners' (quoted in C. Driver, *Tory Radical (The Life of Richard Oastler)* (1946), p. 321.

100 *The Political Register*, 31 December 1831.

101 ibid., 27 August 1831.

102 *Manchester Guardian*, 8 September 1832.

103 *Manchester Guardian*, 22 December 1832.

104 Hope had 257 plumpers and Lloyd 221. Philips had only twenty-eight,

yet he and Thompson shared as many as 1679 preferences and he even picked up 512 shared votes with Cobbett. He was head of the poll by almost 1000 votes.

105   Cobden to Tait, 3 July 1838. Cobden in his *Incorporate Your Borough* (1837) held up the example of the wayward reformers of Manchester: 'Follow the example of the men of Birmingham who are always foremost in the path of reform.'

106   *Manchester Guardian*, 29 December 1832.

107   E. Parsons, *The Civil, Ecclesiastical, Literary, Commercial and Miscellaneous History of Leeds*, vol. II (1834), p. 203.

108   L. Faucher, *Études*, vol. I, p. 401.

109   ibid.

110   *Leeds Intelligencer*, 20 September 1819.

111   *A Petition of Leeds Stuff Operatives*, 15 February 1830, presented to Parliament by M. T. Sadler. It had 500 signatures.

112   L. James, *History of the Worsted Manufacture in England from the Earliest Times* (1857).

113   L. Faucher, *Études*, vol. I, p. 384.

114   As the Lancashire squirearchy had been and still was in some areas in 1832. See W. Cooke Taylor, *Peel*, vol. I, p. 121: 'The Lancashire squires viewed the manufacturing population with a jealousy which may have been unreasonable, but certainly was not unnatural; they saw persons suddenly becoming their rivals in wealth and influence, by a course of industry and economy, which hereditary principles led them to despise; and they feared that these new men would displace the ancient families.'

115   *Leeds Mercury*, 1 July 1826.

116   E. Baines, *Life of Edward Baines* (1859 edn), p. 133.

117   In face of considerable opposition from loyal Yorkshiremen, like Cook and Vavasour, who wanted a Yorkshireman as candidate, and industrialists, who wanted one of their own order to protect manufacturing interests.

118   *Leeds Intelligencer*, 30 July 1829, reports a speech of Sadler at Newark, in which he urged the necessity of securing the support of the working classes on whom national prosperity depended.

119   *Mr Sadler, M.P., His Factory Time Bill and His Party Examined* (1832).

120   29 September 1830. This was the first of a series of letters. They are reprinted in C. Driver, *Tory Radical*.

121   J. Mayhall, *Annals of Yorkshire* (1830); *Leeds Intelligencer*, 10 February 1831; *Leeds Mercury*, 12 February 1831. The *Leeds Mercury* claimed that a reform petition was signed representing 'a large proportion of the wealth and respectability of the town'.

122   *Leeds Mercury*, 1 October 1831, described a large town meeting held on Monday 26 September, at which a reform petition was drawn up which obtained 21,423 signatures in two days.

123   *Leeds Intelligencer*, 24 November 1831. Factory reformers continued to be recruited from all parties.

124 Driver, *op. cit.*, esp. Chapter X.
125 *Leeds Intelligencer*, 27 September 1819.
126 ibid.
127 See E. Baines, *op. cit.*, p. 87.
128 *Leeds Mercury*, 19 September 1829.
129 Cobbett visited Leeds and delivered three lectures in January 1830.
130 There was some support in Yorkshire for the currency views of the Birmingham Political Union. Anti-Peel meetings were held in Huddersfield in December 1829, while at the same time the *Birmingham Argus* was praising Sadler (September 1829). There was a swing of Radical opinion after Cobbett visited the North of England in January 1830 and spoke of 'the present distress and the means to be adopted to alleviate it'. His vigorous attack on the Birmingham currency doctrines appears to have received considerable local support. Nevertheless, Attwood was writing to the *Leeds Patriot* (3 March 1832) attacking the 'deceitful and injurious doctrine of free trade' and describing currency as 'the master-evil'.
131 *Leeds Intelligencer*, 3 June 1830. At a meeting of the Radicals in May 1831 thanks were expressed to the Tory *Leeds Intelligencer* as well as to the *Leeds Patriot*.
132 *Leeds Mercury*, 1 October 1831.
133 *Leeds Intelligencer*, 10 November 1831. Hunt was being a nuisance to the Whigs at this time by arguing that 'the people', far from being 'all run mad with joy' by the Reform Bill, 'think they are deluded by it'. 'They thought they were going to get meat or clothes cheaper by it, but when they found it would have none of these effects, they were naturally disappointed at the whole measure' (*Hansard*, 3rd Ser., vol. III, 1245). For Tory use of this speech, see *The Advantages of Reform as Proposed by the Present Ministers* (1831).
134 See A. S. Turberville and F. Beckwith, *Leeds and Parliamentary Reform* (The Thoresby Society, 1943), p. 52.
135 Baines, *op. cit.*, p. 127.
136 As early as August 1829 it had expressed a strong preference for Radicals rather than Whigs.
137 *Leeds Intelligencer*, 15 September 1831.
138 See D. Fraser (ed.), *A History of Modern Leeds* (1980), p. 277. Sadler also lost ground on the moral issue of slavery to Macaulay.
139 *Leeds Intelligencer*, 26 July 1832.
140 Driver, *op. cit.*, pp. 200-1. It seems somewhat one-sided to suggest, as does Sir George Otto Trevelyan, that Sadler, 'smarting from the lash of the *Edinburgh Review*, infused into the contest an amount of personal bitterness that for his own sake might better have been spared' (*The Life and Letters of Lord Macaulay* (1900 edn), p. 182). The bitterness was not restricted to Sadler.
141 The Radicals in July 1832 thought of putting up a candidate of their own, George Wailes, to work alongside Sadler. Turberville and Beckwith, *Leeds and Parliamentary Reform*, pp. 57-8.
142 *The Tables Turned*, By an Elector (Leeds, November 1832). Cp.

Oastler's comment in Fraser, *op. cit.*, ' "The People" don't live in £10 houses.'

143 *Leeds Borough Election Poll* (Leeds, 1833); Marshall 2011, Macaulay 1984, Sadler 1590.

144 Driver, *op. cit.*, pp. 203-4.

145 A poster of the Leeds Committee of Operatives during the 1832 election stressed that while the benefits offered by the Reform Bill were 'problematical', unless Sadler's proposals for 'bettering the condition of the Agricultural and Manufacturing Poor of England and the Poor Irish are its fruits, the lower orders of society cannot be materially benefitted'.

146 Hill, *op. cit.*, p. 122.

147 Lady Trevelyan (ed.), *The Works of Macaulay*, vol. V (1876), pp. 328-9.

148 T. Pinney (ed.), *The Letters of Thomas Babington Macaulay*, vol. II (1974), p. 361.

149 W. N. Molesworth, *The History of the Reform Bill of 1832* (1865), p. 2.

150 *Report of the Proceedings*, 30 July 1832. Cp. H. Dunckley, *The Charter of the Nations*, pp. 47-8. In Manchester 'parliamentary reform was desired chiefly as a means of breaking the landlord's monopoly of the people's food, and bursting the fetters which bound our trade'.

151 *Report of the Proceedings*, 7 May 1832.

152 When the Commons went into Committee on the First Reform Bill, Russell explained that the ministers proposed as a counter-balance to the 'pure principle of population' to give representation to large towns possessed of 'manufacturing capital and skill' (*Hansard*, 3rd Ser., vol. III, col. 1519). In introducing the Second Reform Bill, Russell divided the newly enfranchised boroughs into those representing great interests like wool, cotton, coal and potteries, and those not immediately representing any interest but perhaps in consequence 'better qualified to speak and inform the House on great questions of general interest to the community' (*Hansard*, 3rd Ser., vol. IV, col. 338).

153 It was not only Brougham and Macaulay who wooed the middle classes as 'the most numerous and by far the most wealthy order in the community'. Grey, in 1831, referred to the middle classes 'who form the real and efficient mass of public opinion and without whom the power of the gentry is nothing' (*Correspondence of King William IV and Earl Grey* (1867), vol. I, p. 376).

154 Richard Fryer, a Wolverhampton reformer, put it very bluntly: 'All fiddle-de-de about Old Sarum – Stick to the Repeal of the Corn Laws and vote by ballot' (*Staffordshire Advertiser*, 11 December 1830).

155 *Birmingham Journal*, 2 June 1832.

156 Flick, *op. cit.*, p. 12.

157 E. Burritt, *Walks in the Black Country and its Green Borderland* (1868), p. 120.

158 See *inter alia* D.C. Moore, *The Politics of Deference* (1976) and J. Cannon, *Parliamentary Reform, 1640-1832* (1973).

159 See Driver, *op. cit.* (1946), Chapters 12-17. See Also J. T. Ward, 'The Factory Movement', in J. T. Ward (ed.), *Popular Movements c. 1830-*

1850 (1970) and J.T. Ward, *The Factory Movement, 1830-1855* (1962).
160 See Kirby and Musson, *op. cit.*, Chapter VIII.
161 *Birmingham Journal*, 12 November 1836.

8 Social Structure and Politics in Birmingham and Lyons, 1825-1848

The rapid increase in the size of towns and cities in the early nineteenth century amazed and alarmed traditional politicians and administrators in all the countries of Europe. They were afraid of large masses of people over whom they could at best administer a distant control – masses of people who did not fit into the traditional social pattern of small towns and predominant countryside. Disraeli, excited as well as afraid, was one of many who contrasted the 'mighty mysterious masses' of the swollen towns and cities and 'that free order and that natural gradation of ranks which are but a type and image of the economy of the universe'.[1] In 1831, after the July Revolution in France and while Britain was still struggling with its Reform Bill, the *Journal des Débats* in Paris warned that 'the barbarians who menace society are neither in the Caucasus nor on the Tartar Steppes; they are in the suburbs of our manufacturing cities.'[2]

The 'free order' was the more highly praised – often, of course, idealised – because it was so difficult to establish from above a satisfactory artificial order. Effective administration was experimental and expensive, effective police control was lacking, and so deep were many of the new cleavages in society that there were frequent attempts from below to meet force or the threat of force by counter-violence. 'Europe is becoming sick', wrote Wilhelm Riehl, 'as a result of the monstrosity of its big cities.'[3]

Since the large towns and cities – some of them new and considered 'without precedent' – provided extended opportunities for political discussion and action, they were often centres of subversive ideas which for Conservatives threatened the bases of constitutional government. 'The popular element will always be stronger in them than the Conservative or moderate.'[4] Some rebels were quite explicit about this, with Karl Marx, in particular, acknowledging in the *Communist Manifesto* that the bourgeoisie in creating enormous cities had rescued a considerable part of the population from 'the idiocy of rural life'. What Marx praised, Andrew Ure in his *Philosophy of Manufactures* attacked. Workers 'little versant in the great operations of political economy, currency and trade' were easily persuaded in an urban environment by 'artful demagogues' or 'leaders of secret combinations', that their 'sacrifice of time and skill' was beyond 'the proportion of their recompense, or that fewer hours of industry would be an ample equivalent for wages'.[5]

Both men's facts were right, though their values clashed. Subject to changed and changing routines, neither workers nor manufacturers were prepared to accept existing conditions without question. Inquiry led to protest, and protest could lead to revolt.

I

Birmingham and Lyons were two of the most important cities in Europe in the period between the end of the Napoleonic Wars and the revolutions of 1848, although neither place was a new product of the eighteenth-century industrial revolution. Lyons was, of course, an important Roman town, and the foundations of its industrial supremacy in the silk industry were laid in the sixteenth and seventeenth centuries.[6] At the beginning of the nineteenth century, the city had an estimated population of just over 100,000, at that time more than that of any English city except London. Although Birmingham was a small village when Lyons was a great town, and lacked corporate status until 1838, the foundations of its industrial importance were laid in the seventeenth and eighteenth centuries, and in 1801 it had a population of over 73,000.[7] The population of the city doubled during the next thirty years, and while that of Lyons and its suburbs increased more slowly (it actually fell between 1821 and 1831), by the 1830s in both cities and their surrounding areas large urban populations pressed closely together, distant from the national capitals.

These large urban populations played a most important role in English and French politics between 1815 and 1848. A comparative study of their development and influence in national politics raises several important problems. We can trace in the two cities taken together the apparently independent formulation of parallel ideas and the evolution of similar political tactics, and to an extent at least we can refer back such parallelisms and similarities to similar features in the social structure of the two cities and to similar dynamic factors affecting their social balance – particularly the impact of economic crises, sometimes the same or related economic crises. The differences and divergences which remain are just as interesting, however, as the similarities and parallelisms and may help to throw light on the bigger problem of the differences between so-called English evolution and French revolution throughout the period.

It is necessary to begin with a picture of the economic and social framework of Lyons and Birmingham and the strains to which it was submitted before examining the emergence of local leadership and the nature of some of the problems local leaders faced in trying to keep contact with their followers. This in turn raises the bigger problem of the relative importance of local initiative and outside stimuli in the working out of political ideas, organisation and action.

The dominating feature of the productive economy of Lyons in the early nineteenth century was its continuing dependence on a single industry – silk – a luxury industry, while the dominating feature of Birmingham was its dependence on the metal industries, a very wide range of industries, many of which claimed to be responding to need. Before discussing the obvious differences which sprang from this basic divergence, it is important to stress four features which the two cities had in common.

(1) Both cities contributed substantially to the national economy. In 1830, for example, the silk and silk products of Lyons are said to have accounted for half the city's income and a third of all French exports.[8] 'Within a radius of thirty miles of Birmingham', Samuel Timmins was to boast later in the century (though it was at least as true of 1836), 'nearly the whole of the hardware wants of the world are practically supplied.'[9] Whether or not these two local claims could be fully substantiated, they pointed to local perceptions of exceptional contributions both to the national and the international economy.

(2) Neither city was distinguished by big enterprises. The organisation of work in the silk industry in Lyons still followed eighteenth-century lines, what Le Play called *'fabrique collective'*, commercial concentration which so far had not brought with it industrial concentration. An attempt had been made in 1817 to found one big factory with 600 workers, but it was an exception during this period rather than the rule.[10] The economic and social structure of Lyons rested upon the small workshop. In 1834 only twenty-six *chefs d'atelier* (master weavers) in the rue Tolozan, packed with 1427 residents and 678 silk looms, out of 232, owned more than four looms: thirteen of them owned five, nine owned six, two owned seven and one owned eight.[11] They employed 227 resident journeymen. In Birmingham also, the characteristic economic unit was the small workshop, where the independent master reigned supreme. As late as 1843, the Commission on Child Labour reported that the typical Birmingham workshop consisted of only 6-30 workers.[12] Both Lyons and Birmingham lacked, therefore, the large-scale factory organisation which had already made such advances in Lancashire. Lyons had the new Jacquard loom, first displayed in 1804,[13] but no steam-engines. Birmingham had been the first centre of Boulton and Watt's great steam-engine partnership, proudly selling power to the world, but its own trades did not primarily depend on steam.[14]

(3) Workers in Birmingham and Lyons were relatively well-off – when in employment – compared with workers in other parts of England and France. Wages were higher in Lyons than they were in Lille or Mulhouse, and higher in Birmingham than they were in Manchester. In 1838, at the annual conference of the Association of All Classes of All Nations in Manchester, it was decided to move the headquarters of the Association to Birmingham on the grounds first that the workers there were enjoying higher wages, and second that they were politically more mature, 'ripe indeed for the sickle'.[15]

Their political curiosity had been commented on as early as 1823 when the *London Guardian* informed its readers that in Birmingham 'many a lean, unwashed artisan' would discourse upon political and economic topics 'quite as rationally as some of the theorists in higher places'.[16] The same maturity is evident in Lyons, where it has been estimated that around 70 per cent of male silk workers were literate in the late eighteenth century, and they played a key role in two insurrections in Lyons in 1831 and 1834.[17] Before dismissing the insurrection of November 1831 as a simple *émeute de faim* (hunger rising), it is important to consider, as Fernand Rude has so thoroughly done, the traditions, the pride and the organisation of the silk workers, their 'relative well-being', as he calls it, 'which favoured the development of action' and the birth of '*conscience ouvrière*'.[18] A 'spirit of independence' was evident there even before the French Revolution of 1789, and after the 1834 uprising two-thirds of the arrested workers could sign their names.[19] One of two working-class papers, the remarkable *Echo de la Fabrique*, a key source, was scornful about 'stupid' peasants and illiterate weavers who were willing to let others rule them.[20]

(4) The voice of the Birmingham and Lyons working classes was more then than the voice of hunger. Very frequently, however, it was the voice of unemployment. The existence of recurring unemployment was the fourth feature which the two towns had in common. Since they both produced for wide markets, they each felt the impact of price and employment fluctuations. The luxury trades of Lyons were often as hard hit as the varied trades of Birmingham, and in Lyons if the silk industry suffered there were few alternative means of employment inside the city. 'The unfortunate position of Lyons', wrote the Prefect of the Rhône in 1833, 'is that it has really only one industry and thus discontent here is never partial, but soon becomes general.'[21]

During the early nineteenth century, we can trace reasonably clearly – in general – the synchronisation of distress and unemployment in different places. In 1811, for instance, over 9000 people in Birmingham were in receipt of poor relief, and over 7000 looms in Lyons were idle.[22]

In 1817 a fall in the price of iron and a sharp rise in the price of wheat – the dangerous social contingency[23] – provided the setting for the first flickers of post-war Radicalism in Birmingham. At the same time, in Lyons, with less than half the looms employed, with the employed workers only working three or four days a week, and the price of wheat up from 46-64 francs a quintal, the town was full of what the Prefect called 'an indefinable uneasiness'. There was talk everywhere of 'meetings, plots and movements'.[24] The *Journal de Lyon* commented at this time on the similar atmosphere of unrest in England and France, the 'conspiracies of obscure men', 'the most gigantic projects and the most narrow means for achieving them, the most extravagant boldness and the most absolute ignorance.'[25]

The synchronisation continued. 1825 was a peak year in both countries. While the King's Speech in London was proclaiming that there never had been a period in the history of the country when all the great interests of the country were in so thriving a condition, a police bulletin in Lyons said that the city had never enjoyed more employment.[26] When the crash came in London, the *mal anglais* was transmitted from English to French markets. While merchants faced bankruptcy and workers unemployment, there was, not surprisingly, a sense of irritation. As the physician and economist L.R. Villermé was to put it, the *canuts* (silk men) 'pass rapidly from an excess of misery to prosperity and back again to distress'.[27] The stagnation was never cured until after the turn of the decade, and in the meantime in conjunction with bad potato harvests and a final rise in the price of wheat, it provoked a social crisis which was an important element in the background of the French Revolution of 1830 and the Reform Bill crisis in England from 1830-2.[28]

Unemployment coupled with the high price of food provided plenty of raw material for agitation in Birmingham and Lyons both at this time and in the period which culminated in 1848. Thomas Attwood always quoted with approval what 'Mr Cobbett used to say: "I defy you to agitate a fellow with a full stomach".'[29] Once the agitation had begun, the government was usually blamed for the existence of unemployment and hunger. As a Birmingham manufacturer wrote to Sir Robert Peel in October 1830, unemployment had produced 'a very general feeling of discontent among the middle and lower classes, and a disposition to attach blame to the Government for the privations they are experiencing'.[30]

The government was the villain of the piece both in England and in France, and this anthropomorphic conception of crisis, as Labrousse has aptly called it,[31] played an essential part in the revolutionary formula. As the first manifesto of the Birmingham Political Union put it in January 1830: 'The general distress which now afflicts the country, and which has been so severely felt at several periods during the last fifteen years, is entirely to be ascribed to the gross mismanagement of public affairs.'[32] Even after the Reform Bill of 1832 had been passed, a Birmingham correspondent of the Bank of England noted that the Political Union would never be dissolved until 'the restoration of the country to a state of permanent prosperity was first accomplished'.[33]

It is at this point that the important difference between the social structure of Birmingham and Lyons should be stressed. While the social structure of Birmingham favoured talk of middle-class co-operation with the working classes,[34] the social structure of Lyons made for social antagonism and conflict in deed as well as in talk.

The key figure in the economic and social life of Birmingham was the small master, owner of his own workshop, entrepreneur and merchant in one. The key figure in the economic and social history of Lyons was the master weaver, the *chef d'atelier*, 'a sort of superintending weaver', as John Bowring called him,[35] who, although he owned and worked looms and employed *compagnons*, only did so under the complete direction of the merchant, the *marchand fabricant, l'industriel véritable*.[36] It was the latter who bought raw material, had it prepared for the looms, furnished the designs, paid a piece-rate to the *chef d'atelier*, and sold the finished article. The *Echo de la Fabrique* put it clearly when it complained of 'the immoral and arbitrary exploitation of the *chef d'atelier* by the *marchand* ... who by virtue of the laws which govern us ... exploits the industry as he chooses'.[37]

This difference in social grouping in the two cities was of great importance. In Birmingham the limits of the class of small masters were not rigid or fixed. In times of crisis they might fail in their enterprises and become journeymen again.[38] Nor was there an established capitalist aristocracy, as there was, for instance, in Manchester.[39]

In Lyons there were many gulfs in a city described locally as 'glorious and unfortunate'.[40] The *chefs d'atelier* constituted an intermediate class between the real capitalists, the *marchands*, and the real dependent workers, the *compagnons*.[41] But the word *class* is a misleading word to apply to them. As Pierre Charnier, the mutualist leader, himself a *chef d'atelier*, said of them: 'the *canuserie* is subdivided, like society. It has its rich and its poor and its aristocrats and its humble subjects.'[42] Some *chefs d'atelier*, owning 8-10 looms, were intermediaries between *marchands* and *compagnons*. Others owning few looms were little better than *compagnons* themselves. There existed a marked hierarchy, with those owning more than four looms constituting an *aristocracie du métier*. 'They have their separate cafés', wrote Norbert Truquin, 'where they gather together and hold their meetings. Their women display incomparable pride'.[43]

This is the background against which we can examine economic programmes, political manifestos and forms of action in the two cities. While the tendency in Birmingham was to try to build up political organisations based on cooperation between the classes, the tendency in Lyons was for different groups to meet and organise separately.

In Birmingham, from 1811 to 1838, joint statements of grievances were often drawn up between masters and men in times of crisis. The propaganda of Thomas Attwood, suggesting currency reform to secure full employment and political tranquillity, which embodied a social philosophy of class co-operation, contrasted with the manifestos of *mutuellisme* drawn up in Lyons, where an attempt was made to secure through a system of lodges a united resistance of *chefs d'atelier* against *marchands*, chiefly to secure and maintain a wage *tarif*. But the early *mutuelliste* organisation, the Society of Mutual Duty, had another side. Although Pierre Charnier's first manifesto of 1827 insisted that 'the man who is poor is not a poor man',[44] it made no concessions to the *compagnons*, who were excluded from membership and denounced for their ever-growing 'insubordination'. The *compagnons* were indeed a volatile element in Lyons at this time, 'a floating population with no family ties with the *chefs d'atelier*'. They were described as 'easy to impress', and as 'adherents in advance to secret societies',[45] and they have their own organisation, the Society of Ferrandiniers, who called themselves 'the sons of Mutualism'.[46] Out of the confusion, Charnier dreamed of the restoration of harmony between all social classes.[47] Instead there was more confusion.

During the Lyons insurrection of November 1831, in some respects a joint working-class struggle against the refusal of many of the *marchands* to honour the wages *tarif*, *chefs d'ateliers* and *compagnons* played different roles. Although the *mutuellistes* had directed the early peaceful agitation, the *compagnons* played a leading part in the fighting, struggling 'with most determination'.[48] When the battle had been won, there were two rival centres of revolutionary leadership, the *Volontaires du Rhône* at the Town Hall, mainly backed by *compagnons*, and the *partie ouvrière* at the Prefecture, mainly backed by the *chefs d'atelier*.[49]

After initial concessions were offered to the workmen, the subsequent defeat of both the *chefs d'atelier* and the *compagnons* by the *marchands* polarised the social conflict. This indeed seemed to be the lesson of a new revolution. 'Businessmen made a revolution for themselves. We want to make a revolution for ourselves.'[50] Everyone tried to discover lessons with social import. For François Guizot in Paris, 'social questions, domestic questions, discussions of society' had joined 'political questions' in the aftermath of the July Revolution of 1830.[51] Events in Lyons fascinated the young Marx, and were seen by later historians as a chapter in the making of working-class solidarity, so that Tarlé could write in 1911 that 'the insurrection in Lyons in 1831 constituted a turning point in the history of the working class, not only in France but also in the whole world'.[52]

The fact that the 1831 rising was followed by a second uprising in 1834, the biggest urban uprising in France between 1830 and 1848, which lasted for six days and accounted for 300 lives, kept the spotlight on Lyons. Once again, moreover, uprising was strongly influenced by economic factors: the insurgent quarters 'tended to be those with working-class profiles'.[53] 'The workers of Lyons', wrote a Polish observer, 'did not rebel as Republicans but as workers united by a mutual interest.'[54] The Orleanist J.B. Monfalcon, a doctor and founder of the *Courrier de Lyon*, who claimed that the 1831 rising was 'industrial' and the 1834 uprising 'political', wrote that nonetheless both uprisings pitted the poor against the rich.[55] 'Our goal', wrote the *Echo des Travailleurs* in 1833, 'is social equality . . . a uniform condition of well-being . . . an integral development in all men of their moral and physical abilities. This does not yet exist.'[56]

Between the two risings there was continued discontent, although in Lyons, as in Birmingham, the years of improved employment and good harvests, 1832, 1833 and 1834, were characterised by economic rather than by political action. As Vidal complained in the *Echo de la Fabrique*, nothing had really changed except that whereas previously 'the big ate the little, now the little were eaten by the big'.[57] If some of the *chefs d'atelier* of Lyons were beginning to talk openly of a republic, it is also true that some of the republican membes of the *Société des Amis du Peuple*, particularly from the time of the publication in December 1831 of their tract *La Voix du Peuple*, were drawing nearer, at least in their propaganda, to the working classes of Lyons. The propaganda was pushed further by the *Société des Droits de l'Homme et du Citoyen* in 1833.

While the economic aspects of class conflict in Lyons were stressed both at the time and by later historians, the economic roots of the Political Union in Birmingham tended to be quickly forgotten. In particular, the social implications of the currency formula of Attwood, which had been the pivot of all his political tactics,[58] were ignored, and the political objectives and organisation of the Union alone remembered. The currency jungle was abandoned by the historians as it had been abandoned by the working classes, and was left only to the economists. Its historical importance as an instrument to help maintain class collaboration can only fully re-emerge in a comparative study of Birmingham and other cities.

II

It would be misleading to abandon a comparative study of Birmingham and Lyons at this point with an over-drawn black and white
contrast between the social tension of the one place, which has
fascinated historians, and the social peace of the other place, which
they have tended to ignore. There are three further paths of interesting exploration: (i) a study of the common elements of leadership,
organisation and ideology in early Birmingham and Lyons, before the
word socialism had passed into current usage; (ii) an account, however
brief, of changing leadership and the challenge of new doctrines;
and (iii) an examination of the interesting problem of the cross-
fertilisation of ideas.

To those in authority in England and France, there was something
alarming about the rise of powerful new leaders in the towns, but while
Englishmen, frightened of great crowds and torchlight meetings,
concentrated on the demagogic clamour of Attwood or O'Connor,
Frenchmen concentrated on the mystery and obscurity of unknown
men working underground in secret societies. Attwood knew, of
course, that English laws of 1795 and 1817 prevented the formation of
branches and correspondence with other societies, and he attached
great importance to openness. All the meetings of the Political Union
were open to the public and their proceedings published.[59] Attwood
welcomed crowds, not only at Newhall Hill meetings, and was happy
to advertise that actual membership of the Political Union had risen
from 2000 in May 1830 to almost 9000 in January 1831, and to over
10,000 two years later. 'The Union', he told a meeting in 1831, 'had
condensed the moral power of this great population and gathered it, as
it were, into an electric mass.'[60]

Effective power was in the hands of a Political Council with a
minimum size of thirty-six. Its *Rules and Regulations* approved in
January 1830 gave it the power to act and speak between annual
business meetings and it could add to its membership at any time. As
for the general membership, it was called upon 'to obey strictly all the
just and legal directions of the Political Council'.[61] At the same time,
obedience clearly rested both on emotional sympathy and shared
enthusiasm, which Attwood knew well how to mobilise.[62] Moreover,
the fact that the Union had taken local power and influence away from
an older Whig 'oligarchy' encouraged its Radical adherents to affirm
that it was 'an engine of great good in a local point of view'.[63]

In Lyons, where the fear of conspiracy was strong, not least because
of the activities of rival groups of revolutionaries and of foreign
refugees, Pierre Charnier's Society of Mutual Duty, often conceived as
conspiratorial by the authorities, was at first a secret society of

'Brothers', a 'worker masonry', and as it grew in size it retained its secrecy: those Brothers found guilty of divulging secrets were immediately expelled. It was formed like a pyramid with four cells headed by 'an Indicator'; and the Brothers recognised each other by repeating the motto 'Equity, Order, Fraternity, Indication, Aid, Assistance'. Two delegates from each of ten lodges formed a Central Lodge, and the Presidents of the Central Lodges formed the Grand Council.[64] A rank-and-file protest against the powers of the Council in 1833 led to the formation of an Executive Council and the election of a number of new officers of a younger generation.[65] It was this body which encouraged the proclamation of a general strike in February 1834. Its collapse – and the arrest of its leaders – led to the resignation of the Executive Council, but within two months it was to be followed by the second great uprising in April.[66]

The Birmingham Political Union, least of all its Council, would never have favoured an uprising in Birmingham. The emphasis was always on 'legality' – 'Peace, Law and Order' – and Attwood consulted lawyers to ensure that 'legality' was maintained, and changed the rules to suspend any member who did not conform strictly to the law.[67] There was a time in the autumn of 1831, however, after the House of Lords had rejected the Reform Bill, when it seemed as if the Political Union would turn to a different pattern of organisation, if not a different set of objectives. Discussions took place in its Council – in the wake of the Bristol riots of October 1831 – about a sub-division of the Union into branches and units (with officers) along quasi-military lines in order 'to render the physical powers of the Union available for the preservation of life and property'.[68] There was even talk of 'fighting for the King' in whom the reformers put their hopes (although there was explicit rejection of 'arming').

The plan was abandoned, yet whether or not it was 'merely a feint in the political warfare waging over the Reform Bill',[69] it clearly represented a threat to constitutional local authority; and in the wake of it, the government issued a proclamation against hierarchically organised associations and their claims. It had been genuinely alarmed by the Bristol riots, the talk of militant Political Unions, some of them far more extreme than that of Birmingham, and writings in the press, including *The Times*, which had called for a National Guard.[70] Political Unions of various types continued to spread, however, after November 1831, not through planned action on the part of Birmingham leaders (except in the Midlands),[71] to such an extent, indeed, that it was suggested that no place would be without one. There was a further burst of development in May 1832 – when the Reform Bill was again under threat – and the Birmingham Union held a massive meeting at which Attwood exclaimed that he would die rather than see the Bill rejected or mutilated. The huge crowd cheered and called out 'All, All.' This was said to have been the largest political demonstration ever held in Britain,[72] and after the King expressed his willingness to create new peers to see the Bill through, Attwood boasted that 'our Meetings in Birmingham have been like claps of thunder bursting over the heads of our enemies'.[73]

Disraeli spoke ironically of Attwood as a brainless Cleon bawling rampant folly at the pitch of his voice on the top of Newhall Hill. 'What', he asked, 'was the Great King on the heights of Salamis, or in the Straits of Issus, what was Gengis Khan, what Tamerlane, compared with Mr Thomas Attwood of Birmingham?'[74] There was undoubtedly an element of conceit in Attwood – and even his whisper was said to be 'theatrical'.[75] Yet such colourful rhetoric is as misleading as the Comte de Chabrol's picture of the emergence of a *conspiration de canaille* in Lyons.[76]

Much of the mystery disappears when one studies the documents. The new leaders of Birmingham and Lyons were often in fact men who only turned to mass politics because they found that that was the only way they could make people listen to them. Attwood began as a Tory, and his brother was a Tory MP at the time of the passing of the Reform Bill.[77] He resorted to mass politics only when the politics of private persuasion failed: 'I did not venture to come forward', he declared, 'until I fancied I saw the very foundations of society giving way, and that storms and troubles were arising.' Throughout the years from 1811 to 1829 he put his faith first in Peel, then in Liverpool, and finally in the Duke of Wellington, whom he was to see as the chief villain in May 1832. 'Our declaration against the Duke of Wellington', he was to say then, 'has sealed the doom of his party for ever.'[78] Disappointment and disillusionment were the instruments which changed Attwood from a Tory into a Radical, and long after he had gained the undisputed mastery of Newhall Hill, he continued to hold essentially conservative views about the nature of English society.[79]

Pierre Charnier, too, as Rude has shown,[80] was a convinced royalist and an adversary of political as well as of economic liberalism, pushed into politics by unsatisfied grievances.[81] At the end of his life, he admitted that he had conceived of *mutuellisme* as 'a working-class freemasonry, created in opposition to revolutionary freemasonry'.[82] His aim at first was not very far removed from that of the right-wing *Société des Amis du Roi et de la Religion*,[83] just as Attwood's aims as late as 1830 were warmly endorsed by the Tory monthly *Birmingham Argus*.[84] But Charnier soon realised, as Cobbett had realised, and as the Yorkshire factory reformer Richard Oastler later realised,[85] that in attacking an abuse, one was often attacking a system. 'Alas', Charnier wrote in 1856, 'the evil was without remedy, because the administration of 1827 was far from willing to back the simple silk-worker Charnier in an enterprise so gigantic as that of guaranteeing wages.'[86] Such dangerous enterprises drew Charnier increasingly into revolutionary circles. On his visit to Paris at the end of the rising of 1831, he mixed with the most republican deputies and agitators, and was regarded by the Paris Prefect of Police as 'really dangerous'.[87] Mauguin, the left-wing deputy, even went so far as to tell him, 'continue like that and you will be shot'.[88]

The story of the emergence and development of Attwood and Charnier is a familiar theme in the history of nineteenth-century Radical leadership. It has been described tersely and brilliantly by G. K. Chesterton in his portrait of Cobbett: 'The fools who put Cobbett in prison probably did believe they were crushing a Jacobin, when they were really creating one.' 'He refused emphatically to let sleeping dogs lie. It is not surprising that in the end he had the whole people in full cry after him.'[89]

Nonetheless, indifference and disenchantment – the fairy tale, to change the metaphor, of lambs turned into wolves or at least of sheep turned into lions – is only the beginning of the story of the leaders. Attwood and Charnier shared certain basic ideas. First, they both saw society, as St Simon did, as composed of *oisifs* and *travailleurs* or in more picturesque language, as a hive of bees and drones. Attwood loved the image, and used it constantly.[90] The *industrious* classes should secure political power. 'The ox is muzzled that treadeth the corn.' 'The public business is now become the best private business for every man to attend to. Without attention to public affairs, indeed, there is no security for private interests.'[91]

Second, they asserted alongside the duty to work, the right to work. Thirty years before the revolutions of 1848, Attwood separated the ideas of charity and the right to employment: 'Let no relief whatever be given to persons who are able to work; but let us have a legal right to demand work from establishments in every country.'[92] The same demand, advocated by Fourier and Considérant, was reiterated in the streets of Lyons. The widespread recognition that charity was not sufficient to maintain the social harmony of the new cities as it had so often maintained the social harmony of the countryside marked one of the biggest landmarks in nineteenth-century social thought. 'Man is at last compelled to face with sober senses his real conditions of life and his relations with his kind.'

It was these basic ideas and the failure of those in authority to listen to the panaceas of currency reform and *mutuellisme* – and not blind demagogy or ambition[93] – which provided the call to local leadership. But here we come across a big problem. Leaders must have followers, and Attwood and the *mutuellistes*, in order to build up powerful organisations in the towns, had to collect very varied materials. They had to fuse together a wide range of economically and socially discontented elements. The result was sometimes disturbing. Uneasy conservatives in Birmingham could dismiss the Political Union as made up 'in greater part of everyone that was in debt and everyone that was discontented'.[94] Attwood himself confessed that they were a 'most unruly flock', but recognised their energy and determination. Muntz candidly acknowledged the risks of handling such material, when he pointed out that it was only bad times which produced powerful popular agitations. 'It had always been an invariable political rule with him never to light a fire while the sticks were wet, for he knew by experience that he injured his lungs and blew the smoke in his face. Wait till the sticks are dry.'[95]

Meanwhile, a Lyons newspaper claimed that all 'associations have always been and always will be the refuge of malcontents', and applauded Fulchiron, a deputy for the Rhône, who had told the Paris Chamber that 'you cannot leave our most important cities and our great manufacturing centres under the dread of the sword of Damocles ... The ancients have said that the Muses need tranquillity, and I affirm that our industry wants it even more.'[96]

For shrewd leaders to handle and control urban material, even when the sticks were dry, emphasis always had to be placed on order, unity, solidarity and discipline. These values were stressed in practice before words like *solidarité* were clearly used as part of a political terminology.[97] The working out by the new leaders of an ABC of political action was far more difficult than the creation by thinkers of a new revolutionary vocabulary. Followers could deviate as well as withdraw from the struggles.

In Birmingham, Attwood imposed upon his organisation a discipline which not only kept it within the bounds of what he called the 'devil-trap laws',[98] but also maintained peace in the city. In Lyons, too, the *chefs d'atelier* needed a framework of social order even in a revolutionary situation, and Louis Blanc was right to note that during the 1831 uprising 'the city was never better guarded than during that astounding day of the 23rd of November'.[99] The workers themselves were unarmed, and they kept the peace. Theft and pillage were punished by death: a large store of francs, discovered in a government office, was locked away in safety: as far as possible the routine tasks of city government were carried on from the Town Hall.

Both Birmingham and Lyons contrasted with the old English city of Bristol, where there was the worst urban rioting in the country since the Gordon Riots of 1780.[100] The citizens there not only refused to enrol as constables before the riot but withheld their support after it had started.

Within the specifically English context, a body like the Political Union could provide order, where the Corporation of Bristol could not. This fact was realised at the time by two very different people: Lord Melbourne, the Whig Home Secretary, and the great utilitarian thinker, John Stuart Mill. 'I have felt much less fear from Birmingham or Manchester than I have from any town where there was a Corporation,' the former wrote, while the latter stated in October 1831 that he was convinced

> that we are indebted for the preservation of tranquillity to the organization of the people in Political Unions. All the other unions look to the Birmingham one, and that looks to its half dozen leaders, who consequently act under the most intense consciousness of moral responsibility, and are very careful neither to do nor say anything without the most careful deliberation.[101]

While leaders in both towns had to place the same emphasis on unity, solidarity and discipline, there was a complete difference in the political atmosphere, which they had to take into account. Birmingham Radicals and even Birmingham Chartists, whatever they wanted to do once parliamentary reform had been won, had a curiously circumscribed picture of parliamentary reform itself, though they fitted it into a continuous picture of English history as a whole:

> God is our guide! no swords we draw,
> We kindle not war's battle fires;
> By union, justice, reason, law,
> We claim the birthright of our sires.[102]

Attwood himself followed in an old tradition when he became Member of Parliament in 1832 after Birmingham won the right to elect two Members, and though he was never happy in Parliament, he never challenged its procedures.

In Lyons, by contrast, however united the *chefs d'atelier* were on their economic grievances, when they turned to politics they were torn by conflicting political philosophies, many of them pointing to new constitutions and new societies. There was a common recognition of a specifically French revolutionary tradition, particularly in and after 1834, but considerable uncertainty as to what form a new revolution should take. Between the July Revolution of 1830 and the insurrection of 1831, and on the eve of the 1834 uprising, tracts were distributed and placards posted advertising the rival merits of Carlism, republicanism, Bonapartism, St Simonism and a variety of miscellaneous programmes. During the insurrection of 1831, a pretender, Louis

XVII, made his appearance in the fighting, 'mixing with the people, directing efforts', as one of his supporters claimed,[103] while in the middle of the struggle a young man asked to be presented to Roguet with the words, 'General, I am the son of Napoleon the Great. Have me proclaimed Emperor and the firing will everywhere cease.'[104] The St Simonians, who were active there in 1832 and 1833, called the city 'the Manchester of the European continent',[105] and when John Bowring, who visited it, brought to the city Manchester's gospel of free trade, he prompted the same kind of attack on liberal political economy as working men were advancing in Manchester.[106]

In short, however much we can generalise about revolutionary situations in two cities, we have to bring in third cities and a spectrum of ideologies too. The colour of politics in Birmingham and Lyons was as different as much of the symbolism – the contrast, for instance, between the famous black flag of the Croix-Rousse bearing the words 'Live free in working or die in fighting' and the blue and tricolour banners which greeted Attwood on his triumphal return to Birmingham after the passing of the Great Reform Bill in 1832. In 1834 there was also a red flag on the steeple of St Polycarpe's Church in Lyons.[107]

Another difference between the two cities was the strongly international flavour of much of the political controversy in Lyons. The nearness of the city to the frontiers, the presence of a large number of foreign workers, the powerful international connections of the silk industry, the influence of the propaganda of the Carbonari, the organisation of the Volontaires du Rhône all provided interesting contrasts with Birmingham. It was the French city which looked forward to a golden age when 'all the peoples will be intimately linked together and will form only one chain in which every manufacturing town will be a link.'[108] Yet there was more internationalism in Birmingham at this time than is sometimes thought. Attwood was in correspondence with Lafayette and helped to found the Birmingham Polish Association. Prominent Poles appeared on the Union platform, and there was a strong anti-Russian flavour to many Union speeches, particularly following the Warsaw rising of 1831, which in any study of nineteenth-century Radical politics should be set alongside the Lyons rising. Some speakers in Parliament compared the Union with the Jacobins and the Carbonari.[109]

III

Attwood's hour of triumph was more long-lived than Charnier's, but both in Birmingham and in Lyons new leaders emerged during the late 1830s and new ideologies were worked out, reflecting disappointment with what had already been achieved. Nonetheless, there was working-class continuity in Lyons, and the working-class/middle-class adherence in Birmingham did not break up completely.[110] The *Echo de la Fabrique* disappeared after the 1834 rising – the *Echo des Travailleurs* had already gone – but new working-class papers appeared within a climate of repression. Attwood retained his hold, despite opposition,[111] on most working-class Radicals in Birmingham after 1832 at a time when conservatives, temporarily won over to the cause of reform, turned aside from 'the continued debates of a hundred petty legislatures ... the Political Unions'.[112]

The Union – in the opinion of one of Attwood's allies 'reposing, not sleeping'[113] – was suspended in 1834, but revived again in more democratic form in May 1837. Once again the economic climate was dark, with 'distress coming like a destroying angel',[114] the angel for whom Attwood was waiting, but this time there was less middle-class support. The Political Union was not 'the same kind of thing as that whose name it bears which had existed in 1832', one commentator stressed.[115] By then, Attwood was completely disillusioned with the practical results of 1832. There had been no change in currency laws and no re-orientation of national economic policy. Already in 1834 he had attacked 'the false, perjured and cruel Whigs', and two years later argued that with a million able-bodied unemployed in the country and a bad harvest or two, 'a further reform of parliament would be a much quicker and easier operation than it was in 1832'.[116]

Attwood, who had not been successful as a Parliamentarian, knew now that he would have to go further to meet the demands of the working classes than he had done in 1830, and consequently he planned his campaign with great care. In January 1836 he claimed that 'in a great cause, he was content to stand or fall with the workmen alone', even if the middle classes were against him,[117] and in December 1837 he demanded universal suffrage: the middle classes were 'strangled by pride and servility' and the working classes were the only hope.[118] In the same month the Union published an *Address to the Country* and joined forces with William Lovett's London Workingmen's Association. Birmingham thus provided part of the main initial driving force of Chartism,[119] and Attwood and the members of the new Council of the Political Union canvassed as hard as they could for the National Petition, drawn up by R. K. Douglas, the editor of the *Birmingham Journal*, which became a major document in early Chartism, as influential as the six-point Charter itself. There were differences from the start on currency questions, but Attwood tried, notwithstanding, in 1838 and 1839 to secure the cooperation of the trade unions and even took over the scheme of a 'Grand National Holiday', what would now be called a general strike.[120]

But there was now a wide and growing gulf in Birmingham between middle-class and working-class Radicals, the latter pushing forward their own programmes and searching for a new theory of the causes of distress. The currency formula, which had been useful in the years 1830-2 as an instrument of class unity, could now become an instrument of class division. The militant tactics of O'Brien, who thought Attwood a paper-money schemer,[121] and the oratorical fireworks of O'Connor, who dismissed currency talk as 'rag botheration',[122] were beginning to attract the Birmingham working classes more than the familiar and always somewhat abstruse talk of their own middle-class leaders.[123] In November 1838, O'Connor was cheered inside the holy of holies itself, the Council of the Political Union, and after the opening of the Chartist Convention, the divisions in Birmingham came to a head with the resignation of the Birmingham delegates. Attwood introduced the Petition to the House of Commons in June 1839, but was 'paralysed' when Russell in reply quoted from a working-class manifesto signed by every member of the Convention, denouncing his currency views. Attwood felt that 'out of my own camp a mortal weapon was directed against my heart.'[124]

In the same year, Attwood retired from Parliament, and Birmingham lost its position of primacy in the Radical movement. Indeed, despite attempts by Joseph Sturge in the early 1840s to build up working-class/middle-class understanding on a new foundation – repeal of the Corn Laws, along with the extension of the suffrage – confidence had been broken. There was working-class drilling in the back streets in 1840, and increasing contact between politically-active skilled workers in Birmingham itself and the impoverished and more militant metal workers in the Black Country just outside. Socialist ideas were current within a Chartist context. Attwood never recovered his influence, though he never stopped writing, and when after a long illness and retirement he died in 1856, it was not easy to collect subscriptions to build him a statue.

By then, Europe had passed through its year of revolutions (and into counter-revolution) with Britain spared both. Between 1834 and 1848 the silk workers of Lyons joined many utopian causes. There was a group of Fourierist Phalansterian Workers, for example, and when Étienne Cabet visited the city in 1844, he was warmly welcomed by dreamers of a new society.[125] There were fewer such groups in Birmingham.[126] The Revolution of 1848 in France, like that of 1789, started in Paris, not in the provinces, but after it had taken place the Lyons uprising of 1834 was hailed as a landmark on the way.[127] A tree of liberty was planted in the Place des Cordeliers, centre of the 1834 fighting, and a speech was delivered by Joseph Hugon, a former member of the Central Committee of the Lyons Republican Society of the Rights of Man. In the wake of 1834 this Society was said (with some exaggeration) to have operated a network of organisations from Lyons.

The attempt completely to appropriate the uprising by mainstream republicans in 1848 was as misleading in 1848, a year when republican left and right clashed dramatically in Paris, as it had been in 1834. Yet very soon the economic and social structure of Lyons had changed, and the sense of fear – and hope – which had characterised its urban politics between 1815 and 1848 was largely lost. The *compagnons* dwindled in numbers, the *chefs d'atelier* became more conservative, the domination of the silk industry came to an end. Even the social topography was different.[128]

V

Far more detailed work needs to be carried out on the pattern of transfers of ideas, concepts and experiences between different places – notably the cities – in Europe in the early nineteenth century. It is already clear, however, from a limited survey of English reactions to events in Lyons that cross-city and cross-national comparisons were made and that general 'lessons' were drawn.

The first English news of the 1831 Lyons rising – 'deplorable disorders'[129] – appeared in London in *The Times* on 28 November: it was based on information and commentary in the Paris newspapers, backed by a letter from a correspondent. 'These scenes of riot and bloodshed', *The Times* began, 'originated in the distress of the work-men employed in the silk manufactures of that city and had no political object. Their formidable character depended on the numbers, discipline and arms of the mutineers.' 'There is one great difference between the days of Paris and those of Lyons,' a French newspaper had already argued.

> The great days of Paris were [days of protest] against political measures and centred on a question of liberty ... At Lyons the insurrection has been caused by misery, the result of the system which we have developed ... There are, therefore, no possible concessions we can make for the purpose of stopping sedition. The most commercial town in France demands employment and bread. Force alone can overcome obstacles which have their foundation in and are the natural consequences of the state of things.[130]

The 'class' aspect of the situation – as well as its basic economics – was noted in London. 'The National Guard of the higher classes was called out to disperse the rioters, but the latter, so far from yielding to the summons of the authorities to retire to their houses, fired upon the

Guard.'[131] A private letter underlined the point: 'the workmen have broken loose'.[132]

As further information arrived, there were some glosses on these initial statements, although in general they were reinforced.[133] The fact that when the working classes had taken over France's second city a new order had been imposed itself seemed ominous. 'Even their surprising order and moderation appears dangerous, from the perfect discipline and resolute purpose which it manifests.'[134] Yet some kind of 'remedy' would have to be offered. 'Men who have gone so far, as under the pressure of distress, to hold the flag of rebellion', wrote *The Times*, 'are not likely to return to obedience without some promise of higher wages.'[135] The difficulty was that such a local promise would defy the universal laws of political economy. 'All the power in the world', wrote a correspondent from France, 'cannot compel a manufacturer or a capitalist to persist in working at a loss.' No government, whatever its 'energy, influence and power', was in a position to secure an effective remedy. And as it was, work would pass in the interim to 'less turbulent cities'.[136]

Trans-national comparisons were drawn. 'The present disturbances, whatever may be their present aspect, had their origin in what at Macclesfield or Manchester would be called a strike for higher wages.'[137] Yet the violence – to Frenchman at least – recalled Bristol rather than Macclesfield or Manchester.[138] Such comparisons even had a transatlantic dimension. 'It has not generally occurred to one class that they can relieve themselves by the pillage of another. A servile war, or a war of servitude and want, upon property and racial superiority, can never succeed, except by general massacre, as in St Domingo.' Such comparisons of cases culminated in generalisation. 'The rising of the lower class united classes above the lowest for their own protection, unless some political cause or pretext be put forward to divide them and to procure a certain alliance of property with the greatest mass of physical force or numbers.'[139] It was the City report on the state of the money market in *The Times* which switched back from such theatrical generalisations to practicalities in France. 'The Paris money-market had seen no collapse of the Funds. Yet 'many persons, who are acquainted with the manufacturing districts of France, seem to entertain very serious apprehensions of what may possibly follow from the singular degree of organization which has been established among the working classes, which will, they fear, lead to unions of the neighbouring towns with Lyons.'[140]

Among the correspondents of *The Times* – or the newspaper sources which it quoted – there were no working-class representatives, and 'the serious apprehensions' would have been strengthened rather than dissipated if reference had been made either to the *Echo de la Fabrique* in Lyons, or to the *Poor Man's Guardian* in London. At a meeting of the National Union of the Working Classes at the Long Rotunda on 5 December 1831, significantly with a Macclesfield man, Smedley, in the Chair, a resolution was proposed, seconded and carried that 'the insurrection in the city of Lyons, proves that the rights of the working classes, in any country, cannot always be withheld with impunity.' 'Lyons was the Spitalfields of France,' the proposer, Mansell, stated, urging that in London as well as Lyons the working classes should trust to their own 'union' and not join other broader unions. The seconder, Julian Hibbert, produced his own generalisation. 'The rich were growing richer and the poor poorer.' Cleave pressed for continuing working-class organisation. 'The Lyonese had suffered much and were likely to suffer still more, because they were not sufficiently enlightened to know their right course ... Had the whole populace of France been prepared to assert their rights when they had the opportunity, these poor Lyonese would not thus have fallen; nor would the city be surrendered to military power.'[141]

At least one Rotunda speaker thought that Birmingham in 1831 was on the 'right course'. Given that the Whigs 'only wanted the working classes to be hewers of wood and drawers of water and to do other dirty work at their base bidding', Birmingham was a continuing warning to them. 'Birmingham first frightened them, Birmingham stands admirably.'[142] In 1834, there were fewer English working-class comments on Lyons, for the mood of 1831 and 1832 had passed, although there were rumours that 'delegates from Lyons and Paris had visited the unions of London and Birmingham, and that deputies from the latter towns had been despatched to Lyons and Paris on similar measures'.[143] In 1848, when the regime of Louis Philippe fell, Lyons no longer seemed to be as interesting to Englishmen as many other European cities, including Brussels as well as Paris. The Chartists then had their eyes more on the capitals than on the provincial centres, and so, too, did their opponents. London itself was more the centre of the action, too, than it had been earlier. It was in 1831, the moment of convergence in the two provincial cities, therefore, not in the year of revolutions, 1848, when lightning sparks were passing from capital city to capital city, that the most interesting observations were made about the common interests of two great European cities.

Birmingham and Lyons provide perhaps the best example of useful early nineteenth-century comparative city studies, but there are many others which should be made – between, for instance, the new textile towns of France and England or England and Germany. It is only by a careful examination of individual cities that we can hope to understand the driving forces of early nineteenth-century history.

NOTES

1 See *Old England*, quoted by H. W. J. Edwards, *The Radical Tory* (1937), p. 148, and *Runnymede Letters, To Thomas Attwood, M.P.*, printed in ibid., pp. 96-102.

2 *Le Journal des Débats*, 8 December 1831.

3 W. H. Riehl, *Die Naturgeschichte des Volkes*, vol. I (1854), p. 75.

4 W. H. Greg, *Reform: Fingerposts and Beacons* (1859), p. 11.

5 A. Ure, *The Philosophy of Manufactures* (1834), Book 3, p. 279. Ure spoke of 'a peculiar Class of men, concentrated in masses within a narrow range of country'.

6 See E. Pariset, *Histoire de la fabrique lyonnaise: étude sur le régime social et économique de l'industrie de la soie à Lyon depuis le XVIe siècle* (1902).

7 See W. H. B. Court, *The Rise of the Midland Industries* (1838); C. Gill, *A History of Birmingham*, vol. I (1952); and A. Fox, 'Industrial Relations in Nineteenth-Century Birmingham', in *Oxford Economic Papers*, vol. VII (1955).

8 C. Beaulieu, *Histoire du commerce et l'industrie et fabrique de Lyon* (1838), pp. 144-6.

9 S. Timmins, *The Resources, Products and Industrial History of Birmingham and the Midland Hardware District* (1886), p. 1.

10 See *Report from the Select Committee on the Silk Trade* (*Parliamentary Papers*, vol. XIX, Session 1831-2): A. Beauquis, *Histoire économique de la soie* (1910).

11 R. J. Bezucha, *The Lyons Uprising of 1834* (1974), p. 18.

12 *Report on Children in Manufactures* (1843), pp. 27, 80. See also above, p. 184.

13 See C. Ballon, 'L'évolution du métier lyonnais au XVIIIe siècle et le genèse de la méchanique Jacquard', in the *Revue de l'Histoire de Lyon*, vol. XII (1913).

14 See G. C. Allen, *The Economic Development of Birmingham and the Black Country* (1929).

15 Quoted in W. E. Hampton, *Early Co-operation in Birmingham and District* (1928), p. 61. The Birmingham petitioners of 1812 (see above, p. 141) referred during the Napoleonic Wars to the economy of high wages. 'Ten shillings a week is enough to exist upon, but it is a miserable existence for men used to thirty or forty.'

16 Quoted in *The Bazaar of Literary and Scientific Repository*, no. 1, 26 June 1823.

17 M. Garden, *Lyon et les Lyonnais au XVIIIe siècle* (1970), p. 311.

18 F. Rude, *Le mouvement ouvrier à Lyon de 1827 à 1832* (1944), p. 733. This important book still remains the major source: it is based in large part on archives in Rude's own possession.

19 See L. Trénard, 'La crise sociale lyonnaise à la veille de la Révolution', in the *Revue d'Histoire*, vol. II (1955), p. 24; Bezucha, *op. cit.*, Appendix B.

20 *L'Echo de la Fabrique*, 5 February 1832.
21 Quoted in Bezucha, *op. cit.*, p. 35.
22 Parliamentary Papers, *Reports of Committees*, 1812 (iii), p. 27; M. Pariset, *La Chambre de Commerce de Lyon* (1889), vol. II, p. 107.
23 See above, p. 152.
24 Le Comte de Chabrol, *Sur les évènements de Lyon au mois de juin 1817*, (1818), pp. 10-11.
25 *Journal de Lyon et du Department du Rhône*, No. 88, 15 November 1817.
26 Quoted in Rude, *op. cit.*, p. 111.
27 L. R. Villermé, *Tableau de l'état moral et physique des ouvriers* (1840), vol. I, p. 361.
28 See E. Labrousse, *1848-1830-1789*, 'Comment naissent les révolutions', *Actes du Congrès Historique du Centenaire de la Révolution de 1848* (1948), pp. 1-20.
29 *Birmingham Journal*, 29 January 1831, 12 November 1836.
30 HO/52/11. B.W. to Sir Robert Peel, 21 October 1830. See above, p. 153.
31 Labrousse, *op. cit.*, p. 10.
32 *Report of the Proceedings*, 25 January 1830.
33 Letter from George Nicolls to the Bank of England, 29 June 1832 (Bank of England/Birmingham Correspondence).
34 See above, p. 139.
35 *S.C. on the Silk Trade*, Q.8925.
36 As Monfalcon called him in his fascinating *Histoire des insurrections de Lyon en 1831 et en 1834* (1834), p. 45.
37 *L'Echo de la Fabrique*, 23 August 1833.
38 See above, p. 184.
39 See above, p. 188.
40 *L'Echo des Travailleurs*, 1 March 1834.
41 It is estimated that in 1830 there were 8000 *chefs d'atelier*, 750 *fabricants* and 30,000 *compagnons*.
42 Quoted by Rude, *op. cit.*, p. 49.
43 Norbert Truquin, *Mémoires et Aventures d'un Prolétaire* (1888), p. 213.
44 Quoted in Rude, *op. cit.*, p. 126.
45 E. Pariset, *op. cit.*, p. 277.
46 O. Festy, *Le mouvement ouvrier au début de la monarchie de juillet* (1908), p. 161.
47 Rude, *op. cit.*, p. 67.
48 Rude, ibid., pp. 426-31.
49 The organisation and role of the *Volontaires du Rhône*, who provided a military force, complicated all events in Lyon during this period.
50 *Le Globe*, 27 November 1831. Letter from Peiffer and François, the two leading disciples of St Simonism in Lyons.
51 *Le Moniteur Universal*, 22 December 1831.
52 E. Tarlé, *The French Working Class at the Period of the Revolution* (St Petersburg, 1909-11), quoted by Rude, *op. cit.*, p. 29. Only the last

chapter was translated into French, 'l'Insurrection ouvrière de Lyon', in the *Revue Marxiste* (1929)).

53 Bezucha, *op. cit.*, p. 163. Bezucha's account is strongly influenced by British and French writing on 'the crowd' and its social composition (see above, pp. 51-2). Bezucha calls the uprising 'the first example of "modern" collective violence in European history' (p. 170).

54 Letter of Count Skarzinsky in Cracow, written by his cousin, and intercepted by the Austrian secret police; quoted in Bezucha, *op. cit.*, p. 174.

55 J.B. Monfalcon, *Histoire des insurrections à Lyon en 1831 et en 1834* (1834); Bezucha, *op. cit.*, p. 186.

56 *L'Echo des Travailleurs*, 9 November 1833. Cp. 23 November 1833, 'Proletarians of all types, you were united for those days by fraternity of arms, by a community of danger. Never forget it! From your union comes your strength.' This periodical first appeared in this month. Cp. the other working-class paper, *L'Echo de la Fabrique*, which first appeared in January 1832: 'Our paper is completely industrial. The single goal in creating it was to promote the amelioration of the working class which is the glory of our city.' (22 January 1832.)

57 *Echo de la Fabrique*, 18 March 1832, 'Une Quasi-amélioration'.

58 See C.M. Wakefield, *op. cit.*, p. 57.

59 See *Birmingham Journal*, 27 February 1830.

60 ibid., 29 May 1830, 29 January 1831, 12 May 1832.

61 *Resolutions passed at the Meeting on the 25th of January 1830, together with the Declaration, Rules and Regulations of the Political Union.*

62 See the comments by George Edmonds, in the *Birmingham Journal*, 24 July, 18 September 1830.

63 ibid., 29 January 1832.

64 *L'Echo de la Fabrique*, 2 March 1834.

65 See Bezucha, *op. cit.*, p. 111.

66 ibid., pp. 123 ff.

67 See C.T. Flick, *The Birmingham Political Union and the Movements for Reform in Britain, 1830-1839* (1978), pp. 43-4.

68 *Broadsheet: Proposed Plan for the Organization of the Birmingham Political Union*, November 1831.

69 See H. Ferguson, 'The Birmingham Political Union and the Government, 1831-2', in *Victorian Studies*, vol. III (1960).

70 *The Times*, 23 November 1831.

71 For a Tory view of conspiratorial action in other places, including Bristol, on the part of Birmingham Political Union leaders, see the *Standard*, 3-5 November 1831.

72 *Report of the Proceedings*, May 1832. There were exaggerated claims that 'at least 200,000 people' were present. Half that figure, huge though it was, was more likely. (See Flick, *op. cit.*, pp. 79-81.)

73 Letters from Attwood to Mrs Attwood, 19 and 26 May 1832.

74 *Runnymede Letters*, *op. cit.*

75 *Monthly Argus* (1821), pp. 71-2.

76 Comte de Chabrol, *op. cit.*

77 A Sub-Committee of the Council of Political Union which demanded pledges from their candidate in 1832 did so on the grounds that Attwood was once 'a great Tory'. (*The Substance of the Extraordinary Proceedings*, 1832.)

78 *Birmingham Journal*, obituary notice, 8 March 1856.

79 Letter to Mrs Attwood, 19 May 1832.

80 See *op. cit.*, and also *l'Insurrection ouvrière de Lyon en 1831 et le rôle de Pierre Charnier* (*La Révolution de 1848*, t. 35, 1938).

81 Rude, *op. cit.*, p. 233.

82 ibid., p. 129.

83 ibid., pp. 64-6, 85-6, *et al.*

84 *Birmingham Monthly Argus*, June 1829. In July 1829 Attwood was described as 'bold, independent, talented and truly patriotic individual'. For the *Argus*, see above, pp. 120ff.

85 For an interesting study of Oastler's development as a passionate reformer, see C. Driver, *Tory Radical* (1946).

86 Rude, *op. cit.*, pp. 139-40.

87 ibid., p. 625.

88 ibid., p. 624.

89 G. K. Chesterton, *Cobbett* (n.d.), pp. 88, 224.

90 The importance of the bees-drone image in early socialist and co-operative thought is shown by the way in which it is used (apparently independently) by many different writers. Mandeville's *Fable of the Bees* (1714) praised luxury as a stimulus to production. Nineteenth-century socialists could see no good in the drone. As St Simon wrote in his *Catéchisme Politique des Industriels* (1822), 'all being done by industry, all ought to be done for industry' (pp. 2-3). Attwood's social thought with its stress on the industrious classes (*les industriels* of St Simon) is very near at times to St Simonism. The bees-drones image was used by him at a meeting of the Political Union in May 1830, a few months after it had been used by the Owenite magazine in Birmingham, the *Birmingham Co-operative Herald*, no. 9, 1 December 1829. From that time onwards, he frequently referred to bees and drones in the social hive, for example at the general election of 1834. Cp. a speech reported in the *Birmingham Journal*, 9 April 1831. 'In natural history it was a well-known fact ... the drones in a hive of bees were often in the habit of encroaching so far on the rights and interests of the community that the bees were at last driven to the necessity of destroying them. In our hive ... we will merely exact justice from the drones and do no more injury to their right for property than we will suffer them to do to ours.'

91 *Report of the Proceedings*, 25 January 1830.

92 *Observations on Currency, Population and Pauperism* (1818), esp. pp. 45-6.

93 Both Attwood and Charnier had to meet frequent attacks on the grounds that they were merely following their own ambitions. Bouvery, for instance, told Charnier in 1827 'You are less concerned with improving our lot than with acquiring celebrity' (quoted in Rude, pp. 127-8). The nature of the panaceas owed a lot to the

day-to-day interests of the leaders – Attwood's banking business and Charnier's work in the silk trade. Both men felt that the political leadership was weakest where it touched their own lives most directly.

94 *Birmingham Advertiser*, 18 June 1835.

95 *Birmingham Journal*, 12 November 1836.

96 *Le Courrier de Lyon*, 12 March 1834: *Archives Parlementaires*, vol. 87, p. 394.

97 The word *solidarité* was only used freely for the first time as a political expression in the early 1840s by Fourier's disciple Renaud. It was not used in English until Hugh Doherty introduced it in 1841. For the history of *solidarité* and other key words, see A. E. Bester, 'The Evolution of the Socialist Vocabulary', in *Journal of the History of Ideas*, vol. IX, no. 3, 1948.

98 *Report of the Proceedings*, 11 May 1830. Attwood had in mind 39 George III, c.79, prohibiting all societies with secret proceedings, and 57 George III, c.19, prohibiting political societies with open proceedings from corresponding or choosing delegates. The main 'devil-trap' law in France was Article 291 of the Penal Code. To try to get round it the *Devoir Mutuel* at Lyons was organised at first in groups of five, and *ateliers* of twenty members. *Le silence le plus absolu* was imposed on all participants.

99 *Histoire de dix ans*, quoted by E. Dolléans, *Histoire du mouvement ouvrier, 1830-70* (1947), p. 66.

100 See S. Thomas, *op. cit.*

101 *Morning Chronicle*, 8 August 1835; letters of 20, 22 October, 1832, vol.I, p. 7, pp. 20-2.

102 Quoted by S. Maccoby, *English Radicalism, 1832-1852* (1935), p. 43. They were, as Professor Tawney has suggested, 'irrepressible constitutionalists'.

103 *Hansard*, vol. XVI, cols 910ff.: Rude, *op. cit.*, p. 363.

104 ibid., p. 384.

105 Quoted in Bezucha, *op. cit.*, p. 115.

106 *L'Echo des Travailleurs*, 30 December 1832. For Bowring's views on free trade, see *The Westminster Review*, vol. 18 (1833).

107 Bezucha, *op. cit.*, pp. 166, 171.

108 *Echo de la Fabrique*, 20 May 1832.

109 *Hansard*, vol. VIII, cols. 106, 913.

110 Wakefield, *op. cit.*, p. 251.

111 Some prominent merchants and manufacturers left the Union as soon as the Reform Act was passed.

112 *Birmingham Gazette*, 16 July 1832.

113 *Birmingham Journal*, 10 January 1835.

114 ibid., 15 April 1837. At a meeting in November 1836, Edmonds had argued that prosperity had generated apathy.

115 *Philanthropist*, 21 December 1837.

116 Letters to his wife, 19, 21 November 1834; *Birmingham Journal*, 12 November 1836.

117 ibid., 17 January 1836.

118 ibid., 23 December 1837.

119 See A.Briggs (ed.), *Chartist Studies* (1959), Chapter I. There was an important foray of the Union into Scotland.

120 Attwood took over the scheme of William Benbow, who wrote his *Grand National Holiday and Congress of Productive Classes* in 1831. Attwood tried to change the idea into one of class cooperation. See G. D. H. Cole, *Chartist Portraits* (1941), p. 127.

121 O'Brien set out his view in *The National Reformer*, 7 January 1837.

122 F. F. Rosenblatt, *The Economic and Social Aspects of the Chartist Movement* (1916), p. 121. An 1839 manifesto to the working classes called 'the corrupting influence of paper money one of the causes of their oppression'. (*Birmingham Journal*, 20 July 1839.)

123 Even the *Birmingham Journal*, the organ of the middle-class Radicals, was compelled to note the difficult appeal of the currency question. On 27 December 1836, it said that the currency question, although first in importance, would have to come last in propaganda if the Political Union were to be revived.

124 Wakefield, *op. cit.*, p. 344. 'Paper money', according to the manifesto, was 'a corrupting influence which had destroyed and robbed labourers of three-fourths of their labour.'

125 Bezucha, *op. cit.*, p. 193.

126 The Owenites, however, had been active in the Political Union from 1830 to 1832, among them Bronterre O'Brien, editor of the *Midland Representative* until the spring of 1832, William Pare and William Hawkes Smith. See E. W. Hampton, *The Early Cooperation in Birmingham and District* (1928). Attwood supported the setting-up of the Birmingham Equitable Labour Exchange in 1833.

127 For the role of Lyons, see F. Dutacq, *Histoire politique de Lyon pendant la révolution de 1848* (1910).

128 See F. Dutacq and A. Latreille, *Histoire de Lyon, 1844-1940* (1952); and C. Leonard, *Lyons Transformed: Public Works of the Second Empire* (1961).

129 It quoted the message to the inhabitants of Lyons on 23 November by the Prefect and the Mayor – 'Tremble at anarchy: think of the welfare of your families and of the city.'

130 *La Gazette de France*, 26 November 1831.

131 *The Times*, 28 November 1831.

132 ibid., 29 November 1831. 'Our notions as to these people are extremely ill-founded when we suppose them destitute of energy', the letter writer went on. 'Hitherto we have not known by experience what these men are like when they fight for bread.'

133 In particular (ibid.), the French Prime Minister's statement was underlined that 'the rebels made war on property and civil order, but not on political institutions'. There were reports later of attempts by Carlists and others to exploit the situation.

134 *The Times*, 29 November 1831. Cp. *op. cit.*, 2 December 1831. 'The city exhibited the strange and anomalous appearance of being at once

loyal and rebellious . . . of maintaining a profound peace between hostile camps.' When the Duke of Orleans entered Lyons after the uprising on 3 December it was noted how peacefully organised was 'the transition of power from the insurgent masses into the hands of its lawful depositories'. (*op. cit.*, 10 December 1831.)

135 *The Times*, 29 November 1831.

136 A private letter from Paris, quoted *loc. cit.*, 2 December 1831, and the message from the Prefect of the Isère to the citizens of Grenoble, dated 24 November 1831. *The Times* gave conflicting reports of disorders in other French cities following the events in Lyons.

137 *The Times*, 29 November 1831.

138 Letter from Lyons, dated 21 November 1831, published in *loc. cit.*, 30 November 1831. For a later contrast with Bristol, see a letter from Lyons, *op. cit.*, 2 December 1831. 'What is strikingly singular in contrast with your Bristol affair is that, although they have burned and destroyed property to such an immense amount, not a single *sou* has been stolen.'

139 ibid., 2 December 1831.

140 ibid., 10 December 1831.

141 *Poor Man's Guardian*, 3 December 1831.

142 ibid., 3 December 1831.

143 ibid., 19 April 1834. A month earlier, after the arrest and imprisonment of the socialist Member of the Chamber, Cabet, the *Guardian* compared the English and French social and political systems. 'In France the Government is made exclusively by the middle class; in England partly by the middle, partly by the higher.' 'This explains the baseness of the French Government, even as compared with our own . . . Without an aristocracy to shed dignity on its usurpation and without "the raw spirit of the people" to impart honesty to it, it works its mole-like way, degrading and degraded.'

Index

241